THE
MANAGER'S
HANDBOOK

THE MANAGER'S HANDBOOK

DR. AMBROSE E. EDEBE, MBA, PhD

To order additional copies of this book, contact:
Xlibris LLC
1-888-795-4274
www.Xlibris.com
Orders@Xlibris.com
550885

ACKNOWLEDGEMENTS

I give glory to God Almighty for making it possible for me to start and complete this book. May His name be praised!

Life has convinced me that we are the sum total of what we have learned from those who have shared their impressive accumulation of wisdom; from life experiences which has provided the influence of both the positive and negative, from the great and the small.

I am grateful for what I have been privileged to ascertain from men and women who have deposited within my soul wisdom that otherwise may not have been taught or experienced.

I acknowledge the unflinching support received from my wife, Josephine, and the ceaseless prayers of my children – Sarah, Mary, Elizabeth, and Samuel- for my success. I would like to thank my father, Senior Apostle Thomas Edebe and my mother, Mother of Grace (Mrs.) Esther Edebe, for their unconditional love. I also wish to thank my brothers and sisters for their support.

Finally, I would like to acknowledge the support and contributions received from my professional colleagues. The book is all the better for their advice, but full responsibility for it rests with me.

PREFACE

As you know, being a supervisor often leaves you sandwiched between the competing demands of subordinates and upper level management. You may be called upon to implement policies that you didn't have a voice in preparing, or you may be buffeted by the questions—both reasonable and unreasonable—of those who work for you.

For most supervisors, it's not the work itself that frustrates them. Instead, it's the wide range of unexpected problems that pop-up on a daily basis. And you're the one that has to have the instant answer.

Coping with the daily dilemmas compels you to deal with problems you haven't confronted before. That's where the Manager's Handbook comes in. Its purpose is to provide ready answers for a vast array of questions that you have to tackle in your supervisory role. You'll find workable solutions for a wide variety of situations, as well as straightforward answers that deal with the nuts and bolts of your daily endeavors.

Contents

Introduction

Does being a supervisor sometimes make you feel like the sixth passenger squeezing into a five passenger car? That is to say, you're not exactly unwanted, but no one would really mind if you weren't there. As you know, being a supervisor often leaves you sandwiched between the competing demands of subordinates and upper level management. You may be called upon to implement policies that you didn't have a voice in preparing, or you may be buffeted by the questions—both reasonable and unreasonable—of those who work for you.

For most supervisors, it's not the work itself that frustrates them. Instead, it's the wide range of unexpected problems that pop-up on a daily basis. And you're the one that has to have the instant answer. You're called upon to be not only a leader of those you supervise, but also a follower of upper management. Unfortunately, this dual role can be a lightning rod for conflict, which brings a steady stream of demands cascading in your direction from both above and below.

But being a supervisor goes beyond being an intermediary between upper management and employees. Questions can come your way every day that propel you into playing the part of counselor, confessor, troubleshooter and negotiator.

How many times have you thought, "My job would be great if ..."? In some way, shape, or form, that big "if" involves other people. Perhaps someone you supervise is the problem. Or maybe your biggest headaches are caused by your boss. It may even be your best friend at work who constantly bombards you with complaints such as, "This place is all screwed-up. I can't wait to get out of here."

The same friend who has been in the same job for five years, and will probably be there another ten—all the while finding fault with everything and everyone.

People problems at work can range from serious, such as racial and sexual prejudice, to seemingly silly, such as favoritism based on old school ties. However, even what seems silly to someone else, is downright serious if you're the one who has to deal with it day after day.

Unfortunately, lots of us think our work problems are both unique and incurable. Yet, most of the situations that cause difficulty at work are neither novel, nor hopeless. There are many tacks you can take to get greater satisfaction from being a supervisor. They may not bring joy when the gong goes off every Monday morning, but at least you won't be longing for Friday by two o'clock on Tuesday—or even worse, job hunting after no longer wanting to cope with the many frustrations that supervision entails.

You may recognize some familiar situations as you read this book. That's because wherever you work, the players may be different, but many aspects of work remain the same. As a supervisor, you encounter people who are lazy, while others are incompetent. There are those who don't carry their own load, while others carry more than their share.

You may know educated drones who don't make decisions, and high school dropouts who do. In short, all kinds of people, some of whom you like, and others you merely tolerate out of necessity. All of this makes being a supervisor not only challenging, but also at times frustrating.

Coping with the daily dilemmas compels you to deal with problems you haven't confronted before, and/or new twists to age-old questions. Since it's impossible to predict the unpredictable, you can be bombarded with questions for which you don't have a ready answer. That's where the Manager's Hand Book comes in. Its purpose is to provide ready answers for a vast array of questions that you have to tackle in your supervisory role. You'll find workable solutions for a wide variety of situations that aren't easily resolved, as well as straightforward answers that deal with the nuts and bolts of your daily endeavors.

But the Manager's Handbook goes beyond this, because an answer may be perfectly valid for dealing with a problem –but not quite your problem. After all, there may be a particular spin to your circumstances that a set answer doesn't solve. For example, let's suppose you have an employee with a drinking problem. Do you counsel the employee yourself, refer them for help, fire the person, kick the problem upstairs for resolution, or ignore the situation completely? As you know, that depends upon a particular set of facts, which includes the employee's performance and personality, company policy, and a number of other variables.

Therefore, instead of giving you a set answer which forces you to adapt it to a particular problem, the Manager's Handbook contains alternative solutions, as well as plenty of points and tips designed to help you zero in on the circumstances of your case. In short, in this book you'll find hundreds of answers and subject matter tips on all of the perplexing problems that you have to deal with.

The topics covered are many and diverse, just as are the real world problems you face on your job. There is, of course, a large quantity of material on managing those you supervise. But leaving it there would be like stopping for a red light half-way through the intersection—not quite good enough, and that's because there are other constituencies you must work with. Therefore, the Manager's Handbook includes additional assistance on how to deal with your boss, other departments and outsiders in your role as supervisor.

Beyond that, you'll find information that helps you to view a supervisory role from your own perspective as a person, not as an organizational robot operating in a vacuum. In the final analysis, being a successful supervisor means adapting the job to your personality, not changing yourself to satisfy the demands of the job. So let's go on to the many questions that you must answer as a supervisor, and explore workable solutions that can supply the answers you need.

1

The Basic Steps for Successful Supervision

Successful supervision starts with learning to manage subordinates without getting trapped by the obstacles that lie in wait for an unsuspecting boss. If you're relatively new to a supervisory role, the initial barrier you face may be your own apprehension about managing those you supervise. However, whether you're a beginner, or a seasoned supervisor, there are many strategies that can aid you in grappling with the daily frustrations of the job.

These tactics include how to handle friendships, which can be a tricky proposition when you're trying to balance rapport with work requirements. In this and other matters, your management style can play a major role in your success. In addition, giving instructions, fielding questions, and overall leadership, are all responsibilities that you have to execute with poise, patience, and perhaps a dash of humor.

If managing people isn't enough of a headache, there are always never-ending interruptions and piles of paperwork to occupy your time – as if you had any to spare. Let's look at some ways of dealing with these burdens that can make your daily duties easier to do.

1.1 GETTING STARTED AS A SUPERVISOR

The most difficult time for any supervisor is when you have to make the transition from being a worker to being a boss. Your first supervisory assignment brings with it a certain queasiness in the pit of your stomach about supervising people. How will they react to you, and will they challenge your authority? How will you respond when workers do test you?

Q: I've just been made a supervisor in my department. The previous supervisor, who was very popular, just retired. How should I act toward the people I now supervise, after working with them for two years?

A: Be yourself. Don't call attention to the fact that you're now supervising people you formerly worked with. They're just as aware of the problem as you are. In fact, they're trying to figure out how to deal with you in your new role as boss. Keep things running as they were under the former supervisor. Even though you may have some good ideas for improving operations, it's wise to ease into your new job, so that subordinates won't typecast you as a "boat rocker."

Q: What's the best way for a supervisor to earn the respect of subordinates?

A: There's no sure-fire way to do this, since many variables are involved. For example, if you're replacing a boss who didn't get along with the group, it's easy to assume that you'll automatically win favor by comparison. However, it might be that an unsatisfactory experience with a former boss has soured people on supervisors in general. That's neither logical, nor reasonable, but you're dealing with people, and the unexpected and unpredictable are part of the human equation.

In the long term, being an effective boss will reflect itself in the level of cooperation you receive from subordinates. That means being decisive, communicating competently, and establishing a working rapport within the department.

If the situation presents itself, one of the most effective ways to gain credibility is to resolve a personnel problem that has been plaguing one of the people within your department. It really doesn't have to be anything significant. For instance, suppose a worker is upset because of an error in accrued vacation time. By taking the initiative to promptly resolve this problem, you're demonstrating an ability to quickly resolve matters that most affect employees – their pay and benefits. This can quickly translate into goodwill.

CAUTION: Whatever the circumstances of your new position, don't attach a sense of urgency to gaining the respect of subordinates. It will come about in time as they get to know you, and recognize that you're both fair and reasonable in your supervisory role.

Q: I've been transferred to a different supervisory position within the same company, and when I told an employee he was doing something wrong, he said "That's the way we always do it." In following up, I found that many things are done differently here. What gives?

A: There's often an inconsistency at the operating level in the way that policies and procedures are implemented. As long as company-wide guidelines are being followed, don't storm in and stir things up. That can lead to confusion and impact productivity – at least in the short term. If you bring better ideas to the job as to how tasks should be performed, implement them slowly after you have gained the confidence of subordinates.

1.2 HOW TO ADJUST WHEN YOU BECOME A BOSS

Some folks are promoted into a supervisory position within their department. This offers several advantages, including a familiarity with how the department operates, as well as knowing the strengths and weaknesses of the employees in the group. However, one obstacle often encountered is adjusting from doing the job to assuming a new role as boss.

Q: I've just been promoted to a first-line supervisory position, but I am still getting involved in doing my old job. How should I phase out?

A: As quickly as you can. For some folks, giving up the work they were doing is as difficult as it is for some parents to recognize that their children have grown up. But there are real negatives involved in clinging to your old tasks.

First of all, it can be a form of security blanket which prevents you from ploughing ahead to master your new supervisory role. You can tend to concentrate on your old job because you have mastered how to do it. However, the end result is that you neglect to tackle your new duties.

This can also undermine your supervisory status in the eyes of subordinates. In effect, you're neither fish nor fowl. It can also present a problem for the person who replaces you in your old job. They may feel, with some justification, that you're continuing to do your old job because you lack confidence in their abilities.

The best thing to do is to give up your old duties as soon as possible. Naturally, you should take time to train your replacement, but this should be minimal since you're around to answer any questions that come up. Incidentally, don't misinterpret this to mean you can't or shouldn't pitch in to help if the workload warrants it. Subordinates relate better to a boss who isn't afraid to get his hands dirty. However, that's an entirely different situation than divorcing yourself from your old duties.

1.3 SIX WAYS TO GAIN CREDIBILITY WITH SUBORDINATES

1. Be yourself. Avoid making jokes about being the boss. On the other hand, don't become aloof and distance yourself from the people you supervise.
2. Be decisive. Don't appear to be wishy-washy about making decisions in front of subordinates. That doesn't mean you always have to respond right away, but do your thinking privately so you don't give the appearance of being unsure of yourself.
3. Keep your cool. Getting angry will alienate employees. You may get instantaneous action if you blow your top, but you'll pay for it in the long run.
4. Always be fair. This sounds simple, however there are many little traps you can fall into. For example, don't overload a

capable employee with work to maintain output, because you (a) don't have enough help and/or (b) other employees aren't meeting standards.

5. Be firm when necessary. Always remember that when push comes to shove, you're the boss. It's great to be well-liked – and also an advantage – but there will be times when you'll be tested by subordinates.

6. Be friendly. Advice on being friendly often causes confusion when we think of it in conjunction with being firm. Sometimes, there's a tendency to think we have to be one or the other. That's not so, although it can be difficult to balance the two traits. The trick is to maintain your composure in difficult circumstances. Let's look at how this can be done. Suppose Chuck, a worker, gets hot under the collar about having to drop everything to work on a rush job and confronts Susan, his supervisor. Chuck, beet-red with anger says, "Dammit, I can't do everything around here." Susan calmly replies, "I understand that Chuck, but unfortunately the 'Whipit' job has to be given priority." Not to be put off, Chuck says, "Well, get someone else to do it. I'm busy!" Susan then replies in a reassuring tone, "The 'Whipit' job is important and I know I can count on you to do it right. However, I also understand that it will cause slippage in completing your other work, so don't worry about that." Susan then starts to walk away which indicates the discussion is at an end.

    In all likelihood, Chuck will trudge back to his workplace, grumble a little bit, and go about doing what he was told to do. And as he cools down, he will realize that Susan has confidence in him that she doesn't have in other people.

NOTE: Avoid telling workers that they can do the job better than someone else. This may be discussed during worker conversations and cause resentment. Susan only said she had confidence in John doing the job. He, on his own may infer that others are less capable.

There are several useful points in this scenario.

    a. Susan remains calm and is firm without being demanding.

b. She listens briefly while John vents his anger, and then repeats her request.
c. Susan lets John know he is good at his job.
d. She counters his only valid argument about not finishing his other work by recognizing it might be delayed.
e. She wisely terminates the conversation by walking away when there is nothing more to say.

Look at what Susan accomplished and guess what? She did all that in fifty words. That in itself isn't important, but it is smart to be as brief as possible in these situations. Otherwise, they become debates, or even worse, shouting matches in which there are no winners.

1.4 WHY YOUR APPEARANCE IS IMPORTANT

In some positions supervisors dress pretty much the same way as those they supervise, while in other jobs a supervisor adopts the more traditional business attire worn by men and women in management positions. Whichever applies in your circumstances, both how you dress and your appearance in general send a signal to others – positive or negative – about you as a person.

Q: In my former supervisory position I dressed casually. I've noticed in my new job that some bosses wear work clothes, while others wear suits. Which way should I go?

A: As a general rule, it's better to dress up than to dress down. The important point is to follow the norm where you work. If no consistent pattern exists – and there are no practical reasons to dress in work clothes – you're better off wearing appropriate business attire.

Dress is a subject that sometimes generates controversy and confusion, and some people choose to do battle over this matter. However, in reality there are only so many battles in life that you're going to win, and using up currency in a conflict over clothing isn't prudent.

To some degree, the way folks dress for work relates to the work they do. If you visualize a banker, hand-in-hand with that image is a dark business suit. Other professionals – in advertising for example – tend to dress more flamboyantly. In addition, some companies like to present certain images, which is partially reflected in the attire of their employees.

On the whole, what you wear for work will be influenced both by where you work and what you do. And not to be overlooked are regional differences. Dress on the East Coast is traditionally more formal than in Southern California. In a nutshell, following the established pattern where you work is less likely to get you labeled as a nonconformist.

Another aspect of clothing that gets bandied about is the "dress for success" fad. That's fine to a point, but it can be overdone. If you're concerned about dressing well, but don't have a budget to match, worry about fit – not price. Inexpensive clothing that fits well is far better than high-priced fashions that don't.

In fact, as well as in theory, a neat appearance casts a favorable impression, and impressions are always important. All things considered, it's preferable not to exercise too much independence in the matter of dress. It's admittedly easy to say, "They're paying me for my abilities, not my clothing," but don't forget that you dress in clothes – not a résumé.

1.5 DEALING WITH FRIENDS WHEN YOU BECOME THEIR BOSS

One of the difficulties of being promoted to a supervisory position is your present department is handling friendships in your new role.

Q: What about my best friend Helen? Should I still go out to lunch with her now that I'm her boss?

A: Yes, and take the initiative to ask her. She may be reluctant to approach you, since you're now her boss. You should deal directly with the changed circumstances while at lunch, by telling Helen that you hope your new position doesn't interfere with your friendship.

There's a balancing problem that comes into play here. In your supervisory role, you don't want to alienate anyone by showing signs of favoritism. On the other hand, you don't want everyone to assume that you're now a snob because of your new job. So if you abruptly stop going out to lunch with Helen, it will make it even more difficult for people to relate to you in your new role as the boss.

Instead, by going to lunch, you send a signal that you're the same person you always were. In fact, this will probably be reinforced after lunch, since Helen will likely be pumped by others to find out what you said about work. As far as favoritism goes, you always went out to lunch with Helen in the past, so this shouldn't be a factor – at least initially.

Perhaps later on, when your supervisory role is solidified, you might want to gradually adjust things so as not to create the perception of playing favorites. However, don't worry needlessly about this type of situation. Remember, you're now a supervisor – not a role model for the world.

Q: I want to ask Helen to lunch, but I'm not sure how to handle any discussion about my new job. I'm afraid we'll both eat and avoid the topic, which will only make the situation worse.

A: To some degree the approach to tackling this topic hinges on the closeness of your friendship. However, even if your past friendship has been such that sensitive subjects haven't been discussed, the circumstances here are different. You and Helen have to work together in the future, so it's better to clear the air at the outset and avoiding the topic won't solve it. Try saying something similar to this: "Helen, I'm pleased about being promoted, but I'm concerned about our friendship. I certainly don't want our jobs to interfere with that." This might generate a discussion in which you talk things out, and jointly conclude that there will be no difficulty in maintaining both a solid friendship as well as a good working relationship.

Let's assume Helen smiles and quickly dismisses the topic by saying, "Oh, I think it's great you got the job. Don't worry about us. The thought of us having problems never crossed my mind." At face value that sounds great, and indeed may be a true expression of Helen's attitude toward the subject.

However, there's a chance that perhaps Helen is trying to avoid dealing with the issue. Given that possibility, try testing the waters a little more with a response such as this: "That's great Helen, but you know I feel funny about having to give directions to you." She then will probably either pursue the topic, and the two of you can discuss any potential problems, or else will just reassure you again. In either case, that's about all you can do. This type of predicament usually resolves itself over time anyway. After you've gone this far, there's little else to do – or worry about.

HINT: Don't look for the right moment to bring the subject of your relationship up at lunch. When tricky topics require discussion, there's a tendency to search for the "right" moment to raise them. However, frequently the "right" moment never comes and the opportunity passes without anything being said. There are of course appropriate times and settings to discuss certain subjects. But in this case, lunch itself is the proper time and place.

1.6 SILENCING CRITICS WHO WANT YOUR JOB

Sometimes when supervisory positions are filled, someone in the department expresses resentment. Frequently, it's an older employee with more experience than the person selected.

Q: Alfred, who is much older and has been on the job longer, was pretty confrontational in remarks to me about my getting the supervisory position. How should I respond?

A: Alfred may be just baiting you and/or openly expressing resentment that you were selected over him. In either case, don't get angry, but don't be apologetic. If it's a one-time outburst, it's best to ignore the remarks. However, if this attitude persists you should respond calmly and factually. Try something such as, "Alfred, I was selected for this position, and I would like for us to get along. I don't belittle you, and I certainly don't expect you to be rude to me."

As a new supervisor, you can aggravate the matter by getting drawn into a debate over the relative qualifications of Alfred and yourself. This type of confrontation often occurs when educational qualifications weigh heavier than experience in a promotion decision. Remember two things. You didn't make the selection, and you aren't responsible for defending it. In addition, in many of these predicaments, unsuccessful candidates for positions have been told in the past to seek further training if they hope to advance within the company.

The flip side of this scenario is when the gripes come from someone with more education than the person selected for the position. Obviously, the selection criteria favored experience – all other factors being equal. In any event, the result is the same. The disgruntled employee is misdirecting his anger at you. Usually over a period of time, either the hostility fades, or the individual seeks employment elsewhere.

1.7 MANAGEMENT STYLE: WHAT IT IS AND ISN'T

One of the quandaries supervisors face is how deeply to get involved in monitoring the performance of subordinates. How much, or how little, decision making should be done by individual workers in determining how they do their jobs? Of course, this is partially influenced by the nature of the work, company procedures, union work rules if applicable, and employee capabilities. But beyond these constraints, there's also the question of your personal style of managing people.

Q: What exactly is management style?

A: It's simply how you operate in managing your job responsibilities. Basically, some people tend to delegate work with ease, which is what's referred to as a "hands-off" style. Other supervisors keep a "hands-on" rein on what's going on within their department, and become more deeply involved in the details of how things are done.

You can probably best view this by thinking about some of the managers you know. They probably range from the person who pretty much lets the department run itself, to the boss who wants to know the last detail on everything that happens. The former type lets people do a lot of the decision making about how they do their job, while the latter type doesn't want anything done without prior approval. Of course, there's a wide range of latitude between these two extremes, and most managers probably fall somewhere in the middle.

1.8 THE BEST MANAGEMENT STYLE IN THE WORLD

Q: What's the most effective management style to use?

A: There is no best way for you to supervise your group in terms of a hard set of rules that can be religiously followed, and expected to yield predictable results. This is so primarily because of all the personality factors that make folks what they are, which for one thing includes a wide variance in the amount of supervision they require.

Furthermore, your own personality plays a significant role in how you manage the people who work for you. If you're the type who has confidence in delegating work to people, or to the contrary, are nervous when you don't know what's going on, this will carry over into your supervisory duties.

From a practical standpoint, the best management style is a combination of "hands-on" and "hands-off" management. For instance, some of the people who work for you may be quite capable of getting their job done with a minimum of supervision. Others may require regular monitoring and guidance. Recognizing these differences, and managing to the capabilities of these individual traits is one of the keys to successful supervision.

As a general rule, encourage your people to use their initiative in getting the job done. However, it's important to follow-up to make sure that tasks are being performed in a timely manner. One of the most ineffective ways to supervise people is to get so intimately involved in details that subordinates won't do anything on their own for fear of being criticized. This leads to lackluster performance instead of loyalty, and boredom replaces interest in the job.

1.9 THE RIGHT WAY TO GIVE INSTRUCTIONS TO EMPLOYEES

Giving instructions to people seems simple enough, but a common refrain often heard when something goes wrong is, "That isn't what I thought you wanted." There's little question that quality problems, work delays, missed deadlines, and a variety of other mishaps are sometimes related to nothing more complicated than a basic lack of communication.

Q: Is there a best way to give instructions to subordinates?

A: The important point is to be clear in what you say. Make sure that the person knows exactly what you want done. However simple this seems, it's not always that easy to execute effectively. A barked order may be perfectly clear, but not necessarily conducive to getting the full cooperation of an employee. So it's not only what you say that counts, but also how you say it.

And after you give instructions, always ask the employee if he has any questions. Then casually repeat what you want done again, since repetition minimizes the opportunity for misunderstanding. If you're asking for something out of the ordinary to be done, try to take the time to explain why it's necessary. Folks respond better when they're aware of the reasons for doing something. This is important so let's look at an example:

Background

Patricia, a supervisor in the claims department of Omnibus Insurance Ltd., has been told that the weekly report on processed claims must be submitted in a different format to be compatible with a new computer system the company has installed. She must now give this information to Bertha, who not only has been doing this report for three years, but also is the type of person who is extremely reluctant to change the way she does things.

How It's Handled

Patricia:	"How's everything going Bertha? Did you have a good time at your nephew's last Sunday?"
Bertha:	"Oh it was wonderful Pat, but I think I gained five pounds from all the food I ate. Is that paperwork for me?" she says, noticing the forms in Patricia's hands.
Patricia:	"Yes, as a matter of fact Bertha it's a new form for the weekly processed claims report. It has to be used, since the current format won't jibe with the new computer system. Here, take a look."
Bertha:	"The information is all the same. I don't see why they can't just use the old form."
Patricia:	"Apparently they've redesigned all the forms as part of a cost reduction program. I have looked the new form over and the data we furnish is pretty much the same. However, you're the expert on this. Do you have any problems with it?"
Bertha:	"It's ok. I guess, but at this rate we're becoming slaves to the computer."
Patricia:	"It sometimes seems that way Bertha. Well, seeing that there's no problem, we'll use the new format starting with next week's report. Actually, we're lucky. Over in Accounts Receivable they don't even have a handle on the data."

Analysis

Notice how Patricia eased into the discussion with a little social banter, explained why the change had to be made, solicited questions, and made sure there would be no problems later. Incidentally, the major difference between this situation and the rush job assignment discussed in Sec.1.3(6), is that here something new is being done. Therefore, it was necessary to take the time to discuss it at some length.

CAUTION: Do not overlook the style you use to give directions. Quite simply, politeness scores points with people, whether it's at a social gathering or on the shop floor. Even when you're under extreme pressure to get a job done, keep calm when communicating requests to workers.

Always try to give directions on a one-to-one basis, not by shouting across the office or factory floor. That approach not only conveys an attitude of indifference toward the worker, but it also increases the likelihood of your message being misunderstood.

1.10 EFFECTIVE TECHNIQUES FOR FIELDING QUESTIONS

Supervisors are often required to spend a good deal of time as a conduit of information on general administrative matters. Workers expect supervisors to have the answers, even when they lack the necessary information.

Q: I must spend about 20% of my time answering questions about overtime pay, personal leave, vacation requests, and so forth. How can I cut this down?

A: There are several conditions that can contribute to an excess amount of time spent in answering administrative questions. First of all, the personnel/human resources department might be lax in distributing directives that cover these policies. In fairness to these folks, it's frequently not their fault. They might be understaffed and/or concentrating limited resources on higher priority tasks. Or the fault may lie with upper levels of management who receive this information through channels, but don't funnel it on down the line.

Another cause for confusion is the complexity of the language used in many directives of this nature. Obviously, interpretation of some of the topics requires skill in translating complex terminology into jargon-free terms that people can understand. Unfortunately, this is a common problem that often leaves the recipients of memos thinking, "Do they mean what they say, or do they mean what I think they mean?" Finally, some companies are just plain careless about giving out this information on a timely basis.

The best way to minimize the amount of time you spend in this area is to hold meetings and go over any changes in policy and/or procedures as they are issued. That way you cover the subject with everyone at the same time, and avoid going over the same ground time and time again.

HINT: Before you discuss anything of this nature, always take the time to make sure you understand it yourself. If necessary, get clarifications for anything that's confusing. Otherwise, a considerable amount of time can be wasted while your group sits around and speculates about the intent of a particular provision.

If a meeting does result in questions, wait a few days before seeking answers, unless it's a matter requiring a prompt reply. The reason for this is basic. As employees go over handouts, and/or discuss new personnel policies, questions will arise. Therefore, you will likely be getting this type of feedback for a couple of days. By waiting before seeking answers to employee's questions, you can consolidate them, and then track down the answer once – not several times.

Incidentally, general material on benefits and the like should be given out to everyone. That's logical enough, but unfortunately it's not always done. It's also a time saver to give the material out first before you discuss it with everyone. There's also a simple timing trick to avoid unnecessary downtime because employees read and discuss handouts instead of getting the work out. To avoid this, distribute handouts just before the end of the day and schedule the meeting to discuss it for the following morning. That way, people will read the material on their time, not the company's.

Another problem frequently encountered is the "shoot the messenger" syndrome. For example, if a fringe benefit is revised to the detriment of employees – perhaps an increase in employee contributions for health benefits – you're likely to be the recipient of employee dissatisfaction.

TIP: Don't waste time trying to defend the indefensible, which from an employee standpoint is anything that adversely affects their pay and benefits. Simply give the reasons for the change, and state that you will forward their concerns to top management.

In summary, you should expect to spend some time in fielding employee inquiries on administrative matters, and although at times it can be frustrating during a busy day, it's not entirely wasted effort. Over the long-term, loyalty and esteem are generated when your subordinates know that you don't give their concerns short shrift.

1.11 HOW TO HANDLE EMPLOYEE CONFLICTS

One of the minor irritants of a supervisor's job is preserving harmony when subordinates don't get along with each other.

Q: Two of the people in my unit are constantly bickering. How can I intervene without alienating either one?

A: Unless the individuals involved are interfering with the smooth functioning of the department, you shouldn't get involved at all. However, if they are, then it's wise to proceed with caution, since dealing with disruptive behavior is always difficult. First of all, look for an underlying cause. It may be that boredom is being translated into bickering, or maybe a misunderstanding over workload has started a feud.

In any event, after discreetly gathering any background information, sit down with both employees and explain that their behavior is having an adverse impact on other people. Ask if there's anything you can do to help, but avoid getting drawn into the debate. The important point is to emphasize that the work place isn't the proper forum for their quarreling. Usually, just the fact that you've dealt directly with the matter will calm things down.

On the other hand, you may discover that the problem centers around some aspect of their jobs. If that's the main thrust of their disagreement, attempt to work out a solution to the problem. Of course, this may turn out to be only a temporary expedient, especially if the real reason for their arguing is simply the fact that they don't like each other very much.

If your initial attempt to control their animosity isn't successful, then eventually you may have to take more drastic action. If it's feasible, reassign them so they aren't in a position to confront each other as often. This might mean transferring someone to another department, but the inconvenience of this will be offset by the restoration of harmony within your own group.

Ultimately, behavior that disrupts the work place must be controlled. In extreme cases, that may mean terminating one or more of the perpetrators if all other approaches fail to resolve the problem. Fortunately, most of the time when you let it be known that disruptive behavior won't be tolerated, the situation usually quiets down.

1.12 THE BEST METHOD FOR DEALING WITH CLIQUES AT WORK

People at work tend to socialize in small groups or cliques. This is insignificant, in and of itself, but it can lead to difficulties under certain circumstances.

Q: I have people working for me who belong to cliques. Can anything be done to keep this from interfering with the teamwork of the group?

A: Every day at work the same groups of people gather to have coffee, eat lunch, and exchange workplace gossip. It's only natural that folks socialize at work with those whose company they enjoy. However, sometimes these groups evolve into rigid cliques based either on outside interests or job status at work.

Managers tend to view cliques as detrimental to the concept of teamwork. Cliques are assumed to be – and sometimes are – groups with informal objectives of their own which conflict with management's theory of the common good. Furthermore, supervisors sometimes believe that a work clique is undermining their authority. Infrequently, the resentment of cliques merely results from a feeling of isolation, by virtue of being in a supervisory position.

On the other hand, unless there's excessive gossiping at the water cooler, extended lunch hours, or other actual interference with job performance, there's little that you can or should do about cliques. Building teamwork is a gradual process that involves trust, feedback, and good communication. Eventually this process will develop teamwork, with or without the existence of cliques within your group.

The only real problem to directly avoid is in joining one of these groups at coffee breaks and lunch on a regular basis. This can generate resentment on the part of other workers. Of course, this doesn't mean that you should be known as a sullen shrew with rolled-up shirtsleeves. However, instead of becoming a cohort of a clique, exercise your independence and be friendly with everyone. After all, the people you work with are associates by necessity; not by choice. And if you think about it, good friends are generally developed at the retail level – one at a time – and not wholesale in the form of a group. The only real group plan bargains at work are in your fringe benefit package.

1.13 WHAT TO DO WHEN YOU ARE BYPASSED BY SUBORDINATES

It's upsetting to be ignored by someone, and even more so when you're their supervisor. This often happens, especially when you're a newly assigned supervisor.

Q: Mary is going directly to Arthur, my boss, when she has problems. What, if anything, should I do?

A: This is a pretty frequent problem, especially when the next level of management is accessible, and/or doesn't discourage people from doing this. Once it's apparent that this is happening, talk to your boss. He should discourage Mary from doing this by telling her to see you the next time she approaches him with a question.

It's important to nip this bypassing problem in the bud, because it can spread like wildfire. If it does, you'll be a supervisor in name only. Then, anytime someone wants an answer, they'll seek the forum where they can get the best result to suit their purposes. If you think about it, this isn't very different from the way children try to play one parent against the other to get what they want.

Actually, when a new supervisor is appointed, the next level of management should introduce the person to the group as their new boss. However, this doesn't always happen, especially in a close knit environment where everyone knows everyone else. What's overlooked, however, when this formality is neglected, is that the purpose of introducing a new supervisor goes beyond letting employees meet their new boss. An introduction also sends a signal to employees that management has vested you with the duties and responsibilities of that position. When that's done, there's less of an excuse for someone to make an end run around you.

Q: How should I approach my boss when someone is bypassing me?

A: Something like "Arthur, Mary seems to be approaching you with problems, rather than coming to me. I thought I'd mention it to you before I say anything to Mary."

The ball is now in Arthur's court. The net result – no pun intended – should evoke a general response that takes one of two forms: (a) Arthur says he'll refer Mary to you if she goes to him again, or (b) He says it's no problem, and not to worry about it. If you get the latter reply, don't accept Arthur's assurances. Worry! It's then obvious that Arthur is either insensitive to the problem and/or incompetent, but in any event, he's of no help.

Therefore, talk to Mary directly, and suggest nicely – but firmly – that you want her to come directly to you on job problems. Unless she's a real troublemaker, she should fall in line. Even if she gets a little huffy when you tell her, keep your cool. You've just discovered one of the reasons they're paying you to be a supervisor.

1.14 WHY FOLLOWING UP ON ASSIGNMENTS IS CRUCIAL

Once tasks are assigned, there's an assumption that they will be completed – both satisfactorily and on time. However, that assumption is unlikely to become reality without periodic follow-up to make sure that subordinates aren't experiencing difficulties.

Q: How closely should I follow-up to make sure employees are completing assignments as instructed? I don't want to hover over people, but I also don't want anything to go wrong.

A: This is a common quandary that supervisors face. How closely you follow-up depends upon several variables. These are

- the nature of the task
- the importance of the task
- the abilities of individual employees
- your own personality
- your workload
- outside influences.

Let's look at these points one-by-one:

The Nature of the Task

The type of task you have assigned may be routine and repetitive, or it may be unusual and complex. This, in and of itself, is a prime consideration in determining how closely you should monitor a subordinate's performance. Ordinarily, conventional assignments need only minimal monitoring.

The Importance of the Task

The degree of follow-up is also influenced by the relative importance of the task in the general scheme of things. Consequently, you might have an employee working on a routine job that can be performed with a minimum of supervision. However, because of some other factor, the task can take on added importance. For example, perhaps work in other areas is dependent upon completion of this job. Here then, even though the task is simple enough, you might want to follow-up more closely to see that it stays on schedule.

The Abilities of Individual Employees

The capabilities of the individual employee also dictate the level of follow-up required. There are people who unfailingly complete assigned tasks on time, while others need a little prodding to keep them moving along. Of course, the longer people have worked for you, the easier this is to evaluate.

Your Own Personality

The amount of follow-up performed also depends upon your own personality. This is a function of your particular management style which was discussed in Secs. 1.7 and 1.8. However, if you're inclined to get intensely involved in what's going on, try to do so without being obvious.

Your Workload

Hands-on supervision often suffers when supervisors are overloaded with work. Care should be taken not to neglect follow-up during such periods. In fact, when you're busy with other chores – extended meetings, special assignments, and so on – it's more important than ever to at least make your presence known. That's because less conscientious workers may take advantage of the fact that you're occupied elsewhere to do a little goofing off.

Outside Influence

Considerations other than those within your own department often require a greater degree of follow-up than would normally occur. For example, perhaps top management wants production accelerated. Even more mundane reasons, such as closer scrutiny by your immediate boss can warrant keeping a careful watch on things to insure that everything keeps moving smoothly.

In summary, all of the above factors will affect the way you follow-up on assigned tasks within your department. Incidentally, another aspect of follow-up involves matters outside of your immediate department. The amount of this activity will vary according to the specifics of your job. However, the uncertainties and hectic pace of your regular duties make it imperative that you note on your calendar, or in some form of tickler file, any outside activity that requires follow-up.

Memory just doesn't work, since it's too easy to get your thoughts derailed by the crisis of the moment. Therefore, jot it down somewhere, and that way you won't be the one getting the phone call who has to say, "Oh! I forgot about that meeting."

1.15 A SURE-FIRE WAY TO FOLLOW-UP WITHOUT GETTING FLACK

Q: How do I follow-up with workers without offending them?

A: Follow-up as casually as possible – particularly with those workers who require minimal supervision. Try to personalize your approach by saying things like, "Hey, Bob! How about those Red Sox last night. Everything ok with the Winex account?"

HINT: Personalizing your approach by talking about someone's favorite subject – baseball team, golf, tennis, children – downplays the follow-up aspect. It also has the additional benefit of showing concern for the employee as a person apart from the job. This helps build the type of loyalty that's needed to foster teamwork.

1.16 TESTED TIPS FOR GETTING RID OF TIME WASTERS

You can't save time, since it just keeps rolling along. However, you can use the available hours more effectively by eliminating time wasters, and this will allow you to give more attention to higher priority tasks.

Q: No matter how hard I work everything continues to pile-up. It seems I'm constantly under pressure. Are there any time-saving techniques I can use to get things under control?

A: There are all kinds of time management schemes offered as the solution for better use of your time. Many of these involve elaborate ways to budget the time you spend on certain tasks. However, if you've ever tried any of these approaches, you may have found them to be impractical. That's because your job can't be separated into neat little blocks – with so much time for this and so much time for that. If you've experiencing time pressures, what you really have to do is not budget time, but cut back and/or eliminate time wasters that clutter up the workday.

But before doing anything, first decide if you're really under time pressures that are preventing you from being an effective supervisor. It may well be that you're busy – but productive – and the desire for more time is only the natural wish of a hard working supervisor. The more detail oriented you are, the greater this yearning is likely to be and in some cases, time pressures can be self-imposed. To overcome this tendency requires a personal adjustment in attitudes, as well as recognizing that you're doing your best without worrying about what comes next.

Aside from personal pressures, people and paperwork are the main culprits that have to be controlled to make more effective use of your time. First of all, let's look at the "people" aspect of the problem.

Just as there are people who sail through the workday with a minimum of supervision, there are others who thrive on hand holding. It's the latter group who consumes most of your time. Of course, it's necessary to assist those who are having genuine difficulty and to monitor laggards.

However, to a large extent, some folks – consciously or subconsciously – shift their work to you. "No way, you say!" Maybe not, but on the other hand you may be an unwitting victim. For example, suppose a subordinate – let's call him Bill – interrupts you on your way to a meeting and says, "We're running low on widgets. What do you want to do?" If you reply, "I'll look into it and get back to you Bill," what has actually happened? Bill's off the hook and the job of digging up more widgets is now yours.

Naturally, in many instances a subordinate isn't in a position to resolve a problem. In these cases, it's entirely appropriate for them to refer the matter to you for resolution. However, often employees pass the buck to their supervisors when they could just as easily do what needs to be done themselves. This only has to happen once or twice a week for you to be spending an appreciable chuck of time doing work more properly done by subordinates.

How can you combat this tendency to assume the workload of subordinates? Actually, just being aware of this possibility is the best deterrent. That's because the best chance of it happening is when you're busy on something else. Therefore, when a worker approaches you with a problem, there's a natural tendency to be helpful which leaves you saying, "I'll get back to you."

Instead of this, always phase your response in a way that leaves the next step to be taken with the worker. For example, say "See what you can do about it." Or if it's apparent that the employee can't resolve the problem tell him to, "Look into this and get back to me with your recommendations." This forces the employee to do the preliminary work that's required before any action can be taken.

By doing this, you can cut back on the time you spend doing unnecessary work. Of course, it also reverses a practice where subordinates are in effect assigning work to you, rather than the other way around.

1.17 THE SIMPLE SECRET THAT SHUTS UP CHATTERBOXES

Q: I've got a guy who's a good worker, but he's a motor mouth and it drives me crazy. Is there an easy way to deal with this?

A: A chatterbox is often a real time waster. They'll consistently interrupt you when you're busy with something else. Even though this irritates you, there can be a hesitancy toward bluntly telling the person not to bother you when you're busy. However, suffering in silence doesn't get your work done. What to do? Simple. Assign persistent pests projects when they bother you needlessly. It's amazing how effective this tactic can be in curing the culprit.

1.18 HOW TO CONQUER YOUR PAPERWORK BURDEN

Q: I'm pretty good about using my time effectively, but the piles of paper I have to deal with leave me working late several days a week. Is there anything I can do about this?

A: Along with people, paperwork is a time consuming pitfall if it's not handled properly. One concept that frequently overwhelms people is the philosophy of "leave clean, start clean." This is the overplayed notion that you should clean up your paperwork burden by the end of every day, so you start fresh the next day with an empty in-basket.

On the surface that seems like a sensible thing to do. In fact, you've probably seen dozens of tips on how to get everything done. However, there's an assumption made in these recommendations, which is valid in theory but not in the real world. That assumption is that every piece of paper you receive should be read. After all, so the theory goes, if it wasn't important it wouldn't be sent to you.

The cold, hard truth is that there's a lot of useless paper generated that should never have seen the light of day. In addition to this, paperwork that does have a useful purpose is often sent to an extended list of people who shouldn't receive it. A partial list of reasons for these paperwork foul-ups would include:

- Distribution lists aren't carefully checked to make sure only those with a need for the documentation receive it.
- Some people arbitrarily use a "cover all the bases" strategy and send memos to everyone.
- People and/or departments justify their jobs by pushing out paper.
- No one culls lists of periodic reports and directives to determine which reports may no longer be needed.

All of this means that an overflowing in-basket may indicate that you're a victim of one or more of these practices. If so, the first thing to do is to weed out what you don't have to read at all. The best way to do this is to sort the paperwork you get into groups. Try to do this at a set time every day. Incidentally, if you generally arrive early for work, that's a good time to tackle your in-basket without interruption.

Quickly scan your paperwork and sort it into piles. You can vary how you do this to meet the particular requirements of your job. But in general, the following grouping is useful:

1. Priority items. Those action items that must be attended to right away.
2. Non priority action items. Documentation that requires some action, but not on an immediate basis.
3. Read and forward. Informational matter accompanied by a routing slip, which requires sign-off and forwarding to the next person on the list.
4. Read and retain. Usually generalized information for future reference which requires no action on your part.
5. Useless. Anything that shouldn't have been sent to you in the first place.

If you sort your paperwork in this, or similar fashion, you'll have a system that will cut back considerably on the amount of time you spend on paperwork. Actually, only categories (1) and (2) require a complete reading. Much of the category (3) "read and forward" material can be quickly scanned. The category (4) "read and retain" information can be put aside and read when more important business isn't pending.

The useless paperwork could conceivably be deposited in the trash can. Although, if you're reluctant to do that, toss it into an empty drawer. That way, you're safe in the knowledge that you have it in the unlikely event that you ever have to pull it out and read it.

2

How to Master Commonsense Communication

Your responsibilities as a supervisor can be far less troublesome if you make an effort to improve your communication skills. Doing this can help in identifying problems and reaching decisions, which can go a long way toward earning you recognition from superiors and respect from subordinates.

Communicating effectively will also allow you to combat rumors, control interruptions, and keep your people fully informed. However, expressing yourself effectively is only one side of the coin for a good communicator. The flip side is learning how to listen to people – a task that isn't always enjoyable.

2.1 THE PRACTICAL APPROACH TO PROBLEM SOLVING

Solving problems isn't easy, especially when they are thrust upon you without warning and require immediate resolution. As a supervisor, the range of problems can be both diverse and complex, or seemingly simple, yet difficult to resolve. Therefore, each and every problem has to be dealt with effectively in order to keep things running smoothly.

Q: Is there a certain technique that can be used to solve problems?

A: There are no set rules for solving problems, but in deciding what to do about a problem, it usually helps to answer these questions:

- What is the problem?
- Who and/or what is causing the problem?
- What are the choices available to resolve the problem?
- Who can resolve these problems?

Let's look at each of these steps more closely.

What Is the Problem?

It's sometimes easy to overlook the real problem and this can cause you to come up with the wrong solution. For example, suppose someone – let's call him Herb – is showing a noticeable decline in output. Arthur, his supervisor, has also noticed that Herb has been late for work recently. "Ah ha!" Arthur thinks, "If Herb came in on time, he'd be able to get his work done."

A seemingly simple problem (falling productivity), an obvious cause (tardiness), and an easy solution (tell Herb to start getting to work on time). Therefore, Arthur does just that, but lo and behold, although Herb's tardiness is cured, his productivity is still subpar.

Two weeks later – before Arthur figures out what to do next – Herb, who used to be an excellent worker, quits to go to work someplace else. The bad news is that Arthur needs to replace a worker. Arthur thinks the good news is that he's solved the headache over Herb's productivity.

Let's look at what Herb knows and Arthur doesn't. Herb was late for a couple of weeks because his wife was in the hospital, and Herb had to get the kids off to school in the morning. However, he had been making up the time by either skipping breaks and/or working through lunch. Sure, he should have discussed this with Arthur, but he didn't for two reasons.

1. The first day he was late, Herb phoned and Arthur was at a meeting, so Herb told a co-worker that he would be late

for the next few days. Unfortunately, the co-worker never gave the message to Arthur.

2. Herb was too mad to say anything when Arthur finally reprimanded him for being late. Herb also knew that his production was down because Jack – who performed a preliminary process on the units before Herb worked on them – was making too many mistakes. This was requiring Herb to correct these defects before doing his own job. Herb didn't tell Arthur this because, (a) he didn't want to get someone else in trouble, and (b) he was unhappy about being chewed out by Arthur.

As a result, what seemed to be the problem (Herb's productivity) wasn't the problem at all. Actually, it was Jack's inattention to quality that should have been dealt with. What went wrong? Arthur, the supervisor, jumped to a hasty conclusion without getting the facts.

It's easy to think that a problem such as this isn't likely to happen. After all, if Arthur had been supervising more effectively, and/or the co-worker didn't forget Herb's message, and/or Herb told Arthur about his problems, then things might have worked out differently. Unfortunately, unexpected and unexplained events such as this constantly cause problems, and that's why common sense day-to-day communication is so important.

CAUTION: Never assume that you have a particular problem based on appearances. Get all of the facts that might bear on the situation. Then, and only then, can you make a sound judgment about your problem.

What Is Causing the Problem?

After you have a handle on a problem, be sure you understand what is causing it. This avoids disastrous results such as what happened with Herb. You may find that in some cases there are multiple factors contributing to the problem.

Choosing a Solution for the Problem

Once you identify the problem, and the cause or causes, the next step is to decide what to do about the problem. Often, there are a number of alternatives available. Depending upon the nature of the problem, a decision on a course of action can affect anything from costs to morale. Therefore, always be sure to assess the impact of alternative solutions before making any decision.

Who Should Resolve the Problem?

Resolving a particular problem may not be within your power because of its nature. Under these circumstances, all you can do is alert the person with the authority to act, and identify the problem, the causes, and alternative solutions. You may also want to recommend a particular course of action based on your knowledge of the facts. However, when doing this, make certain you're not going to be seen as butting into someone else's business, since some people resent unsolicited suggestions.

 HINT: You can deal effectively with most problems by a adopting a "walk and talk" approach to problem solving. That's simply a shorthand way of remembering to get all of the facts when a problem arises, which means you have to discuss the situation with other people, both inside and outside your department.

 Q: This sounds silly, but how can I tell if a problem is really a problem?

 A: That may sound silly, but it isn't, and the answer may sound simple and it is. If you think you have a problem, or a subordinate approaches you with what they think is a problem, then accept the fact that there is one. It will remain a problem until the cause is identified and a solution implemented.

 It's easy to get bogged down in theory and semantics in the business world – often to the exclusion of common sense. In practical terms, this often leads to "analysis paralysis." This can sometimes put you in a bind, particularly when you're dependent upon other departments and levels of management for cooperation in resolving problems. In short, anytime you think you have a problem, treat it as such, and don't waste time trying to decide whether it's fish or fowl. To your misfortune, you will have to deal with other people spinning their wheels doing just that.

In fact, the biggest hurdle some people face in solving problems is worrying too much about the end result. As long as you get the facts (unlike Arthur) don't be afraid to act. One in a while you may make a poor decision, but these can be readily reversed.

Q: Is there anything in particular to avoid when solving problems?

A: Primarily the extremes of acting impulsively as in the Arthur/ Herb case, or failing to act in the hope that a problem will go away.

2.2 HOW TO DECIDE WHAT THE REAL PROBLEM IS

Sometimes a problem is brought to a supervisor's attention and the more the problem is looked into, the more complicated it becomes to pin down the cause. People trying to duck responsibility for mistakes are common contributors to this type of dilemma. Some folks can be pretty clever at erecting smoke screens that prevent you from getting at the facts.

Q: On more than one occasion I've been led on a wild goose chase while trying to get to the bottom of a problem. Can anything be done to avoid this?

A: The best prevention for this type of situation is to develop a good working relationship with subordinates. To do this successfully, it's important to have a constructive rather than a critical attitude when an employee makes a mistake. As you know, this is easier said than done. After all, when someone makes an error that fouls things up, it's natural to get irritated.

However, if a supervisor gets emotional, acts accusatory, and in general makes an employee feel stupid when an error is made, a message is sent. The message workers receive is that, (a) mistakes shouldn't be made, and (b) if they are, the worker is going to be embarrassed by his supervisor. This approach has inevitable consequences, none of which are good.

First of all, employees may slow the pace down to minimize the chances of making errors. What this does to productivity is obvious. Eventually, the supervisor will notice the slackening in output, pressure will be applied to speed things up, and errors will increase again.

However, not wanting to be humiliated when mistakes are discovered, employees will not have answers when the boss starts berating them. They'll come up with ingenious excuses to pin the blame somewhere else. This leaves the supervisor scurrying about trying to solve a problem, without being able to pinpoint what is wrong.

The best way to handle mistakes is to reassure workers when something goes wrong. Let them know that mistakes are inevitable and that you don't hold them responsible. Put a positive spin on the error. Most people feel bad about making blunders, so reassurance will relieve their anxiety and encourage them to be honest about what's causing the mistakes. With this type of strategy, it's a lot easier to work out solutions to problems.

Incidentally, this method of sowing the seeds for two-way communication is a general one to be used on a continuing basis. However, it only gets you to the point of fact finding when problems arise. The solutions will vary according to what you discover. For example, it you find someone making repetitive mistakes because of a bad attitude, it's certainly not sufficient to reassure the worker and let it go at that.

NOTE: Dealing with difficult people in specific situations is covered in Chap. 3.

2.3 WHEN TO DO NOTHING ABOUT PROBLEMS

Although it's common for people to avoid problems in the hope that they will disappear, that's generally wishful thinking. Therefore, as a general rule, problems should be identified and dealt with. However, sometimes there are reasons for not doing anything about a problem.

Q: One of the people I supervise isn't performing too well lately. A co-worker told me in confidence that the person is going through a divorce proceeding which has her upset. Should I say something to her about her work in view of her personal difficulties?

A: Occasionally, as in this instance, you might receive information that leads you to believe a problem will resolve itself. Virtually everyone experiences personal problems that might temporarily affect their work for a short period of time. Some people will let you know what's bothering them, while others won't.

In this particular case, you might want to wait a few days to see if the problem resolves itself. If it doesn't, you will have will have to speak with the employee about her performance, but don't mention the person's pending divorce, since that is a private matter. However, if the employee volunteers the information about a personal problem, be as supportive as you can in assisting the person to work through the problem.

Anytime a supervisor becomes aware of personal problems that are interfering with job performance, there's an inevitable conflict between sympathy for the individual and concern about job performance. Many of these predicaments work themselves out without any necessity for the supervisor to intervene. However, if you must take action on a matter of this nature, do it based on the facts of the particular problem including

- the nature of the personal difficulty
- the extent of the employee's subpar performance
- the length of time the employee's performance has been affected by the problem
- the impact on other workers and the department as a whole

The key point here is to maintain a proper balance between empathy for the individual and the demands of the job.

Another type of hassle where no immediate action may be necessary is when a problem calls for temporary avoidance. Under certain circumstances, some problems are best dealt with after the passage of a period of time. A common case in point is when an employee simmers over a work-related incident. Often, rather than continuing a heated discussion, it's better to wait a day or two until the employee cools down.

WARNING: There's a distinct difference between temporarily avoiding a problem because it's more effective to handle it later and avoiding problems so as not to have to deal with them at all. Since problem avoidance can become a convenient habit, use it only when you're convinced it's the best answer. Otherwise, you will develop a reputation for being indecisive.

2.4 THE NECESSARY STEPS FOR MAKING THE BEST DECISION

Decision making is basically thinking through what you're going to do about a problem. Of course, many decisions are routine and you simply have to follow company policies and procedures, for example, approval of sick leave and vacations.

When you must deal with complex problems, the following steps are helpful in making decisions.

1. Explore your options. There are usually many choices available to solve a problem. The more you think about it, the greater the possibilities are likely to be. Discussions with subordinates, other supervisors, your boss, various staff functions and common sense all play a role when you're exploring alternatives. This fact gathering should include the pros and cons of alternative decisions including ease of implementation, costs, the effect on others – subordinates, other departments, and so forth.

2. Estimate the risk involved in a decision. This includes thinking about how certain you are that a particular decision will have the desired result. How much thought

you give to any one decision will depend upon how important it is in terms of its potential impact.

3. Determine how you will implement the decision. How you go about implementing a decision can be just as important as arriving at the decision. In fact, a good decision can backfire if it's not handled properly. Therefore, it's important to clearly communicate your decision to everyone who will be involved in implementing it.

4. When you do this, it's helpful to explain why the decision was made. This is especially true when a decision changes the way things are being done on the shop floor, in the office, or elsewhere. The old dictatorial answer to the question, "Why are we doing this?" which is "Because I said so," can quickly turn a good decision into a bad one. Why? Because a lack of cooperation from your subordinates can prevent successful implementation.

Although telling employees why a decision is being made won't always be met with yelps of joy, knowing why something is being done can lead to cooperation and understanding. That alone can carry the day in getting the decision implemented. Of course, some decisions will require follow-up to make sure they are being implemented properly. (See Secs. 1.14, 1.15 in Chap. 1.)

SUGGESTION: In making decisions, always ask yourself, "What do I need to know in order to make a decision on this matter?"

2.5 EFFECTIVE METHODS FOR KEEPING EMPLOYEES INFORMED

The information flow at work is a two-way street. First of all, you have a responsibility to keep subordinates informed. Likewise, they have an equivalent duty to advise you of work-related problems. In addition, you should communicate effectively with your boss and upper levels of management – starting with your boss – should relay information top to bottom in a timely in a timely manner. A failure to furnish information by any of these parties breaks the chain of effective communication. This can result in everything from botched work to bizarre rumors.

Q: I supervise five people. Is this too small a group to hold weekly meetings?

A: Neither the number of people you supervise, nor the frequency of meetings is of great consequence. What does matter is that you have a free and easy flow of dialogue within the group. The method you use will depend upon a number of variables, such as the quantity of information to be transmitted and the type of operation you supervise. You may want to experiment a bit to find out what works best in your circumstances. The essential requirement is to be sincere in your desire to encourage employees to discuss matters openly with you.

Regular meetings with your group are one way to encourage feedback. They don't have to be a formally scheduled event. A quick ten-minute once-a-week meeting might do it. On the other hand, regular meetings may not be practical. If that's true, then you can forego meetings on a regular basis. (Sects. 2.14 to 2.17 discuss meetings in greater detail.)

Q: The problem I have isn't in communicating with the people I supervise. It's getting Beth, my boss, to tell me what's going on. Frankly, I sometimes feel like a fool, since people in my department often get information that I'm not aware of through the grapevine. They then ask me about it, and I'm stuck with saying, "I don't know."

A: This is a common problem which may be the result of your boss not keeping you informed, either through her own failure, or because she just isn't getting any information from her own boss. Many managers fail to pass the work on to lower levels of management. The reasons are varied, but include

- Insecure bosses who think that withholding information gives them job security. They operate on the assumption that if everyone knows what they know, they won't be needed.

- Some managers place a strict "need to know" interpretation on information. Obviously, everyone doesn't need to know everything that's going on, however, a manager who draws too fine a line leaves people in the dark about matters that concern them.
- There are managers who place a very low priority on keeping people informed. This is more prevalent in companies where top management doesn't encourage open lines of communication.
- Some folks are just poor communicators and consequently aren't good at identifying information that should be passed on to the next lower level in the company.

If you're not getting sufficient information from your boss, sit down with her and discuss this problem. Raise the issue in the context that a lack of information is hampering productivity and damaging morale. However, don't be accusatory. In fact, you may want to infer that the information isn't coming down from topside to you and your boss. (This may or may not be true.) Let's try a trial run between Carol, the supervisor, and Beth, her boss.

Carol: "Beth can you help me out? The past few months I've been spending a lot of time knocking down rumors about everything from layoffs to adding a second shift. Morale is pretty low. Management may have good reasons for keeping us in the dark, but I'm afraid it's going to start affecting productivity. Can you find anything out?"

Beth may respond in several ways.

1. "Aw, your people are just crybabies. There's nothing they need to know that they don't know already."
2. "Gee, Carol, I didn't realize that. I'll see what I can do."

3. "I know your problem Carol, but I'm just as uninformed as you are. Management just doesn't see the need for better communication."

Response (1) indicates that Beth may, or may not, be the bottleneck, but she certainly doesn't believe in keeping people informed. Her reply in (2) may mean that she is sincere and will attempt to open up the communication pipeline. Conversely, she may be faking it because she is the bottleneck. If it's the latter, she may start passing things on now that you have confronted her. In (3) she's also either covering up for herself, or honestly admitting that it's a company problem over which she has no control.

Assuming you can't get information from your boss – even after raising the issue as Carol did – then you can still keep posted on what's going on by networking within the company. Cultivate other knowledgeable sources to get the information you need to keep both yourself and your subordinates informed.

Q: I'm from the old school that says people are getting paid for doing their work, and all they need to know is how to do their job. Why should I waste time trying to be a great communicator?

A: First of all, establishing good lines of communication is time well spent. In fact it can be a time saver for a supervisor in the long run. Keeping people informed builds both trust and teamwork. It also improves morale, can reduce labor turnover, and increase productivity.

But you can look at it in a much more basic way. Take it out of the work context and think about it from a personal angle. Do you expect your friends to be open and honest with you? If they treat you as inferior, do you still want to maintain the friendship? Who will you go to bat for when crunch times rolls around? Will it be someone who doesn't level with you?

Sure, employees are paid for working, but don't forget that they can also get paid for working someplace else where they'll be treated with more respect. Even those employees who hang on because of seniority, or simply convenience, won't be motivated to do any more work than they have to. The fact is that good communications are just as important in maintaining a productive work force as they are in preserving a solid marriage.

2.6 A COMMONSENSE WAY TO COMBAT THE RUMOR MILL

The quickest way to promote a gathering around the water cooler is to start a rumor. Therefore, it's a distinct advantage to keep the rumor mill as quiet as possible.

Q: My people spend more time discussing rumors than working. How can I overcome this?

A: The two main conditions under which rumors flourish are (1) where the company doesn't keep people informed and, (2) when you have an employee who delights in starting rumors.

In either case, the best rumor control technique is to keep the dialogue flowing within your department, both on a group and individual basis. If you do this, you'll quickly be a party to the latest rumblings, and when you hear a rumor, knock it down fast to limit the scuttlebutt.

By keeping yourself well-informed and accessible, employees will see you as the source for sorting out fact and fiction. That, in itself, will minimize the birth of rumors within your department.

2.7 THE NEED TO CONTROL YOUR TEMPER

Anger begets anger, and/or silent resentment and bitterness which can devastate the workplace. The simple truth is that people don't respond well to a nasty boss. Therefore, a supervisor who maintains control by fear is doomed to eventual failure.

Q: I have a tendency to yell at people and no one seems to mind within my unit, but my boss recently told me to tone it down. Who's right?

A: Your boss. On the surface, a supervisor may not get any feedback about berating people and in general displaying a bad temper. However, just because subordinates don't respond directly doesn't mean they either like, or accept, being treated that way.

It's easy to forget that as a supervisor you have a great deal of power over the fate of subordinates. Their jobs, performance evaluations, pay raises, and promotional opportunities are all under your influence. Even when they actively search for employment elsewhere, they're ever mindful of the need for a good reference. To put it bluntly, they could hate your guts without you ever knowing it.

Your supervisory authority brings with it a responsibility to treat employees with decency and respect. It's not always easy to control your temper, but maintaining control of your emotions allows you to handle things on an intellectual, rather than an emotional basis.

2.8 WHEN IT PAYS TO GET GROUCHY

Although control of your temper is critical to your success, not only with subordinates, but also with anyone else you interact with at work, there are occasions when you should register your disapproval in strong terms.

Q: I've got a problem with the supervisor of another department who always responds to any type of request by being loud and nasty. I can't ignore him, since my department relies on his technical support. Is there a reasonable way to deal with this sort of mayhem?

A: Everyone faces predicaments where they "bite their tongue" rather than speak out. Controlling your emotions in these circumstances is generally an admirable trait, but some people at work will always try to kick sand in your face. Therefore, on occasion, you'll have to redline your emotional tachometer and let it all hang out. In fact, feigned anger is often used as a technique by skilled negotiators. Let's look at how and when displeasure should be expressed so as to work to your advantage.

First of all, success in solving disagreements requires an awareness of why there's a misunderstanding in the first place. The real cause may not be readily apparent, even though you may be convinced that it's purely the result of the other person being obnoxious.

Analyzing the cause of someone's anger is important in determining your course of action. If you've been the victim of misdirected anger, a cooling off period of a day or two ought to get things back on course. However, if the hostility was just a tactic, then you'll have to counter with some shrewd strategy of your own.

Anger resulting from an out and out personality conflict requires a still different approach. Maintain your self-control, and if possible support your argument with information from objective sources. This helps diffuse anger by lessening the "me vs. you" competitive aspect. Stick to the issues and avoid getting drawn into a shouting match. Whatever the circumstances, if you just fly off the handle, you're a sore loser.

Once you understand the cause of the other person's anger, think about the best way to handle it.

- Are you communicating properly about the subject matter of the dispute?
- Does the other person fully understand your position?
- Are you or the other person letting emotions control the discussion?

Let's go back to the supervisor in the question who is being unreasonable despite earnest attempts to reach agreement. Should you get angry? Yes and no. You may be reaching the boiling point, but losing control won't win, since any angry outburst won't solve anything.

However, if you've been reasonable to no avail, you don't have to continue to suffer in silence. The trick is to keep your emotions in check, while outwardly appearing to be upset. When you do this, avoid bringing personalities into the discussion, and simply stick to the facts of the subject in dispute.

Raising your voice and becoming more assertive is likely to have one of two probable reactions. The most likely is that the other party will back off. Why? Perhaps they were just faking it to gain the upper hand, or maybe they were simply trying to bully you into submission. When they see you're not intimidated, they'll realize their strategy isn't working. Since they then have nothing further to gain by remaining angry, you should then be able to résumé discussions aimed at a reasonable conclusion.

On the other hand, the person may get even madder, and sometimes they'll even storm away in a huff. Of course, if they don't break off the discussion, but start to engage in a shouting match, then you should quietly depart. However, don't despair if you fail to back a business bully down. After all, you only became aggressive after trying to be calm and rational in the face of hostility, and your alternative would have been capitulation.

In the final analysis, after you have tried everything in an attempt to be reasonable with surly people, you're basically stuck with three choices.

1. Work around them as much as possible.
2. Ignore their attitude when you must deal with them.
3. Let your boss know about the difficulty, especially if other people are experiencing the same problem.

2.9 FIVE TESTED TECHNIQUES TO CONTROL INTERRUPTIONS

One of the petty annoyances for every supervisor are the constant interruptions that occur on a daily basis. Although many of these are justified, others aren't, and mastering the art of limiting unnecessary interruptions within your department can increase efficiency and perhaps sooth your frazzled nerves. Basic techniques that can help include

1. Be alert for "gossip grazers" who wander into your department and distract workers from doing their job. Just as cows meander about in a pasture in search of grass to chew on, "gossip grazers" wander around a company looking to chew the fat. Just as farmers shoo the cows from where they don't belong, you should chase these malingerers out of your department. If you're dedicated in doing this, they'll soon learn to do their wandering in greener pastures.

2. You may have one or more people in your group who are social butterflies and tend to attract people to their area – from both within and outside your department. If it's a constant headache for you to break up these gatherings, you may want to relocate the culprits so they're within your sight, sound, and mind. (Also see Sect. 1.17 on assigning projects to pests.)

3. The layout of your working area may encourage interlopers. Water coolers and copiers are notorious for attracting crowds of chatterers. The flip side of the coin is that a remote area, hidden from view by machinery or partitions, attracts the folks who want to goof-off without being seen. Therefore, give some thought to practical changes that can lessen these problems. Frequently, the solution is as simple as taking down or putting up a partition.

4. If you're constantly victimized by interruptions when you have a deadline to meet – such as a weekly report for your boss – find yourself a "great escape" spot where you can complete deadline projects. It may be a conference room or just any empty desk in another department. But don't issue an "all points bulletin" as to where you'll be, since that just serves as an open invitation to be interrupted. To be on the safe side, you can let one person know where you are in the event that you must be contacted.

5. Use a "make them a messenger" approach. You can partially convert the negative aspect of interruptions into positive results by using pests as personal couriers. It's simple enough to do by saying something such as, "Hey Bob, do me a favor and drop this off in the mailroom on your way back." It not only edges the culprit along, but it also saves you, or one of your people, a trip.

2.10 WHY LISTENING IS THE KEY TO SUCCESS

The most effortless way to communicate is also the most underrated. Listening, whether it's to subordinates, your boss, or others, isn't generally given its due as a means of communicating. Yet, listening effectively allows you to pick up on the details of what's going on in your department. A willingness to listen to bad news as well as good lets you hear about problems that need solving.

Q: I've put my foot in my mouth a couple of times lately. I try to be a good listener, but I've had people tell me on more than one occasion that I've forgotten something they've said to me. My memory is good, so perhaps I'm not listening. Frankly, if listening is so important why can't it be taught? I had public speaking in school – not listening.

A: You can, of course, say the wrong thing for a lot of reasons, only one of which is a failure to listen attentively to what other people are saying. On the other hand, many more blunders are made by talking rather than listening. Even casual greetings can communicate greeter sincerity with silence instead of speech. For instance, a wave of the hand and a bright smile says, "Good morning," much better than the same words mechanically dispensed like candy from a vending machine.

So why don't we place more emphasis on listening? Because instinctively we've been taught from childhood that intelligence is demonstrated by speech rather than by silence. The subconscious commandment of communications that's instilled in us throughout life is, "The powerful talk, and the meek listen."

As a toddler, parents tell children, "Do this Fred," or "Don't do that Sarah," and children listen – even though parents might not always think so. As children go off to school, once again they're primarily listeners. Later on in life, as adults at work, the company president addresses employees at meetings and everyone listens – or at least that's the assumption. All of this listening to power figures throughout life conditions people to prefer being the talker than the listener.

The mechanics of listening are simple, so it's taken for granted that people listen when we talk. They likewise assume that we listen to them. To add to the problem, it's not easy to know whether someone is listening, or is just going through the motions. The end result is that two-way communication becomes a one-way street.

As a supervisor, becoming a good listener not only enables you to get the information you need to perform your duties, but it also encourages your subordinates to listen to you. All of which can mean fewer mistakes, greater harmony, and a better functioning unit.

2.11 HELPFUL HINTS FOR BECOMING A GOOD LISTENER

Effective listening requires undivided attention to the speaker. The main difficulty is that people tend to treat listening as casually as a side order of french fries ordered with a meal. However, listening, unlike the fries, is a main course in and of itself.

The following steps are keys to being a good listener. Try working on any that you feel you're weak on and can improve.

1. Don't make assumptions about the value of what someone has to say. For example, "Joe is a dud, so anything he has to say isn't important." Remember, no one is always right or wrong.
2. Listen with an open mind and don't draw conclusions while someone is talking.
3. Don't interrupt people in the middle of a thought.
4. Show that you're listening by eye contact, nodding, and an occasional "Yes" or "No."
5. Don't take the offensive just because you don't agree with what is being said. This is especially important with subordinates, because if you shoot them down in midstream, they'll avoid discussing things with you. As a result, you won't hear about problems at an early stage.
6. Everyone can't make their point quickly. So fight to keep from being bored when people ramble on endlessly.
7. Avoid distractions such as phone calls and paper shuffling. Give your complete attention to the speaker. In some circumstances (when an employee is angry) make sure that the location for the conversation is private.
8. Be certain that you understand what the person is saying. Ask questions if necessary.

9. When the person is finished speaking, summarize the position, but don't put words in his or her mouth. Close the conversation by giving an indication that the person wasn't talking to a brick wall. You don't have to agree or disagree with what was said, but at least let it be known you were listening.

HINT: Always keep in mind what someone doesn't say. For example, if a worker is promoting a cause that's to one's benefit, that person will pitch all of the advantages and conveniently leave out any negative aspects.

All in all, effective listening isn't difficult to master, but it does require some degree of self-restraint. Just remaining silent doesn't always suffice. For example, if your boss is telling you about his exploits on the golf course, look at him, nod your head periodically, and in general follow the tale of the bouncing ball. Keep in mind, that even though you may hate golf, being bored can be beneficial. After all, listening to the boss, and indicating your interest makes him feel good. Priming his ego can be rewarding, since he's the one who evaluates your performance. Besides, while you're following the travels of his golf ball, you're getting paid for it.

2.12 THE FOOLPROOF WAY TO GO ONE-ON-ONE WITH ANYONE

There's an inconsistency in business that finds technology expanding rapidly, while the practice of competent one-on-one communication continues in benign neglect. Meetings, memos, computer printouts, telephone calls, and the all too familiar second-hand edict such as, "Hey Ken, Phil said to...," are all used as substitutes for discussing things face-to-face. Therefore, if you sometimes feel like a potted plant, don't despair because you're not alone.

Although mastering the skills of one-on-one discussions isn't hard, the techniques you use will vary with different people. And the first group of people to improve communications with are those you supervise.

Q: I have someone in my section who intimidates me to the point I avoid talking to the person unless it's absolutely necessary. Even then, I get a knot in my stomach. It seems as if he's trying to prod me into blowing my top and making a fool of myself. How can I overcome this?

A: Once in a while – always more than you would like – you'll run into someone who persistently tests your tolerance. In some instances, you'll just have to accept the fact that there are a few people who are seldom pleasant. So as long as they do their job and follow directions – no matter how reluctantly – it's best to basically ignore their attitude.

On the other hand, it's sometimes possible to get through to this type of individual with good results by direct confrontation. The tactic is pretty much that used to back down a bully. Let's look at how this can be done.

Background

Martha, who works for a large service organization, is told that she is being promoted to a supervisory position in the accounting department. She has mixed emotions, since she will now be supervising Mike, who has a company-wide reputation for being miserable. He's also considerably older than Martha, is independently wealthy, and has the physical size to match his mouth. All in all, he's an intimidating individual.

Sure enough, shortly after the formal announcement of Martha's promotion, but a few days before she is scheduled to take over her new job, Mike confronts her in the hallway.

The Encounter

Mike:	"So you're going to be a big shot now?"
Martha:	"What do you mean?"
Mike:	"Aren't you taking over the 'B' group?"
Martha:	"Yes I am, and I think we'll make a good team."
Mike:	(in abrupt tone) "What makes you so smart?

	Why are you being promoted?"
Martha:	(replying in a firm tone of voice) "I was selected for the position by management. You'll have to ask them about that. All I know is that I intend to do my best and I'm sure I can count on you."
Mike:	smirks, says nothing, and walks away.

The Outcome

During her first two weeks as Mike's boss, he constantly brings Martha work-related problems. She answers his questions effectively each time, but notices that a certain pattern is developing. As Mike talks with her, he eventually switches the conversation to his children and his interest in gardening.

Martha listens attentively and shows a genuine interest in Mike's anecdotes. She also notices that his gruff attitude is slowing disappearing when talking with her; although not so with other people. Finally, several weeks later, Mike does something that convinces Martha that he's on her team. As she is sitting at her desk talking to another employee, someone from another department starts to interrupt when Mike sitting three desks away barks, "Can't you see she's busy?"

Martha, by being forthright and patient had discovered what prior supervisors hadn't noticed. Mike, a widower with two children living in a distant city, was essentially lonely. Martha, by doing a little listening soon discovered this fact, and turned what could have been an unpleasant association into a solid working relationship.

Obviously, face-to-face encounters will vary based on personalities, setting, and the subject matter under discussion. But you can establish a good track record in dealing with people by being forthright, sincere, and a good listener. Most important of all, make the effort to communicate on a one-to-one basis, rather than avoiding unpleasant issues, and/or by relaying messages through third parties.

2.13 PRACTICAL GUIDELINES FOR BEING PERSUASIVE

Persuading people isn't always easy, particularly if you're trying to convince them to perform an unpleasant task, or accept an unpopular decision. When we think of the ability to persuade others, it's often in the context of dynamic speakers who have a talent for selling anything to anyone. However, it's possible to be an effective persuader in your day-to-day activities without being a human dynamo.

Q: By nature, I'm a pretty quiet person. Does that mean I'm less persuasive than some of my more exuberant peers?

A: Just as with your car radio, clarity is more important than sheer volume. The fact that you're not outgoing doesn't mean you're less convincing. Being persuasive with folks on a regular basis depends upon skills that have nothing to do with a knack for tossing out funny one-liners. The most important guidelines to follow are

1. Clarity. For any message to be effective, it's most important for the other person to understand what you're saying. So always simplify what you say, especially when you're using technical terms or jargon that others may not know.
2. Consistency. How people view you over the long term will depend to a large extent upon your prior dealings with those people. If you're honest, keep promises, follow through on employee requests, and in general project a reliable image, your ability to persuade others will be enhanced.
3. Positive attitude. Always emphasize the positive aspects of anything, but be honest and don't try to sell someone a bag of hot air. Putting a false light on a subject may work once in a while, but over the long haul it will destroy your credibility.
4. Empathy. Be willing to look at things from the other person's viewpoint. If employees know that you'll listen

to the negatives from their point of view, then they'll more readily accept the fact that an unpleasant task has to be done.

2.14 TRIED AND TRUE WAYS TO CONDUCT EFFECTIVE MEETINGS

When you're responsible for conducting meetings, you will have to approach this duty from a different outlook than as a participant. While attendees can pick and choose their spots for speech or silence, leading a meeting requires constant control. Your primary task is to keep everyone working on the agenda to accomplish the purpose of the meeting.

Q: I really get nervous when I have to hold a meeting with my people. Is this natural?

A: Many people don't like to run meetings; however, stage fright can be overcome by a little thought and preparation. Perhaps you're insecure about your knowledge of the subject matter. If so, rest easy. Since you're running the meeting, you can control the proceedings and direct or deflect questions toward other attendees. This insecurity is senseless anyway, since most of the time you know more about the topic than anyone else.

There's a persistent myth in the working world that equates credentials with job knowledge. A well-educated manager is presumed to know more about a specific subject than the person doing the job. In actuality, the higher in management a person is, the less they know about specifics. Therefore, don't be gun-shy about demonstrating your knowledge at meetings or anywhere else. No one knows your job better than you.

TIP: Whenever you're arranging a meeting, even if it's just with one other person, try to schedule it in your office or some other location of your choosing. This alone will give you greater confidence and control.

Q: What's the best way to keep a meeting from wandering off-course?

A: A constant problem facing anyone chairing a meeting is keeping it on a steady course. It's hard enough in a one-on-one discussion to coax folks to get to the point, and with more people at a meeting, it becomes harder.

There's a natural inclination to invite anyone and everyone to meetings in an attempt to "cover all of the bases." This is wrong. For one thing, inviting people on the assumption the meeting may be of interest to them reveals a lack of preparation in thinking about: (1) Is a meeting really necessary? (2) What will it accomplish? and, (3) Who is essential to the meeting's success? This type of planning is rare, and as a result meetings often have too many people, saying too much, about too little.

The fallout from a lack of planning, not only includes botched meetings, but also unhappy people grumbling about wasting their time. If there are power people in attendance – including your boss – the finger points at you for being the guilty party who invited them. So remember, "the more the merrier" applies to parties – not meetings.

Q: How can I keep someone from dominating a meeting?

A: When you're leading meetings, don't let tedious talkers monopolize the conversation. Try to cut in with questions directed at someone else, and if you get a persistent dissenter who objects to everything, then suggest they put their thoughts in writing after the meeting. This accomplishes two things. It keeps the meeting moving, and it also discourages those who like to talk but contribute nothing.

2.15 THE GOLDEN RULE FOR GETTING YOUR POINT ACROSS AT MEETINGS

As a participant at meetings, there's nothing quite as frustrating as failing to get your ideas across to other attendees. However, timing is important, so just jumping in with your thoughts when someone pauses isn't wise. Often, it's not what you say, but when you say it that counts.

Q: Many times, my ideas get lost in the shuffle at meetings. I'm having trouble overcoming a couple of people who monopolize every meeting. Is there a way to outwit them?

A: Even when you're well versed on a meeting's agenda, don't participate too early for a couple of reasons. First of all, by holding back, all of the know-nothings will have their say and run out of gas, although one or two may continue to participate by running on a tank of hot air. This strategy makes it less likely that you'll be interrupted when you make your pitch. By the time you speak up, everyone will likely be ready for some sound ideas.

Another benefit of not participating too early is that you get an opportunity to listen to what everyone else has to say. If ideas different from your own are expressed, you can note the weak points in these positions and counter them when it's your turn to talk. Naturally, the right time to inject remarks at a meeting will depend on the ebb and flow of the conversation, the structure of the meeting, and your position with respect to the others in attendance. Needless to say, never make your boss look bad before a gathering, or you may prove that being right isn't always bright.

TIP: If you're going to a meeting on a subject that you know little about, be careful. If you must make any comments, make them early in the meeting before the focus and direction of the discussion takes shape. Later on, as a subject is discussed in greater depth, an attendee without detailed knowledge of a topic can look foolish.

2.16 WHY SOME MEETINGS ARE USELESS

One of the biggest time wasters of the business day is useless meetings. The major causes include

- meetings called without a clearly defined purpose ("Hey, Helen, what was that meeting about?")
- regularly scheduled meetings that continue to be held, even though the original basis for the meeting ceases to exist ("I know we don't manufacture gizmos anymore, but it's still worthwhile to have gizmo get together.")

- the meeting agenda that is not controlled and the discussion dissolves into inconsequential matters ("Can anyone tell me where I can get a good pastrami sandwich?")
- a key participant that isn't invited and/or doesn't show up ("Mr. Adams couldn't make it. He went out to lunch for a pastrami sandwich.")
- too many unnecessary attendees that make the meeting unwieldy ("This place looks like Mardi Gras in New Orleans.")
- an unsatisfactory meeting site. ("Can you believe it? It's 95 degrees in here, he's touting a hot product, and all I want is a cold beer.")

Q: How can I determine whether or not I should hold a meeting?

A: Before scheduling any meeting, decide whether or not a memo, phone call or personal discussions with other people might be more effective. Think about what you plan to accomplish, who should be invited, and where the meeting will be held. Try to roughly estimate the costs involved and the productive time that will be lost by attendees. Then, and only then, make your decision. You don't have to go through any extensive exercise in making these judgments for run-of-the-mill meetings. Usually, you can figure out the best method with a little thought.

Q: When I hold meetings, they often drag on longer than I had planned. Is there anything that can be done to prevent this?

A: If you're doing your best to keep meetings moving without too much success, you may want to try a timing trick. When possible, schedule your meetings before lunch and near the close of the workday. This discourages talkers who tend to drag out meetings. You'll also receive subtle support from attendees in the form of peer pressure on anyone who is delaying the wrap-up of the meeting.

2.17 HOW TO SKIP MEETINGS WITHOUT GETTING CRITICIZED

You may be in the unfortunate position of having to attend numerous meetings which are of little or no benefit to you. Often, this is just a minor irritant, while at other times it's a real burden which can interfere with getting your work done. Many people silently stew about this, since it can get a little dicey if you try to beg-off from these gatherings. However, there are ways to avoid meetings without suffering any adverse reaction from superiors.

Q: The cliché, "When in doubt, hold a meeting," is the unadvertised slogan at my company. How can I justify skipping some of these meetings so I can get some work done?

A: Getting out of a meeting on a one-shot basis isn't too much of a hassle. Any solid excuse about priority work should do it. The real trick is in being able to dodge meetings on a regular basis. The best way to do this is to convince your boss that (a) some aspect of your work is more important than attending regularly scheduled meetings, and (b) you have a capable substitute to fill-in for you.

Your boss is unlikely to buy a simple story about being too busy to attend meetings. After all, that's implying that you're too busy to go, but he isn't, and that's probably exactly what he'll think if you try that angle. What you really want to pitch is a temporary problem that requires your absence for a few weeks.

For example, perhaps you have two new hires who need constant supervision for a while. Actually, any solid excuse will do with a reasonable boss. You then delegate one of your people to take your place at the meeting. Now, if you're lucky, your replacement will become a permanent fixture at these events. That's because people get used to seeing the same faces at regular meetings, so hopefully, after a couple of weeks you won't even be missed.

At the worst, your boss may eventually remember your "temporary" substitute, and ask when you'll be back again. At that point, just string it out as long as you can without being obvious. When your luck finally runs out, start going to the meetings again until you can come up with another creative idea. Incidentally, if you're a creative genius, be patient and don't spring another reason for your absence for a couple of months. That gives your boss a chance to forget about the last time you begged-off.

Q: I'm afraid of getting knifed behind my back if I skip meetings, even when they are a waste of time. Does that make sense, or am I just being paranoid?

A: Actually, an absent person is very vulnerable if there's blame to be placed at a meeting. Therefore, unless a capable substitute is there to defend you, you're ill-advised to skip meetings just because they're boring. A better tactic is to take some work along to minimize your downtime.

In fact, even if a meeting is run efficiently, you'll have a few minutes to work while everyone is settling in before the meeting starts. Don't be obvious by carrying an armful of material with you. This may irritate the person chairing the meeting, and if they're thin-skinned, they'll think you don't place much importance on their meeting.

They may be right, but ego bruising doesn't pay. Therefore, just bring along a pad of paper that you'll need anyway, and stick a memo or letter that needs answering inside. You can work on it both before the meeting, and also while it's going-on if you do it so that it looks like you're taking notes. This apparent attentiveness may even impress whoever is chairing the meeting, while at the same time you're getting something constructive done.

2.18 SIMPLE STEPS TO AVOID WRITING MEMOS

One of the hardest tasks many supervisors encounter is writing answers to a steady stream of memos. The requests are often unreasonable, generally burdensome, and occasionally just don't make sense, and struggling to keep up with this workload can be a real chore.

Q: I think my boss is a robot programmed to say, "Send me a memo on that." All I seem to do is churn out memos. Is there a way around this? I can't simply say "No" to my boss.

A: The best way to deal with this problem is to reduce the opportunity for your boss to ask for a memo. Three major reasons bosses ask for memos are

- they don't understand what you're telling them.
- they're busy, so asking for something to be put in writing postpones having to deal with it.
- They feel more secure in seeing something on paper. There's a sense of finality to the written word that doesn't hold true for discussions. (Example: "I didn't say that." "Yes, you did. It's right here in the memo.")

The easy route to cutting down on your memo writing is to understand how your boss operates. If he habitually asks for memos, then it's wise to think about what triggers these requests. One or more of the following steps should help to reduce the number of memos you have to write.

1. Don't go to your boss with hard-to-explain dilemmas when he's busy. Catch him when he has time to talk.
2. Always present things as simply as possible. Think through what you're going to say before you see your boss.
3. Whenever possible, offer a solution. Otherwise, your boss has to think about how to deal with the problem which often results in asking for a memo.
4. If your boss is the type who relentlessly asks for memos, avoid bringing minor matters to his attention.
5. If you're being victimized by written requests, try to answer them with a phone call or personal meeting. Just because you get a written request doesn't mean it has to be answered in writing.

CAUTION: Be careful here to avoid getting booby-trapped by not documenting in writing your response to controversial subjects. It also is sensible to reply in writing when you're dealing with people you don't know well, and/or those with a reputation for memory lapse when it suits their purpose.

TIP: Although your boss will be the typical source requesting memos, the steps listed are equally effective for coping with anyone who is a persistent paper-pusher.

2.19 HOW TO HURDLE WRITTEN COMPLAINTS – FROM ANYONE

Written complaints are difficult to answer, since they cast problems in concrete which makes them much harder to finesse. This is one reason people put gripes in writing in the first place. They expect to force you to respond and, of course, you must. But that doesn't mean you have to either agree with them, or be on the defensive.

Q: Should written complaints be answered in writing?

A: Regrettably, in most instances, the answer is "Yes." However, the secret to success lies in how you respond. The best approach to put a written complaint to bed quickly is to get the facts fast. Then talk to the person who sent the complaint; preferably in person, but by phone if necessary.

In general, don't give a blow-by-blow account of what went wrong. Sympathize with the other party without necessarily agreeing with them. Reassure them that the situation won't be repeated. Then, sit down and answer the complaint using something similar to the following format.

Dear Mr. Jones:

This is to confirm our telephone conversation of this morning, in reply to your letter of May 16. It was nice chatting with you, and to be able to so amicably resolve this matter to your satisfaction.

Regards,
Fred Finesse

This method puts most complaints out to pasture without too much fuss. Most folks are pretty mad about something if they take the time to sit down and bang out a gripe in writing.

So if you respond quickly, that alone may give them satisfaction. Otherwise, they may sit and simmer and be harder to eventually pacify. Furthermore, by handling these complaints this way, you avoid putting things in writing that may make them madder. By limiting your written reply to acknowledging that the matter has been resolved, you dodge confirming a mistake in your response.

Although it's unlikely, if the person complaining has second thoughts later, and wants to continue the dispute, the complainer, not you, is on the defensive. That's because the written record now shows the matter has been resolved. Therefore, for that person to pursue it further requires getting over the hurdle of your reply. No matter how you look at it, that essentially involves calling you a liar and any objective party seeing this will question the credibility of the complaining party.

RED FLAG: This approach is for run-of-the-mill complaints that are common in business. Serious matters of any consequence should be brought to the attention of your boss for resolution.

2.20 SEVEN PROVEN WAYS TO ELIMINATE REPORTS

You may be in a position where reporting requirements consume a good chuck of your time. If so, try these techniques to reduce your burden.

1. Obsolete requirements. Many reports continue to be produced long after their usefulness has ceased. If you have a report whose purpose is questionable, follow-up to see who uses it. If it turns out to be of little or no value, recommend its elimination.
2. Consolidation. Look to see if two or more reports can be combined into one. For example, is information in a computer data base being duplicated manually?
3. Substitution. Look for opportunities to substitute other reporting methods. For instance, if you attend a weekly

meeting on a topic for which a written report is also required, see if an oral briefing can be substituted for the report.

4. Change reporting periods. Changing reporting periods from weekly to bi-weekly or monthly can significantly reduce your reporting chores.

5. Maximize computer technology. Talk with your data processing people, or other in-house experts, about programming changes that can simplify report preparation. If you sit down with them and explain what you need, they can probably come up with something to make your life easier.

6. Reassign report preparation. You can reduce your personal reporting workload by delegating it to a subordinate. In addition, you may be doing reports that should be done by other departments. This is especially true where more than one group furnishes input for a report. If the bulk of the data comes from another department, perhaps they should be responsible for preparing the report.

7. Fine-tune reporting procedures. Often, even when a repot can't be entirely eliminated, segments of it can be deleted. By fine-tuning the format of your reports, you can significantly reduce preparation time. So even with reports that must be done, take a look to see if you can restructure them.

3

Successfully Supervising Difficult People

The luck of the draw – in supervision as in life – means that you sometimes have to cope with problems you didn't bargain for. In a supervisory capacity, one of these unwelcome assignments is the misfortune of having to deal with difficult people.

Your roster of subordinates may include everything from gossips to goof-offs, know-it-alls to know-nothings, as well as folks who are just plain disagreeable. Such a wide array of personalities can mean handling hassles ranging from bad attitudes to employee theft. Since these kinds of problems are both time consuming and stressful, it's worthwhile to explore ways of minimizing the damage that difficult workers can create.

3.1 FIVE POSITIVE WAYS TO COUNTERACT NEGATIVE ATTITUDES

One of the irritants of being a supervisor is having to contend with people who are constantly negative about their job in particular and the company in general. However, rather than shrug your shoulders, it's important to try and modify their behavior, since negative attitudes can affect other employees. Good ways to cope with bad attitudes are as follows:

1. Be positive yourself. If you're essentially upbeat about matters, this in itself can help to modify a negative attitude.

Even if it doesn't have any impact on the "group grouch," it will encourage other employees to ignore the rumblings of a malcontent. This helps to maintain group loyalty and limit the spread of job dissatisfaction.

2. Be a sounding board for complaints. It's not pleasant to listen to gripes, but being a good listener pays dividends. Employees are going to air their gripes anyway, and if they feel at ease in doing so with you, they're less likely to grumble amongst themselves.

3. Delegate responsibility. Someone with a bad attitude isn't likely to change ones behavior if that person feels what is bothersome can't be controlled. Therefore, if an employee is unhappy about some aspect of the job over which he or she has no influence, there's little home for improvement. However, if you can give the person more responsibility in the troublesome area, this can help to eliminate the difficulty.

   For example, incorrect information in the office, or defective parts on an assembly line, can create real headaches for an employee. However, if the worker is given the authority to reject poor data or parts, that person won't be frustrated over having to live with someone else's mistakes. This can quick turn a bad attitude around.

4. Show respect. It's pretty easy when you're supervising someone who has a bad attitude to become tense and irritable when talking with the offender. Yet, this just makes a bad situation worse. It can also influence other employees to form a judgment that the worker's bad attitude is attributable – at least in part – to your behavior. This may not be fair, but don't forget that you're the boss, so subordinates aren't going to judge your actions with a great deal of sympathy and/or objectivity. Therefore, it's important to be calm and matter-of-fact when confronted by people with bad attitudes.

5. Be realistic. If a bad attitude is caused by a job-related problem, do your best to resolve it. Having done that, you may find to your dismay that the person's attitude doesn't improve. If that happens, don't feel that you have failed. Attitudes are learned from others and can be formed over a long period of

time. Furthermore, even when they appear to be job-related, the root cause may be much deeper than that.

For instance, someone who has developed a deep-seated disrespect for authority over a lifetime isn't going to change that attitude overnight. Therefore, in some circumstances, the solution is simply to ignore a bad attitude. Naturally, this assumes that the worker is performing satisfactorily, and not exerting a disruptive influence in the workplace.

3.2 LEARNING TO LIVE WITH DISAGREEABLE EMPLOYEES

One of the things that can make your life miserable is a disagreeable employee – but only if you let them get under your skin.

Q: I've got a person working for me who is a pain in the neck. Why am I the one who always seems to get the nasty people assigned to me?

A: It might be that (a) your boss doesn't like you, or (b) the boss feels that you can handle this type of person better than other supervisors. On the other hand, it might just be that you have unrealistic expectations when it comes to people. No one in a management position for any length of time can avoid supervising people they consider to be disagreeable.

First of all, it depends upon your viewpoint. For example, consider Kenny and Chris who work in the same department and are equally well liked by most people. Over a two week period Fred, their supervisor, had each one complain to him about the other's personality.

Kenny to Fred: "That Chris is tough to work with. She's a real snob. Trying to carry on a conversation with her is an exercise in futility."

Chris to Fred: "I don't know how you do it, Fred. Kenny doesn't seem to bother you, but his ear-bending drives me crazy. Doesn't he ever stop talking?"

The simple fact is that Kenny is outgoing and Chris is reserved, and their respective personalities grate on one another. As a supervisor, it's inevitable that you will find some folks not to your liking. Nevertheless, it's part of your job to be as objective as possible in working with everyone in your group. Therefore, it helps to lower your expectations as to the personal traits of your subordinates.

You may think you have someone in your unit who is the most unpleasant person in the world. In reality, many other supervisors feel the same way, therefore, concentrate on making your people productive and forget about reshaping their personalities. You're getting paid for the former, not the latter.

3.3 HOW TO LIGHT A FIRE UNDER GOOF-OFFS

Goof-offs not only waste a lot of their own time, but they can also require an inordinate amount of supervision. Everyone will do a little goofing off from time to time, therefore, concentrate your efforts on those few individuals who tend to slack-off every time you turn your back.

Q: I've run into a lot of goof-offs and I've always wondered who they manage to get away with it. What's the secret to their success?

A: Goof-offs come in several different forms. There are the obvious individuals who just aren't going to do any more work than the minimum required for survival, and survive they do for several reasons. First of all, some goof-offs are quite clever at creating the illusion of being busy. Many a magician could learn a trick or two from a goof-off.

In addition, some supervisors are reluctant to fire a dud. It's not unknown for a goof-off to land a better job somewhere else, partly because of a glowing reference from their present employer. After all, it's a hassle-free way of unloading deadwood.

Other goof-offs survive because of a mentor mentality that corrodes manager's minds. A supervisor that hires someone is often reluctant to admit a mistake, or may just like the individual, so personal feelings cloud the fact that a buddy isn't hacking it.

Some incompetents survive by operating in obscurity. The best breeding ground for poor performers is often a large company where inadequacies either go unnoticed or are compensated for by other people taking up the slack.

Q: I supervise a couple of people who are always clowning around. Yet, they are good workers when they're kept busy, so I don't want to come down on them too hard. How can I cut their downtime without alienating them?

A: Most people will do what they have to do with a minimum of supervision, a few will work hard whether or not you're around, and there are those who will seize every opportunity to avoid work. The first step in goof-off prevention is to make sure that people always have work to do. Some jobs have sharp peaks and valleys in their workload. A good supervisor will have low priority tasks on the backburner to occupy people during slack periods.

Another less obvious reason that can encourage workers to goof-off is lax supervision. No one wants to be thought of as a tyrant and a dictatorial boss can do much more harm than good. However, that doesn't mean you have to make everyone happy all of the time. A supervisor who constantly plays the role of "happy Harry" can be just as ineffective as a tyrant.

The bottom line that you shouldn't worry about prodding goof-offs. Happiness shouldn't be confused with productivity. Being firm – but fair – is what counts. Some workers need to be prodded more than others, therefore, don't worry about hurt feelings and alienating people who are goofing off. To the contrary, you may actually arouse resentment in subordinates who have to pick-up the slack if you fail to make goof-offs toe the line.

TIP: If you have employees who goof-off at every opportunity, try using what we'll call "progressive prodding" to get him going. A typical step-by-step procedure would be as follows:

1. Monitor the employee closely to eliminate the opportunity to goof-off.

2. If the employee claims to have nothing to do, assign other work. It's good to place a deadline for completion on these tasks so time can serve as a motivator.

3. Make a change in the person's workload and/or work location if it's feasible to do so. Some jobs offer more opportunity for downtime than others. People who aren't self-starters are often better in positions that leave them little opportunity to slow down.

4. Sit down with the culprit and explain how much time is wasted and that you expect immediate improvement.

5. If nothing else has succeeded, give the employee a formal warning in accordance with company policy. This should be a last resort, but once you start a step-by-step disciplinary action follow it through. Sometimes a stubborn worker doesn't get the message until a formal warning is given. Then he starts working when it hits home that his job is on the line.

3.4 USING THE OFFICE GOSSIP TO GOOD ADVANTAGE

Workers who gossip may drive you up the wall, but the hard truth is that even though you may be able to control the disruptive effects of gossip, you'll never be successful in stopping it completely. Therefore, instead of agonizing in frustration about gossip, learn to use it to your advantage.

Q: I've got a guy named Ron working for me who I have silently dubbed "Ronny Runningmouth." He's always spreading rumors which usually don't even make sense. How can I shut him up?

A: Habitual gossips are a lost cause, but you can control their impact at work. (See Sect. 2.6 on controlling rumors.) The principal way, as we've mentioned before, is to keep everyone posted on what's going on, so you can minimize the damage a gossip can cause. That usually controls the problem, but it doesn't muzzle a seasoned gossip, since facts seldom outrun a rumormonger.

Despite the annoyance a gossip can cause, there are occasions when you can make them an unwitting messenger. The circumstances will vary and you can create your own opportunities as conditions warrant. Here's one example:

Background

Lou, a supervisor in a large electronics plant, wants to send a message to his group about taking too much time during their midmorning break. He doesn't feel that circumstances are bad enough to hold a meeting on the topic and read the riot act to his people. Don, the chronic gossip in Lou's department, happens to enter Lou's office at that moment.

Sending a Subtle Message

Lou: "Hey, Don, just the guy I want to see. Are you one of the people who's trying to stretch midmorning break into an all-day siesta?"

Don: "Huh? What do you mean Lou?"

Lou: "I mean midmorning break is fifteen minutes and if that isn't observed I'm going to get ticked-off."

Don: "Gee, Lou, it's not me. I'm right back to my work station on the button. Hey! I'll see you later. I just wanted to drop off this lunch pail I found. It probably belongs to someone on the night shift."

Lunchtime

Don is eating lunch with the other workers in Lou's department.

Don: "Ha Ha! Guess what I heard today? Old Lou is all burned-up about us taking too long at morning break. He's about to lower the boom."

Ed: "Sure Don, you know everything. I guess Lou's thinking about making you acting honcho."

Don: "No kidding guys. You know that lunch bucket I found. I brought it to Lou, and that's when he told me we were taking too long for break."

Peg: "Well, I'll just watch you tomorrow Don. When you go back to work from break, I'll go back."

Don: "For crying out loud. I give you people the inside scoop and you don't even believe me."

The Result

The group starts observing the time limit at breaks. Lou, by using the group gossip, has accomplished what he set out to do without having to say a word to the group.

WARNING: Be careful about using an office gossip, since they may completely distort your message. In addition, any matter of significance should be transmitted directly by you to your subordinates. However, on occasion you can try this tactic when things haven't reached the point where you're forced to act.

3.5 WHY INTIMIDATION DOESN'T WORK

The age-old practice of browbeating subordinates is no longer effective for a number of reasons. Yet, some managers continue to badger people unnecessarily.

Q: Some of the supervisors in my company use a "If you don't like it, that's tough," manner in managing subordinates. Others tend to communicate more and promote teamwork. Which is the better model to follow?

A: The use of adversarial management practices is no longer the accepted way to do things, although for some managers, old habits die hard. The old-school method of management comes from an era when, (1) people weren't as mobile in switching jobs, (2) workers weren't well educated, (3) management/union relations were largely hostile, (4) the United States had little world-wide competition, and (5) working couples were the exception rather than the rule.

Today, workers won't tolerate being treated as second-class citizens, and companies tend to realize that worker participation and cooperation are a necessary ingredient for greater productivity. Therefore, intimidating workers is no longer an acceptable practice.

Q: I'm a second-level manager with four first-line supervisors reporting to me. I inherited these people when I took over the department. I'm getting complaints about one whose workers are treated as if they're military recruits in basic training. What should I do about this?

A: As the number of progressive managers increases, there are fewer supervisors who treat workers with hostility and distrust. However, problems will continue if people are placed in supervisory positions without adequate evaluation and training.

What you should do in this case is sit down with the supervisor and explain your point-of-view as to how workers should be treated. It would also be helpful to schedule this person for some supervisory training. In fact, periodic courses in supervision should be regularly scheduled for all supervisors. The daily operating environment can obscure some of the basic principles of managing people, so refresher courses are useful.

3.6 MANAGING GOOD WORKERS WHO HAVE BAD ATTITUDES

One of the requirements of effective supervision is the ability to set aside personal preferences and prejudices and treat everyone equally.

Q: Some of the people who work for me aren't very friendly toward me and actually border on being hostile. They do their job, so I'm wondering if I should do anything about this?

A: Everyone is sensitive – some of us more so than others. The best way to handle this matter is to ignore it. But it won't hurt to think about anything you might be doing to bring about the apparent hostility that exists. If your honest soul-searching reveals nothing, don't worry about attitudes that don't interfere with job performance. Unless people go beyond the bounds of decency, forget it. In the final analysis, you're not being paid to promote friendships.

NOTE: Sometimes folks end up supervising people they used to work with. This can create resentment by workers who, in their minds, are more deserving of a supervisory position than you. This jealousy can manifest itself in their relationship with you as a boss. Don't be paranoid about this, as time alone tends to heal these wounds.

3.7 HOW TO FINESSE LOADED QUESTIONS

Are you still cheating on your wife (husband)? That's a standard example of a loaded question. A simple "No" answer implies that you used to, but have stopped. As a supervisor, you occasionally have to field loaded questions. They may be less personally provocative than the example, but can be equally challenging to answer.

Q: The question I most often get and always dread is, "When am I getting promoted?" How can I waltz around this one?

A: Loaded questions can get you into trouble because of one basic mistake – rushing to answer them off the top of your head. It's an all too common habit to answer questions without thinking through the implications. At the other extreme, is the equally futile attempt to evade the issue by making a promise for some indeterminate future date. Example: "When am I getting promoted?" Answer: "Probably next year."

This may dispose of the problem on an immediate basis, but the year will speed by, you'll have forgotten your off-hand remark, but guess what – here comes Sally looking for her promotion.

CAUTION: Never make promises that can't or won't be kept. This can happen unintentionally when an employee is up for a promotion that requires a higher level of approval. Refrain from telling employees they're getting promoted until you have the papers in hand. This saves you the embarrassment of explaining what happened if a promotion is shot down during the approval process. Of course, frequently an employee knows a personnel action is in progress, but even here, make no verbal assurances while a decision is pending.

Back to the, "When am I getting promoted?" question, which along with pay raise requests, are the most popular topics that you have to learn to finesse. A simple and logical answer to this question is, "When an appropriate position opens up for which you are the best qualified candidate." This closes the door firmly but politely. Of course, the natural follow-up question to expect which is, "When is that going to be?" can be nimbly disposed of by a simple, "I don't know."

The major trap to avoid in this area is getting drawn into a debate over the employee's qualifications and job performance. It's a "no win" situation, since if you agree they're qualified, they'll prod you for a commitment. Conversely, if you tell them – no matter how diplomatically – that they're doing lousy work, dig in your desk for an aspirin, as a headache inducing argument is likely to erupt.

The correct time to discuss promotion prospects at length is during an employee's formal review. It's also important to discuss at that time what training and other self-development the employee has to undertake to enhance promotional prospects. If you are diligent in doing this, you'll frequently find that between reviews the employee hasn't followed-up on any of your recommendations. That being the case, a griper has little ground to stand on when he's bypassed for promotion.

Q: The people who bug me the most about promotions are usually the ones with the least prospects of ever being promoted. Is this prevalent?

A: Unfortunately, it's often the folks with the poorest promotion prospects who push the hardest. One reason is that they continually see others getting promoted ahead of them. In addition, they fail to see and/or remedy the reasons why they're bypassed. Many times these people are unwilling to put forth the effort to get the necessary training that would qualify them for advancement. Consequently, they stake their claim to promotions primarily on having been on the job longer than other people. (See Sec. 4.16 for more on this topic.)

3.8 SUCCESSFUL WAYS TO DEFLATE A KNOW-IT-ALL

Know-it-alls are never wrong in their own eyes, and seldom can be convinced otherwise. If you present them with facts that prove them wrong, they tend to shrug them off with an attitude of, "Don't confuse me with the facts," or "That wasn't what I said." If this sounds like someone you supervise, don't be surprised. Know-it-alls in the world of work are as common as beer in a barroom.

How do deal with a know-it-all? The best solution is two-fold. Buy them a muzzle for their birthday and wear earmuffs to work. Sadly, practicality always wins, and other more mundane tactics are possible.

Q: One of my subordinates is an obnoxious know-it-all. He questions every decision I make and constantly belittles other workers. What can be done about this?

A: Nothing teaches humility faster than hard work. Give the person the most undesirable tasks you can find. Not the most technically difficult, but the most boring. If he challenges the assignment by saying something such as, "Why me? Any moron can do this job," you could avail yourself of the opportunity to say, "Then I'm sure you could handle it Joe." But if you're kinder than that, just ignore the comment to tell him that's what he's paid for.

TIP: You might think that it would be better to give a know-it-all the most difficult tasks to solve by assuming, "If he's so smart, let him prove it." That's not a good idea for one reason. A know-it-all will adopt an attitude of, "I was given this job because no one else can do it." But your objective isn't to further feed an over-inflated ego. Instead, it's to put some starch in his sails and you do this by assigning him plenty of tedious, routine tasks.

Q: How can I tell the difference between a know-it-all, and someone who is just plain bright, but perhaps not too diplomatic?

A: You'll learn this fast enough over a short period of time. That truly bright person will come up with good ideas that make sense.

On the other hand, a know-it-all will never admit to being wrong, and will usually claim expertise in everything except his own job.

At first blush, many know-it-alls are deceptive. They come across as intelligent, aggressive individuals, which are certainly characteristics that bode well for success. However, the very fact that a know-it-all tries so hard to convince you of his wide-ranging knowledge is a warning to beware. Following a know-it-all's advice is a losing proposition, since they generally have difficulty in distinguishing between what they really know and what they think they know.

Know-it-alls are usually perceived to be snobs, and the reason is simple – they are. They see themselves as a cut above everyone else and if they're not contained can cause a great deal of disharmony in the workplace.

3.9 FAILPROOF WAYS OF PUTTING DOWN THE PUT-DOWN ARTIST

The put-down artist is closely related to the know-it-all. The basic difference is that a put-down artist doesn't generally claim self-knowledge. He simply concentrates on belittling everyone else's accomplishments. From a supervisory standpoint the major difference both types of individuals cause are a damaging impact on morale and teamwork. They persistently annoy co-workers, provoke arguments, and are in general a source of dissension.

Q: I've got a real jerk working for me. He's continually putting people down. He attends Charts and Graphs University part-time and his specialty is telling co-workers that they're stupid because they didn't go to college. I've already intervened once to keep him from being punched-out. To be honest, I wish I hadn't. Should I just fire this guy?

A: Take him aside in private and lay the facts out as follows:

- smart folks don't need to tell folks about it.
- he's being rude and arrogant.

- his attitude is affecting the morale of your department.
- he should take a course in manners before he graduates.
- If he thinks he's better than his co-workers, perhaps he ought to pursue his studies full time where he'll be in a more intellectual environment.
- He can immediately (1) watch his mouth, (2) quit, or (3) be fired. Tell him the ball is in his court and end the discussion.

Any variation of the above theme will do the job, which is to let him know that his nonsense won't be tolerated. Incidentally, the above procedure is equally effective for coping with know-it-alls. You don't, as a rule, want to be harsh with people, but know-it-alls and put-down artists display little consideration for the feelings of others. Hence they have little claim on receiving kid-glove treatment.

Furthermore, you're a supervisor with set responsibilities, one of which is the smooth functioning of your department. There's little time for you to waste in the role of counselor for people who don't adapt well to a group environment. Therefore, the best way to deal with both know-it-alls and put-down artists is to calmly – but firmly – let them know that you won't tolerate their behavior.

3.10 WHEN TO CLAMP A LID ON HORSEPLAY AND KIDDING

It's easy enough to rationalize that horseplay and kidding don't belong in the workplace. If people are fooling around, they're obviously not working. However, in practice, a certain amount of frivolity is healthy if it doesn't get out of hand.

Q: My boss told me to "lighten up" in my supervisory role. This confuses me since the productivity of my department is high. But apparently several of my people have gone to my boss and threatened to quit. Quite frankly, they characterized me as a hard-nosed s.o.b. I'm fair, but I expect people to produce. Am I wrong?

A: The workplace shouldn't be the site for a three-ring circus. On the other hand, it's not a forced labor camp for criminals. The difficulty raised in the question most frequently occurs when managers try to squeeze greater productivity out of workers than is either practical or realistic.

As you know, work can get hectic and tensions can run high. That's why a limited amount of humorous by-play is useful in relieving the pressure. Often, when managers push workers too hard, output does increase initially. But over the long haul, problems will surface. The most common manifestations will appear in the form of poor quality work, and a higher than normal amount of labor turnover as harried workers seek employment elsewhere.

So there are benefits to be derived by mixing a little fun with work. How much horseplay is enough depends in part on your own temperament. Other influences include the attitude of upper management in this regard. In short, a little common sense goes a long way in determining the acceptable limits for frivolity.

The following guidelines are useful in controlling silliness so it doesn't get out of hand:

- Clowning around can easily go too far. Assert yourself promptly to call a halt when necessary. By doing this, you also give people a feel for how much you will tolerate.
- Never condone ethnic or sexist remarks and don't tolerate them even though the recipient doesn't object. Prejudice is prejudice and humor is humor, and prejudicial remarks disguised as humor aren't funny. (See Sec. 11.10 for more on this.)
- Discourage workers from playing pranks on co-workers who aren't receptive to a little clowning around.
- Keep the kidding within your group. A lot of folks don't have a sense of humor. They'll quickly complain that your department isn't very businesslike if given the opportunity.
- Use good judgment in deciding when to let a light-hearted atmosphere develop.

3.11 INSTILLING CONFIDENCE IN INDECISIVE INDIVIDUALS

Confidence-building is one aspect of your job where you'll receive dual reward for your efforts. By increasing the level of confidence of shy and indecisive workers, you'll eventually have people who require less supervision. Along with that accomplishment will come the personal satisfaction of knowing that you helped to improve another person's capabilities.

Q: A couple of my people are good workers, but they're in my office every two minutes asking if they should to this, or shouldn't do that. Mind you, these are experienced workers; not trainees. How can I get them to make more decisions on their own?

A: Encourage them to assume more responsibility a little at a time. However, don't stress them out by berating them. One way to do this is to assign minor tasks for them to handle when you won't be around to hold their hand. Perhaps you will be out a day on vacation, or out of the work area for an extended period of time. Try to assign chores that have to be completed by a deadline which coincides with your absence.

Another technique is to ask them to fill in for an absent worker. Profess ignorance about the duties of the absentee. This leaves the indecisive person without anyone to go to. However, reassure them with a comment such as, "Do the best you can." In all of these cases, be sure to bolster the person's confidence with praise as you see them becoming increasingly independent.

In any event, when you're encountering reluctance by employees to make decisions, you should see if you can identify some underlying cause that isn't apparent on the surface. Things to look for include the following:

1. Was the person properly trained? Someone who isn't trained properly may appear to be indecisive when actually they were never trained in the fundamentals of their job. (See Sects. 6.4 to 6.9 on training.)

2. Have previous bosses held the reins so tightly that the employee has become conditioned to be indecisive? If that's true, the indecisiveness will gradually disappear as the employee realizes you are willing to delegate responsibility.

3. Are co-workers being uncooperative when legitimate questions are asked, shunting the employee off with a "Go ask the boss," response?

4. Is your own manner such that you dominate people without intending to do so? This might intimidate someone to the extent that they feel it's necessary to get your "ok" on everything.

3.12 FOUR STEPS TO INCREASE THE CONFIDENCE OF SHY PEOPLE

When new employees are assigned to you, it's important to get them settled in as soon as possible. This is especially true for people who are on the shy side. The sooner they are accepted into the group, the quicker they will become fully contributing workers. The following steps will help to speed this process:

1. Let new employees know they are a welcome addition to your department.

2. Introduce them around to everyone. The blur of faces won't mean anything initially, but other people will remember them and acknowledge them in passing. Spend a few minutes in conversation with key people you want a new employee to know.

3. Line new employees up with a friendly mentor to guide them the first few weeks on the job.

4. Take a little extra time to get to know them personally and reassure them that they should feel at ease about seeing you at the time.

3.13 HOW TO CONTEND WITH AGGRESSIVE EMPLOYEES

Aggression can take many forms at work, ranging from sporadic temper flare-ups to enduring "fight-at-a-flash" temperaments. As a supervisor you're uniquely positioned in the middle between workers and upper-level management. That means contending both with the normal range of aggressive tendencies in subordinates, as well as aggress directed at upper management by unhappy workers. Are you the one in the middle? You bet you are.

Q: We've been working full tilt for two months and my people are on edge. Staff members in the scheduling department aggravate matters by constantly badgering workers with questions about job completion dates. This morning, Ben, who works for me, blew-up at Angelo, a particularly pesky staffer who habitually asks the same question over and over. At any rate, Ben screamed at Angelo on the phone to "stop bothering me," and then literally smashed the phone on the floor. Angelo's boss complained to me. What should I do about this?

A: What's described – other than the smashed phone – is a fairly common example of clashes between staff people and line departments. Differing responsibilities within an organization can result in priorities that are in conflict. Here, the scheduler is concerned with reporting the progress on the job that Ben is working on. Ben, for his part, is pushing to get the work done, and Angelo's interruptions are interfering with that. There are a couple of problems that have to be dealt with in a difficulty such as this.

Ben's supervisor – let's call her Ann – has to (1) respond to Angelo's boss who complained about Ben's behavior, (2) keep the schedulers from interfering with the work process, and (3) react to Ben's behavior. Let's look at how this can be done.

Given the facts, a gut response by Ann might be to tell Angelo's boss to have Angelo stop bothering people in her department. That won't work, since it would only increase the overall level of hostility.

A better course of action for Ann is to suggest that people in the scheduling department come to her, instead of going directly to her subordinates. This allows her to control interruptions and it should be acceptable to Angelo's supervisor, since Angelo will no longer have to work with Ben.

NOTE: Although it may appear that Ann is pacifying Angelo's supervisor, she is in fact resolving the larger problem of staffers going directly to workers. By having them come to her, she regains control of their access and can prevent unreasonable interruptions in the future.

TIP: Always insist that staffers contact you. It's a bad practice to let personnel from other departments go directly to your subordinates. You lose control, unnecessary interruptions take place, and downtime, misinformation and conflict are often the end result. That's not to say that going directly to workers isn't ever appropriate, but it should only be done with your prior knowledge and concurrence.

Having already responded to Angelo's boss, and at the same time solved the problem of Angelo bothering people, Ann's remaining tasks is to talk with Ben. All that needs to be said is that staffers will come directly to her in the future. This will resolve Ben's frustration over interruptions.

Why not say anything about Ben's outburst? Because it was a temper flare-up under stress which only arose after a series of interruptions. It's easy to say that Ben shouldn't have blown his top, but we all do that on occasion. Since this was an isolated incident provoked by frustration, it's senseless to make an issue out of it. The important point is that Ann has taken steps to eliminate the cause.

Q: How much aggressive behavior should take place before talking to employees about their actions?

A: To some extent it depends upon the circumstances, but four common problem areas are as follows:

1. Temper flare-ups. A temper flare-up is when someone such as Ben loses his temper in a fit of frustration. Unless it results in physical or verbal abuse and/or serious property damage, it's best to ignore this type of behavior. However,

if it's caused by a job-related event that's likely to repeat itself, look into the possibility of eliminating the cause.

2. Fight-at-a-flash personalities. This type of person needs talking to for getting angry at the slightest provocation. If such an employee doesn't respond by toning down the aggressiveness, then inevitably disciplinary action culminating in termination is the best course to take. Usually – unless you have a hard-core antagonist – culprits will control their anger in the work environment.

3. Bullies. Most bullies proceed with their aggressive as far as it will take them – which isn't very far if you keep them in line with a friendly chat about their behavior.

4. Borderline types. This category would include those whose aggressive actions are for the most part positive. For example, what is usually termed a "go-getter" who barges ahead to get a job done. The major difficulty you face in this regard is that this behavior may dominate someone's thinking to the extent that they irritate others. This may result in complaints to you from those they work with. In severe cases, you might want to caution this type to tone it down a little and not run roughshod over others. In other words, put them on a short leash, but give them enough room to maneuver.

Controlling aggressive behavior boils down to using good judgment in preventing disruptive actions from interfering with an orderly work environment. It's an area where unusual behavior must be handled on a case-by-case basis as it arises.

3.14 WHAT TO DO TO SNIFF OUT SNEAKS

Collaring sneaks isn't easy, but it's necessary to maintain supervisory control. How you go about this is important, since at best it's a thankless task, and at worst can make you look foolish.

Q: I've got a couple of people who I know take advantage of every opportunity to duck work. I haven't been able to catch them

in the act, because I don't have the time to look over their shoulder
every minute of the day. Is there an easier way to do it?

A: There's no easy way to catch a sneak, but there are adequate measures you can take that don't require time-consuming monitoring on your part. In fact, the first mistake a supervisor can make is to engage in a follow-them-around sleuthing exercise. Sneaks aren't easily caught by doing this, and even when they are, you're only half-way home. That's because any sneak worthy of the designation has a ready-made excuse in the event of being caught. Even after you think you've nabbed this person, you then will have to hurdle a rather ingenuous alibi before you hang this person out to dry.

The best method of isolating and controlling sneaks is two-pronged. The first link is to be unpredictable in your movements. Sneaks are most successful when a manager follows a set pattern day in and day out. They then know when the boss will be in the office, goes to lunch, and in general, where and what the boss will be doing throughout the day. Counter this attempt to pinpoint your activities by randomly roaming the floor. You don't need to spend a lot of time doing this. The key to success isn't the amount of time, but rather the unpredictability of your actions.

The other tool of your two-pronged course of action is to forget about trying to catch them, since that can become a sophisticated game of hide and go seek. As your participation becomes common knowledge, your subordinates may snicker at your efforts with a resultant loss of respect for you.

So instead of playing the sneak's game, let them disappear and then leave them a note to see you. When they show up, present them with a project to work on. After this is done a few times, the message will filter throughout the department.

Of course, you'll get the inevitable beef about doling out work like this. Nonchalantly toss these arguments aside with, "I checked with everyone else and they were busy. Unfortunately, you weren't here at the time so that left you as the only possibility." This off-hand turn of the screw will soon have sneaks sticking around.

3.15 ATTACKING THE PROBLEM OF EMPLOYEE THEFT

A pervasive problem of business is controlling employee theft. Although much of the effort requires top management initiative, in both setting policy and establishing procedures for theft prevention, you're the first line of defense in this endeavor. Even if the company is lax in this regard, you can still manage to control theft within your own department.

Q: My company is pretty poor in theft prevention. They only give it lip service, with little being done in the way of prevention, and even less in the form of enforcement. Given this attitude, why should I get all worked-up about theft? I've got other things to worry about.

A: Did you ever stop to think that perhaps the other things you have to worry about may be directly or indirectly tied to theft? Everything from inventory shortages, to lower productivity, to customer complaints, can result from employee theft. These directly affect the operations of individual departments.

Recognizing this fact is a prerequisite to taking theft within your department seriously, no matter how weak company policy is on the subject. Let's face it. If your department's inventory shortages result in criticism from your boss you can't say, "People are stealing things blind, because the company doesn't do anything about it." Most likely, your boss would respond by telling you it's your job to control what happens in the department. Tough? Sure, but who ever said being a supervisor was an easy job?

Q: I can see how inventory shortages resulting from theft can affect operations, but aside from that it's pretty hard to visualize a direct impact. How about some examples in other areas?

A: Types of theft and their impact are limited only by the ingenuity and creativity of thieves. However, here are a few examples that illustrate the scope of the problem in several areas.

Customer Complaints

- Rebuilt items are substituted for new items stolen by an employee.
- Accessories don't accompany shipment because they were stolen.
- Customer receives less than quantity ordered.
- Customer billed for items not shipped.

Company Productivity

- Workers wasting time on the telephone with personal phone calls.
- Employees using copiers to reproduce documents for a sideline business.
- Production schedules not met because a "rush order" to replace stolen parts wasn't received on time.
- Productive time lost by a worker searching for hand tools that were stolen.

Department Budgets

- Travel budget for fiscal year is used in nine months because of expense account padding.
- Office supply budget is exceeded by 20% because of pilferage.

This list could go on and on, but quite simply, theft has no limits and affects every part of a company. Therefore, whether you're a supervisor in an office, warehouse, or manufacturing environment, theft can influence your operation.

Q: I supervise a group of field service technicians who are on the road a lot. Expense account padding is my problem. How can I control it?

A: Expense account padding can put a great deal of pressure on a supervisor. You don't want to be thought of as tightfisted by your workers, and even worse, you can't be inconsistent in the treatment of expense vouchers, since that can raise all sorts of havoc with your subordinates. But unfortunately, to a large degree, controlling expense account padding is dependent upon the reimbursement guidelines set down by the company.

As a supervisor, about all you can do is consistently apply company policy across-the-board. Travel expenses are a bread and butter issue with employees who travel frequently. This puts you in a tough position if you're the sole approval authority. Companies should always require two signatures for approval of travel expenses. Besides yourself, there should be someone else from the accounting or payroll departments who is also responsible for signing payment requests.

In fact, the best method is for the immediate supervisor to only be responsible for signifying that the travel was authorized and performed. The actual validity of the expenses should be verified by someone else. The reason is simple. It's totally unrealistic to expect supervisors to incur the wrath of an employee over a ten dollar item on an expense report.

In any event, no matter what company policy is, you should insist that expense vouchers be submitted promptly. When employees are allowed to delay submissions, errors – both intentional and inadvertent – will be significantly higher.

3.16 WHY LITTLE THINGS MEAN A LOT IN CONTROLLING CRIME

Theft prevention is an on-going proposition, and the security and record-keeping requirements may seem to be a nuisance from an operational standpoint. However, constant vigilance sets the standard for the effective control of theft.

Q: I supervise a ten-person office and during August and September office supply usage skyrockets. What's happening?

A: Your office is making an "off-the-books" contribution to the education of American youth. The start of every school year sees employees lugging home anything they think is needed for school by their children, nieces, nephews, and the neighborhood kid who mows the lawn. Surprisingly, many employees don't consider this to be theft. The same can be said for such things as long distance personal phone calls from work, expense account padding, and various other items.

Some businesses benignly accept this as a cost of doing business. The theory is that rigid controls and poor morale resulting from stringent enforcement aren't worth the effort. In other companies, the necessary controls just aren't in place. However, the crux of the matter is that condoning petty pilferage creates an atmosphere where major theft can thrive – and in fact may be inevitable.

You can control the disappearance of office supplies by implementing a couple of modest measures. First of all, limit access to the supplies. Keep them in a locked cabinet or file where you can retain control. It's also worthwhile to have workers sign for supplies. This gives you an audit trail of excessive use, and it keeps folks wondering about getting caught if they take supplies home.

There are two other abuses that are common in an office environment. The first is excessive personal telephone usage. Record keeping and auditing can easily control long distance calls, but even more important is getting a handle on nonbusiness local calls. The simplest way to control this is to (1) limit availability of company phones to those who need them, (2) keep workers busy so you limit the opportunity for this form of downtime, and (3) provide public phones with easy access for employee use.

The other form of chronic abuse is the use of copying machines by employees. This practice is particularly prevalent with workers who have sideline businesses or are part-time students. Controlling this usage may seem like small potatoes, but if your department is a high volume user of copiers, as little as 5% or 8% personal usage is a significant sum over a year's time.

Assuming copiers aren't located in a central area where full-time employees attend to reproduction needs, the best strategy is to have the copier located within your view. The problem of using sign-off sheets for copiers – as well as office supplies – is that unless you control it personally, people won't sign off when personal use is involved.

TIP: Enforcing personal phone usage, as well as the unauthorized use of office supplies and copiers, is a subject where you may feel squeamish about strict enforcement. This is particularly true if company-wide control is weak or nonexistent. The mental hurdle you face is, "Why should I enforce rules if no one else does?"

One good reason is that you are – and should be – the keeper of your own standards. An even more practical justification is that it's not only the direct expense involved, but also the lower productivity of your group when workers engage in personal business on the job.

NOTE: The same need for controls that exist in the office applies equally to manufacturing jobs and other positions. Scrap and small tools should be subject to record-keeping requirements, and if someone needs a new tool, they should be required to turn in the old one. In short, wherever you work, accountability and control are necessary to prevent petty pilferage.

3.17 DID YOU KNOW A WORKAHOLIC MAY BE STEALING YOU BLIND

When we think about character traits of individuals there's an inclination to generalize behavior based on our observations. This can be disastrous when it comes to controlling theft.

Q: Someone has been stealing electrical components in my department. I'm not sure who it is, but it's definitely not Al, whom I appoint acting supervisor in my absence, or two other loyal, long-time workers. That only leaves three people. How can I catch the culprit?

A: You can start by forgetting your blind assumptions. The most successful thief is the one you would least suspect. With six people in your unit, there are six possibilities. Just because people are hard-working and trusted associates doesn't mean they're not stealing you blind.

On the contrary, the trusted records clerk who never takes a vacation, or the shipper/receiver who works late every night, may be diligent only because it's necessary to further their thievery. The records clerk may not want anyone else getting a look at the books, and the shipper/receiver may be stealing goods after everyone else has left for the day.

Theft prevention and control requires an open mind, which means that there shouldn't be any predetermined innocents or suspects based on personal judgments rather than facts.

3.18 A SIMPLE DEVICE TO DRASTICALLY REDUCE PETTY THEFT

The "big hit" in terms of embezzlement or theft is headline generating. But on an overall basis, the dollars go down the drain from recurring petty pilferage. Although you may not want to be viewed as a nitpicker, it's important to control this theft at the department level.

Q: Aside from theft prevention policy, which has to be set by top management, is there anything specific I can do to discourage petty theft?

A: Surprisingly, the most effective tool for preventing petty theft is no further away than your own attitude toward the problem. You set the tone for your employees by your example. If you couple this with telling workers that taking company property is theft, and also let them know you won't condone it, you've gone a long way toward preventing petty theft in your department.

However, just because you respect company property doesn't mean everyone else will. You may have employees who view your attitude as that of a "stuffed shirt" or "company lackey." Although these folks may not be impressed by your ethical values, they may well be influenced by knowing that petty theft will be punished.

The long and the short of success as a supervisor in controlling petty theft is an attitude of, "It's wrong and I won't condone it." If you do that, then no matter what formal company policy is, you'll have done your best in this regard.

4

The Art of Overcoming Employee Complaints

Have you ever thought of answering your phone with a greeting of, "Complaint center, … speaking." If there's one thing that can wear you down faster than anything else, it's the constant stream of complaints that land in your lap. If that's not bad enough, you also have to deal with excuses by the score, buck-passers, and critics who challenge your every decision. This chapter explores how many of these problems can be overcome.

4.1 COPING WITH COMPLAINTS ABOUT COMPANY POLICY

One of the headaches every supervisor must cope with is defending company policy. Top management sets policy BASED ON CORPORATE GOALS AND OBJECTIVES. This policy then comes down the line for implementation. That's pretty basic, but difficulties arise when policies are set that are good for the company, but aren't in the best interests of individual workers – at least from their point of view. This forces you to defend the policy when workers complain – even when you don't agree with it yourself.

Q: My company is implementing cost-reduction measures to offset increased competition and falling profits. I'm starting to get complaints from workers and I don't know what to tell them. How can you defend a 3% cap on pay raises?

A: Cutbacks are sometimes necessary even though they may be painful. Many companies try to avoid laying off workers by putting across-the-board measures such as hiring freezes and pay caps into effect. When cost-reduction actions are taken that affect the work force, it's prudent for top management to hold all-hands meetings to explain these actions. Whether or not this happens, it's necessary for you to do your best in explaining the need for these measures, but be straightforward in your answers. As an example, let's say Marty in your unit complains about a salary cap.

Marty:	"Joe, what's with this 3% salary cap? You mean I'm only getting a lousy 3% raise? That stinks."
You:	"Marty, it's only a temporary measure. As soon as business picks up everything will get back to normal."
Marty:	"Hey, why should I get penalized? I work hard and you know it."
You:	"I know that Marty, but the company either has to cut costs this way, or lay people off."
Marty:	"I don't care about layoffs. I've got seniority."
You:	"Look at it this way. By doing this, no one gets laid off. After all, if the company hadn't always handled hard times in this fashion, you probably wouldn't be sitting here with all that seniority."
Marty:	"A 3% raise isn't helping to feed my kids."
You:	"OK Marty, put yourself in the same position. If your household budget got tight, would you buy less steak and more pasta to feed your family, or would you say, `I'll stop feeding one kid.' The company is doing its best to keep everyone on the payroll just like they did for you in the past. If you think about it, I know you'd do the same thing Marty."
Marty:	"Yea, I guess you're right, but it still stinks."

Generally, workers such as Marty will accept company actions that they don't like if you take the time to explain them. Incidentally, if you don't understand the basis for a company decision, touch base with your boss to get the answers. Otherwise, you're in the awkward position of having to defend a policy that you know nothing about.

WARNING: When a worker starts to grumble about company policies, it's important to identify precisely why the person is upset. A worker unhappy over some job aspect may be making general complaints that conceal the real reason for dissatisfaction. By talking to the employee, you may be able to identify and resolve the true cause of unhappiness.

Q: The company has put in place a policy that I don't agree with. How can I defend something that I don't like myself?

A: Often, top level decisions are made that don't make a great deal of sense on an individual basis. Yet, they can be perfectly rational and reasonable from the perspective of achieving company-wide objectives. There will be times when corporate decisions don't meet with your personal approval. Nevertheless, as a manager, it's your responsibility to uphold the company's position if it's challenged by subordinates. Even when you don't possess the facts to support your position, say something such as, "I'm sure there are valid reasons for what the company is doing."

PRECAUTION: When a supervisor doesn't agree with company policy, there's a temptation to take the easy way out and side with subordinates. This is wrong and shouldn't be done. You're a full-time member of the management team; not a part-time opponent when it suits your purpose.

Furthermore, agreeing with workers that a policy is wrong will weaken your future authority with the group. Needless to say, if a lack of loyalty is discovered by superiors, your future may be pretty bleak. Stick to your guns and take the heat from workers even when you silently agree with their objections. If you feel strongly enough about a topic, discuss your position with your boss, and leave it at that.

NOTE: Although it's essential to defend company policy, there are limited circumstances where it should be ignored. These are discussed in Sec. 11.3, but even then, you shouldn't plant the idea in employee's minds that the policy is wrong.

4.2 PROVEN METHODS TO BEAT BACK CHALLENGES FROM CRITICS

It's annoying to break your back doing the best job possible and still have second-guessers criticizing everything you do. Self-appointed critics are everywhere in an organization, ranging from insecure bosses, to supervisory peers, as well as subordinates who question your authority. Controlling this problem requires differing approaches when the source is the boss, or the criticism originates in other departments. Dealing with a boss in this regard is discussed in Chap. 10, while handling outsiders is discussed in Chap. 8. Here, the focus is on the criticism right in your own backyard – from subordinates.

Q: There's a guy in my department who never misses an opportunity to say, "I told you so," when something goes wrong. This really gets under my skin. How can I clamp a lid on this guy's second-guessing?

A: First of all, never let critics get the best of you. The world is full of Monday morning quarterbacks. After all, it's great to be right and there's no easier way than hindsight. In addition, never get drawn into a debate with a subordinate over second-guessing. Either ignore it or cut it short with a response that dismisses it for what it is. Second-guessers thrive on the "if" word, but your response is very easy. For example:

Sal: (the critic)	"If we'd done it my way, it would have worked."
You:	"If 'if' worked, I wouldn't be here right now."
Sal: (the critic)	"What do you mean?"
You:	"If I could sing, I'd be a star," or, "If I could hit a fast ball, I'd be a major league ballplayer," or, "If I was wealthy, I'd be in Tahiti."

There's no limit to possible putdown for an "if" critic. Should you choose to avoid the scent of sarcasm in your reply, then casually remark, "Wait until you're a boss," or, "Anyone can be right after the fact."

You can prevent most second-guessing – except for chronic critics – by having an open door policy which allows for the exchange of ideas. If workers feels they've had an opportunity to contribute beforehand, there will be less after-the-fact criticism. In any event, don't overreact to critics. It's one of the minor irritants that goes along with being a decision maker.

4.3 HOW TO BAILOUT GRACEFULLY WEN YOU'RE BEING BAITED

There are a few people who delight in baiting others. If such a person works for you, it can be pretty annoying. However, in most cases it's relatively harmless – unless of course, you lose your cool and rise to the bait.

Q: "I've got several people in my department who are always needling me with comments such as, "Hey Joe, how come Quality Control people get to leave early on Fridays?" or, "Joe, whey do the Final Assembly grunts get 9% raises when we only get 5%?" Are my workers just needling me, or is there more to it than that?

A: That depends upon the circumstances. On the one hand, the comments could be factual and a real irritant to your people. The flip side of the coin is that you're just being baited by subordinates to get your reaction.

If you want to avoid being baited, you have to learn to refuse to bite the bait. Although it's important to communicate effectively with workers, and to argue on their behalf when necessary, there are limits. That means you can't spin your wheels chasing down every gripe to sort out fact from fiction. By doing that, you open yourself up for continuous baiting. It's possible to get inadvertently drawn into this trap if you're conscientious about checking out employee questions.

However, you have to be careful to separate the real concerns from the nonsense.

A sure sign that you're going overboard is if you chase around knocking down allegations such as those posed in the question. If that's happening, rein yourself in. That requires giving short-shrift to endless comparisons with other departments. Once you start saying, "That's nonsense," and/or "Don't worry about other people," the baiting will subside.

4.4 THE BASIC SECRET FOR CONTROLLING BUCK-PASSING

One of the subtleties every supervisor must contend with are folks skilled in the fine art of buck-passing. Though it's often treated as a trivial matter, and is even fodder for wisecracks, buck-passing can create real headaches if it's not controlled.

Q: I'm getting mixed up in a lot of Dick and Dolly controversies. The kind where Dick said Dolly didn't give him the right information, while Dolly contends she did. How do you handle this sort of thing?

A: Buck-passing is regularly treated as something that happens somewhere else. Regrettably, it's a lot more prevalent than most people care to admit. And if it's allowed to thrive, it can cause difficulties ranging from worker hostility to poor productivity. The cornerstone to coping with buck-passing starts with recognizing that it can happen anywhere and anytime. The best prevention is to let people know that you won't tolerate it.

Most buck-passing within a department takes the form of an employee pinning the blame on someone else when something goes wrong. In fact, buck-passers are simply covering up for their own mistakes.

From your standpoint, the difficulty lies in deciding who is right, since you don't want to point the finger at someone who is an unwitting victim. Buck-passers operate on the assumption that (1) you'll accept their claim at face value and/or, (2) circumstances are such that there's no proof of who's guilty even if you do investigate the buck-passer's assertion.

Therefore, keeping a lid on buck-passing means getting involved by not letting claims go unchallenged, and if possible, setting up procedures to prevent any future repetition of a buck-passing incident. Let's look at how this can be done.

Background

Dick and Dolly both work for Francis in the shipping department of a midsize manufacturer. A crisis has developed because size "C" cartons are needed for a priority shipment to a customer and none are in stock.

The "Who Done It" Mystery

Francis: "Dick, how could we run out of size "C" cartons? You and Dolly are supposed to reorder when the inventory level hits 500."

Dick: "Dolly told me two weeks ago that she sent a requisition to purchasing. It's only a seven day turnaround so we should have had them a week ago. No sweat, she just forgot. I ran a requisition up to purchasing yesterday, and they called the vendor to expedite delivery. We'll have the cartons in two days."

Francis: "Add a day to pack and ship. We'll be three days late with the delivery. I'm going to get flack about this from Hodges (the plant manager)."

Dick: "Hey, so Dolly forgot. We've been busy and we're only human."

Francis: "Yeh, well Hodges ain't human when it comes to late deliveries. This better not happen again."

Dick: "No sweat boss. I'll watch inventory levels like a hawk."

Francis: "Well, just watch it from now on. I'll talk to Dolly when she comes in tomorrow. She's out sick today."

Dick: "Aw, forget about it boss. You know how dedicated Dolly is. She already feels bad enough."

Francis:	"Not as bad as I'm going to feel when Hodges rakes me over the coals. Oh well, let's get back to work."

The Next Day

Francis:	"Can I see you in my office for a minute, Dolly?"
Dolly:	"Sure Frank, what's up?"
Francis:	"We ran out of size 'C' cartons yesterday. Do you know why?"
Dolly:	"That's strange. About three weeks ago Dick and I inventoried all of the cartons. Sizes 'A', 'C', and 'M' needed reordering. Dick said he'd take care of it. I know he did because I saw him filling out the requisitions."
Francis:	"Did we get the 'A's' and 'M's' in?"
Dolly:	"Yea. They came in about a week ago. Want me to check on the size 'C's?"
Francis:	"No, that's ok I'll talk to purchasing."

Decision Time

Francis checks with purchasing and it turns out that Dick had prepared a requisition for sizes "A" and "M" about three weeks ago, and had requisitioned size "C" the previous day. Francis knows that the cartons are always reordered at the same time. It's apparent that Dick goofed and forgot to order size "C" when he ordered the others.

Although Francis is convinced that Dick goofed and then blamed Dolly, he decides not to pursue the matter directly, since Dick will likely stick to his story, or make some other excuse. That will also lead to open conflict between Dick and Dolly. However, Francis decides that Dolly should be given sole responsibility for future reordering. He also knows that Dick isn't in a position to object, therefore, he calls them both into his office.

Francis:	"Look, Hodges chewed me out today about the late delivery because of the size "C" carton shortage. That's not going to happen again. From now on I want you, Dolly, to handle all reordering. Furthermore, copy me

on each requisition that you send to purchasing. Any questions? No, good. That's all for now."

Francis has identified the buck-passer and has taken steps to make certain that this type of incident doesn't repeat itself. He also is savvy enough to know that there's little to be gained by confronting Dick about trying to pin the blame on Dolly. This way, Dick and Dolly still have a good working relationship.

You might think that this isn't being fair to Dolly. Well, when the shipping department expands and needs a supervisor, guess who it will be? Francis had adroitly started to groom Dolly for the job by giving her the exclusive responsibility for reordering inventory items.

Obviously, pinning down buck-passers isn't always this easy, nor does it have as positive a result. Under any circumstances, if you take the time to tactfully follow-up assertions that try to pin the blame elsewhere, you'll have better control over buck-passing.

4.5 HOW TO STOP SUBORDINATES FROM USING SCAPEGOATING

Scapegoating is a close relation to buck-passing. The principle difference is that buck-passing generally refers to passing the responsibility for making a decision to someone else, while scapegoating is primarily associated with looking for someone to wrongfully blame for some form of blunder. Actually – as in the Dick and Dolly case – the difference is often blurred. As a supervisor, you will usually find scapegoating taking the form of employees placing the blame on other departments when problems occur.

Q: My department, which is Final Assembly, has frequent squabbles with the people in Quality Control. I'm not sure whether QC is rejecting items because of quality problems, or for spite because of the hostility between the departments. However, my people blame QC. How can I get this resolved?

A: It's certainly not unusual in a manufacturing operation for disagreements to arise between manufacturing and quality control.

The latter function is to catch other folk's mistakes, and no one wants to admit they did subpar work. In essence, minor scapegoating is nothing more than the normal grumbling about something over which a worker has little or no control. This type of carping should be essentially ignored once it's identified for what it is.

The interdepartmental scapegoating that causes difficulty is when workers claim that their performance is suffering from the actions of other departments. The only way to cure this problem is to get the facts, and then talk to your counterpart in the other group. By working together, the two of you should be able to identify what's wrong. Once you have the problem spotted, correct it and let your people know the results.

For example, let's assume you're the supervisor in the question who is having the problems with Quality Control. You meet with Ken, the QC supervisor, and discuss the controversy. Ken then agrees to tell his people to let him know the next time there are rejects from your unit. This happens, and Ken shows you the defective items which obviously don't meet specifications. You then call your people together for a meeting.

You: "I've got a couple of items here that were rejected by QC. If we want to lower the reject rate, we'll have to pay closer attention to tolerances. Incidentally, in talking with Ken in QC, I learned they don't like rejects either, since reworked items have to be QC'd all over again. So I don't want to hear any more griping about them doing it on purpose.

Of course, not all problems will turn out this way. The difficulty may actually be in the other department, or it may be that the cause originates somewhere else. For instance, in the QC case, the supervisors might have discovered that an engineering drawing was in error, which was the reason behind the rejections. Whatever the cause, the major thrust in dealing with scapegoating is to get the facts and then eliminate the cause.

CAUTION: Don't be accusatory when working with other supervisors to solve a scapegoating dilemma. Even if you're fairly

certain that your people are correct, remember that your role is to be
a fact-finder; not a finger-pointer. Accusations will only cause other
supervisors to become defensive, and that alone makes it much more
difficult to resolve the problem.

4.6 THE WAY TO OUTMANEUVER MANIPULATORS

Subordinates may try to manipulate you in any number of ways to
get what they want. They may also do this to protect themselves by
covering up problems instead of bringing them to your attention.

*Q: I don't like to be conned. How can I distinguish between
subordinates who are buttering me up for their own benefit, and
those who are just plain friendly?*

A: Why bother to try? If a teenage son volunteers to put the
trash out, is he just being helpful or will he later ask to borrow the
car to take the gang for pizza? However, even if he does ask for the
car keys, are the two events related? It's important to accept people
at face value. As long as you remain objective in your dealings
with subordinates, they'll soon learn that you don't play favorites.
Therefore, any overt manipulator trying to get on your good side will
realize that you're impressed by performance alone.

The main danger with manipulators is that they'll fail to level
with you when something goes wrong. The only way to counter this
trait is to establish an environment of trust and honesty within your
department. If you don't blast people when they make mistakes, but
instead seek solutions, people will keep you posted on what's going
on – both the good and the bad.

4.7 WINNING THE CONTEST WHEN WORKERS PLAY GAMES

A few workers try to make careers out of challenging their supervisor
at every opportunity. Instead of channeling their creativity into the
job, they concentrate on testing your self-restraint.

Q: There's one person who works for me who seems to delight in playing work-avoidance games and coming up with complaints by the carload. I'm tired of his mind games, so how can I end this nonsense?

A: First of all, as far as work-avoidance goes, apply the same techniques you would in handling goof-offs (Sec. 3.3) and sneaks (Sec. 3.14). The difficulty with game players is that they aren't as easy to control as other types of shirkers. They seemingly accept any action you take as a challenge. In fact, a worker skilled at playing games can go undetected for a considerable period of time. At other times, game players adopt an attitude of, "I'm yanking your chain. I know it and you know it, but you have to prove it."

Whereas, goof-offs and other shirkers are mainly trying to avoid work, the game player's focus is to challenge your authority. The kinds of games played are limited only by the imagination of the culprit. A few examples include

- On-the-job absence. There's always a reason for this character to be somewhere other than working. Such lines include, "I have to take this down to fabrication," or, "I wasn't late. I stopped off in payroll to check on my vacation time."
- The organization organizer. Always takes up collections, organizes parties, or attends luncheons for someone leaving the company.
- The working environment critic. "It's too cold in here," which is quickly followed-up with a two-day absence with a cold, and a comment upon return, "I told you it was too cold in here. No wonder I got sick."
- Self-promoters. These people perform duties that they aren't authorized to do. If they get away with it, they'll later use this as a reason why they deserve a promotion. (This is one of the few instances where a game player does any work without being prodded.)
- Boss knockers. This type of person will contradict you in front of your boss, screw things up that you have to answer

for – they have a ready-made excuse – and do anything else they can get away with to make you look bad.

The long and the short of winning the battle with a game player is to lay it right on the line in a private meeting. Tell this person in so many words, "I know what you're up to, so don't think you're being cute." Naturally, they'll look shocked and adamantly deny what you're saying. Therefore, ignore them, keep the meeting brief, and don't get drawn into a discussion with a glib game player who will just try to gloss over what you're saying. Once game planners are directly confronted, they usually will, (1) try to transfer within the company, (2) leave the company for another job, or (3) knock-off the nonsense.

In the event the encounter doesn't have any impact, eventually you may have to take disciplinary action.

CAUTION: Document deficiencies carefully, and keep your boss and personnel staffers informed as difficulties arise with game players. They tend to be experts at denial, so it's prudent to follow the rules carefully if you are forced to take formal action.

4.8 WHAT YOU CAN DO ABOUT JEALOUS WORKERS

Jealous workers are usually more of a nuisance than anything else. However, they do have the potential for undermining cooperation within your department. It's certainly not personally insignificant when they get on your nerves.

Q: One or two people who work for me are consumed by petty jealousy. They spend more time worrying about what everyone else is doing, instead of trying to improve themselves. All I know is that it irritates me. Can this sort of envy be dealt with?

A: If you're fair in terms of pay raises, promotions, and work assignments, consistent in your interaction with subordinates, and don't play favorites, then there are no valid reasons for someone to be jealous of others within your department – at least as far as work is concerned. That doesn't mean you won't have someone working for you who is jealous by nature. Some folks are never satisfied, so the standard in dealing with jealousy is not to pander to this trait. In effect, react to jealousy by telling the person to, "Worry about yourself, not Jane or Julie."

The reason that consistency is so important in this regard is that jealous workers will pick up on and amplify any inconsistencies. For instance, one worker will say to another, "Look at that. Every time there's an easy job to do, she gives it to Jim." In fact, jealous people excel in creating inconsistencies where none exist.

There is one form of envy that can be more widespread, and that's interdepartmental jealousy. This happens when there's a real or perceived notion that certain groups of employees are treated better by upper management. There will always be a little bit of comparison griping in any organization based more or less on "the grass is always greener" cliché.

However, if the jealousy gets out of hand, try to offset employee concerns with facts that counteract their erroneous impressions. Of course, if employee perceptions of favoritism appear to be justified, let your boss know about it. Sometimes inadvertent or unthinking actions by management can create this problem. If you see this developing, alerting management to the impact on morale may get the situation turned around.

4.9 CRAMPING THE STYLE OF CONSTANT COMPLAINERS

Have you ever told a subordinate, "I don't want to hear about it?" Even if you haven't mouthed the words, chances are that the thought has flashed through your mind on more than one occasion. Even though chronic complainers can engender these thoughts, it's not a good idea to shoot them down before you hear what they have to say.

Q: My most irksome griper is a guy who never has personal complaints, but persistently badgers me on behalf of other people. For example, last week he came into the office and said, "Poor John, he ought to be promoted. Just because he's not personable doesn't mean he's not a good worker." He's doing things like this all of the time. What gives with this guy?

A: You're faced with what could be called a "good Samaritan" complainer. This type of individual will haunt you on behalf of other people's interests. Their reason for doing this can vary. They might be the kind of person who is easily led, which leads other workers to use them as stooges. It doesn't take long to discover this sort of practice. When you do, admonish these people with comments such as, "I'm sure John can speak for himself."

Another reason for a "good Samaritan" to tout the skills of someone else isn't as charitable as it appears to be. For instance, what they're trying to sell for a co-worker may be a second-hand way of making a pitch for themselves. Actually, the complainer in the question may be pushing John for promotion on the assumption that what's good for John is good for him. Nevertheless, it's not your job to play amateur psychologist and try to discern motives. Here again, merely ease the complainant aside with the suggestion that the person under discussion is quite competent to handle his own affairs.

Q: There seems to be as great a variety of complaints in my company as there are cereal brands in the supermarket. Are there any general guidelines that are useful in disposing of complaints?

A: A few helpful rules to follow are:

1. Always listen to complaints, since even a chronic complainer may have a legitimate gripe.
2. Don't participate in gossip, since this encourages workers to complain if they decide you have a willing ear.
3. Think about the complaint, instead of the complainer. Is there a real basis for the complaint? If so, take the necessary steps to resolve it.
4. Pay particular attention when you get a gripe from someone who seldom complains. It may signal a serious concern that needs attention.

5. Never minimize any complaint. There may be more to it than meets the eye.
6. Be alert for situations that could escalate into complaints, and take preventive measures. For example, aggressive and alert supervisors can prevent sexual harassment or prejudicial behavior from developing by letting their people know it won't be tolerated.
7. General complaints about company policy shouldn't be ignored. Keep your boss informed when these gripes go beyond petty grumbling.

TIP: No one wants to listen to complaints. You know this from your own life experiences apart from your job. Even if you are by nature a willing listener, the crush of daily duties doesn't allow the luxury of extensive hand-holding. Despite this, it's of vital importance to at least spend long enough listening to even trivial complaints so workers know that you will listen to their concerns.

In fact, it's easy enough to discourage complaints by being harshly critical when you hear them. However, if you get to the point where you no longer get any complaints, you're either in utopia, or have discouraged subordinates from complaining. If it's utopia, try to recall if you recently received a sharp blow to the head, since you may need medical attention. Otherwise, start listening, since if you're not hearing occasional complaints, the chances are that you're out of touch with your subordinates. When that happens, disaster may be lurking in the wings.

4.10 WHY THE WORST WORKERS COMPLAIN ABOUT FAVORITISM

One of the most perplexing tasks a supervisor must manage is the fact that less capable subordinates may do the most griping. The focus of these complaints often centers on favoritism.

Q: Freda, a marginal worker in my department, isn't very prompt about completing assignments, but she's pretty swift in complaining about favoritism whenever someone is promoted. Is there a way to handle this without having to just tell her that she's not promotable?

A: Less capable workers, by-passed for promotion, often fall back on a charge of favoritism. From your viewpoint, this is pure nonsense. However, it's not really surprising if you think about it. Workers whose performance is poor can't logically lodge a complaint about being by-passed because of their ability. Therefore, to justify it in their own minds, they link it to favoritism.

When employees come to you with claims of favoritism, simply point out that it's not true. Of course, try to encourage these individuals to improve their performance, but make no promises about the future that can come back to haunt you.

There are essentially two levels to this type of complaint. The first consists of workers who only want a willing ear to listen to their frustrations. In more severe cases, a worker may insist on pursuing these charges with the personnel office and/or through union representatives if your company is unionized.

In either case, if there's no substance to the charge, let the facts fall where they may. When workers persist in a charge of favoritism against all odds, it's quite likely they will quit or transfer once their appeal has run its course.

The important point in this regard is not to blame yourself for the incident. There's no way you can prevent a problem of this nature if a worker is inclined to complain. No matter how hard you try to be the best boss possible, you'll never be 100% successful at pleasing everyone. So do the best you can and let it go at that.

4.11 HOW TO UNRAVEL RED-TAPE COMPLAINTS

Generally speaking, the larger a company is, the more cumbersome are the policies and procedures that have to be followed. To some degree this is understandable, since you can't run an organization with thousands of employees by word of mouth.

On the other hand, a single bottleneck in a small to midsize business can cause more confusion than any detailed policy and procedures manual. Wherever you work, in one form or another, cutting through "red tape" may be the only way to complete a project on schedule.

Q: Here at Bottleneck Bottling Corp., they seem to be striving for a "red-tape" award. It's at the point where getting anything done is an exercise in futility. This has my people constantly fuming. It is possible to cut through this kind of mess without getting in hot water with the power structure within the company?

A: Actually, the more hidebound an organization is with rules and regulations, the easier they are to circumvent without any negative repercussions. That's because, first of all, many other people will share your frustration. This makes them willing accomplices in bending the rules.

Furthermore, the more procedures there are, the less likely it is that anyone understands them all, and this lessens your chances of being challenged for non-compliance. How you go about getting around "red tape" is to a large degree dictated by the particular hurdle you have to overcome. Several methods that will succeed under differing conditions are

1. *Avoid "paper pusher" personalities.* These are people who always seem to brush you off by digging up obscure regulations that essentially say, "You have to do this before you can do that." Inevitably, the "this" requires some action to be taken before you get to "that," which involves work for the person who is shunting you aside by hiding behind a procedures manual. Work around these people as much as you can, since they're a sure-fire impediment to getting anything done in a hurry.

2. *Outsmart "job justifiers".* You may run into folks in the approval loop who never make a decision on the first pass. They justify their existence by questioning everything they see for the first time. Unfailingly, anything you give them will require more work to be done before they'll buy off. Here again is a situation where you have to work around these roadblocks as much as possible. The

difference between these people and "paper pushers" is that "job justifiers" essentially agree with what you're doing, but insist on minor changes, while "paper pushers" won't make any commitment.

Naturally if your immediate boss is a "job justifier" you can't easily take him out of the loop, but you can make things more bearable for yourself by anticipating the objections. Often, "job justifiers" have pet peeves, and once you discover what they are, you can become more effective at counteracting these petty annoyances. Usually, "job justifiers" don't go into any great depth in their review. They're only looking for one item to question which will justify their job – to themselves and to you.

Once you peg someone as a "job justifier," leave out something easy that they can pick up on. That way, they won't delve too deeply and cause you greater grief. Nothing illustrates this practice better than the case of Alonzo, the artful dodger.

Alonzo knew that his boss nit-picked the first page or two to death. It didn't really much matter what the subject was, the first couple of pages were the boss's sole obsession. Other supervisors were driven up the wall by this trait, but not Alonzo. He never got the first page right, which meant he had to spend a few minutes doing it over.

In the meantime, other supervisors took great pains to make sure the first couple of pages of any document wouldn't raise any questions. Did this solve their problem? Of course not. Howard, the boss, would comb everything in detail until he could find something to criticize. Frequently, what he found would require a lot of effort to correct. Alonzo, on the other hand, could sail anything by Howard once he corrected the planted errors in the first couple of pages. Obviously, this is an unusual situation, but it does demonstrate one valuable lesson: "Know thine enemy."

3. *Adopt a "paperwork will follow" strategy.* Just because procedures say do things in A, B, C, order doesn't mean

you can't speed things along by doing them concurrently, out of sequence, or in the case of paperwork, after-the-fact. If you have a rush job to get out, a lot of internal paperwork can be done later. To facilitate this practice, network with people in the company who can help you speed things along. Being friendly with people can go a long way toward getting you through the gristmill in a hurry.

REMINDER: Don't forget that there's a quid-pro-quo involved here. If other people do you favors, be sure to reciprocate when the time comes. If you don't you'll see how quickly cooperation can evaporate.

4. *Interpret procedures to your advantage.* The more complex rules and regulations are, the more subject they become to interpretation. Look for the loopholes and plow on through to get the job done. If and when you're challenged, reply by saying, "that's the way I interpreted the procedure."

5. *Plead priority.* The simplest way to get something done quickly is to plead the urgent priority of what you're doing. However, you can't overuse this technique or eventually you won't be taken seriously, so reserve its use for rare events.

Q: It's nice – and perhaps even necessary – to find ways to get things done in a hurry. What bothers me is the ethics involved in breaking the rules. Is that proper?

A: We're not talking here about being unethical, and it's a question of bending and interpreting rules – not breaking them. Procedures are set forth so everyone has a standard set of guidelines to follow. Every circumstance won't fit the guidelines, so you have to make exceptions.

Furthermore, the guidelines assume that everyone is doing their job as they should. However, it can be argued that it's not very ethical for incompetents such as "job justifiers" to unreasonably impede the orderly flow of work. When the crime is incompetence, the best crime prevention policy is circumvention.

4.12 PREVENTIVE MEASURE TO AVOID MISUNDERSTANDINGS

There are two things that are likely to survive for future generations to endure – roaches and misunderstandings. Fortunately, both can be minimized by concentrating on prevention and control. Although as a supervisor you don't have extermination as an option to eliminate misunderstandings, there are other preventive measures that work. These include

1. First of all, follow the steps for effective listening in Sec. 2.11 and persuasion in Sec. 2.13.
2. Don't give off-the-cuff answers to employee questions. If you're not sure of the correct answer, look into the matter before you respond. This is especially true when workers ask questions about pay and other pocketbook issues.
3. Don't relay messages through others, since they may be altered in the process.
4. Don't promise what you can't deliver.
5. Strive for objectivity when dealing with subordinates.
6. Let people down gently when you don't agree with them. For example, "I see what you're saying Vincent, and although it has merit here's why we can't do it that way..." Then explain your reasoning.
7. When a misunderstanding takes place heal the wound as quickly as possible. Even when an employee is wrong, take the initiative in letting this person know that there's no ill-will. Letting hostility fester only leads to future misunderstandings. (See Sec. 5.6 on preserving goodwill for tips on how to do this.)

4.13 OVERCOMING PERSONALITY CLASHES

When personalities clash at work a great deal of friction can result. This can affect job performance, so it's necessary to maintain some semblance of group harmony despite individual differences.

Q: What can I do to inspire employees who don't get along with each other to become better friends?

A: Your job as a supervisor is to promote teamwork so as to get the most productive effort from your unit. You shouldn't concern yourself with promoting friendships. There are people who won't like each other no matter what you do. All you should care about is that aggression and hostility are suppressed within the workplace.

If people argue, that's their business. However, if they want to do it at work and disrupt other people then it becomes your business.

The main issue to avoid is taking sides, or becoming a "kiddie counselor" by trying to mediate petty quarrels. For instance, visualize two children that a mother has told not to argue, but instead to tell her about disputes. Assume it's a Saturday morning about 11:00 A.M. and Dennis, age eight, and Darlene who is nine, are playing in the backyard.

11:01 A.M. Dennis and Darlene run in the house.
Darlene: "Mom, Dennis hit my ball over the fence."
Dennis: "No, I didn't. She threw it over." (Mom mediates.)
11:09 A.M. Dennis and Darlene are back in the house.
Dennis: "Mom, Darlene called me a jerk.
Darlene: "That's because he called me a big baby." (Mom admonishes the kids about calling people names.)
11:15 A.M. Guess what? Here comes Darlene and Dennis.
Darlene: "Mom, Dennis won't let me ride his scooter."
Dennis: "She won't let me use her things, so I'm not letting her use mine." (Mom discusses sharing and not being selfish.)

Within a span of fourteen minutes the two kids have come to Mom three times with their gripes. Dependent upon her degree of patience, she will soon reach a state of apoplexy. What does this childish bickering have to do with supervising people who don't get along?

Aside from the fact that some folks never grow up – they just get a job – the children's actions demonstrate two points. The first, and most obvious, is that if you start mediating between two workers who don't get along very well, you're going to have your hands just as full as the kids' mom.

Perhaps less obvious, but equally telling, is that the children are in the process of learning to relate to one another. The folks who work for you are adults – even though you may doubt it on occasion – and have a responsibility to get along with others, whether they like them or not.

Therefore, if two people don't get along to the extent that they're a disruptive influence, sit them down and let them know you won't tolerate their behavior. This usually settles things down on the surface, but if it doesn't, you may eventually have to get rid of one or both.

4.14 EXCUSES: THE GOOD, THE BAD, AND THE UGLY

The closest thing to certainty in this uncertain world is that as a supervisor you're virtually guaranteed to hear at least one excuse within the next week. Excuses can range from funny to foolish, and from sincere to silly. The bottom line is that they're either a valid reason, or a shallow alibi, for something that didn't go quite right. When you hear one, it's your job to separate fact from fiction.

Q: Excuses, excuses, excuses. That's all I hear. My problem is how to tell the acceptable from the phony.

A: Most folks don't know too much about legal matters. However, one legal principle is readily understood in the workplace and that's "Innocent until proven guilty." This basic fundamental of our system of justice is exercised wholeheartedly at work in the form of excuses.

The nub of the matter when it comes to excuses is whether or not the reason given for some form of misdeed is valid, or merely a cover-up. In deciding this, it's helpful to consider the following factors:

- Is the excuse reasonable? "I'm late because of the traffic snarl on the freeway caused by an overturned truck."
- Is the excuse unreasonable? "I was halfway to work when I remembered that I forgot to feed Yapper, my pet parakeet, so I had to go home."
- Are you consistent in accepting or rejecting excuses? If you tell the first two people that are late on Monday morning that it's alright, it's not reasonable to nail the third person just because your tolerance has terminated for the day.
- The impact of company policy and its implementation. If company policy states that an employee who is late three times in one month gets a formal warning, that's pretty clear-cut. However, you can't ignore the extent to which this policy is followed throughout the company.
- Individual circumstances. You have to consider the consequences of the action which generates an excuse. For instance, a clerk fifteen minutes late may not cause problems, while a delivery truck driver may have a rigid time schedule to meet.
- The need for flexibility. People to encounter real problems, so it's important to be flexible about accepting excuses. A strict policy of, "I don't want to hear excuses," penalizes good workers as well as bad. It's better to let a shirker get away with something occasionally, than to penalize good workers by a rigid "no excuses" attitude. You'll catch up with the shirkers eventually.

4.15 HOW TO COUNTER EVERY EXCUSE IN THE BOOK

What's your reaction to excuses? It's valuable to think about this, since the pattern you set can either encourage the use of excuses, or reduce their frequency.

Q: Is there a standard to apply in determining when enough is enough? Some people can reel off one excuse after another and they all seem pretty reasonable.

A: In responding to excuses, a rigid rule would be to treat all of them as unacceptable. That means going strictly by the book. Applying this kind of policy might be fairly easy in some areas, such as unauthorized absences. Here, company policy may state that a worker doesn't get paid if the absence wasn't approved beforehand, or if an ill employee doesn't notify the supervisor by a set time.

But even though such a policy seems simple enough to adhere to, it's not necessarily wise or practical. For example, what if there was a death in the immediate family and a grief-stricken worker forgot to call. Do you go by the book and dock the employee a day's pay? What kind of reaction would that have on your subordinates? The truth is that every circumstance can't be covered by rules and regulations. So accepting or rejecting excuses requires some discretion.

Sure, being flexible about excuses may allow a laggard to be late a few times. However, sooner or later, you'll be able to pinpoint the one or two people who specialize in "the devil made me do it" practices. Your real concern is when to call a halt to these shenanigans.

Once you target an employee who uses phony excuses, develop the habit of putting the ball in his court. The essence of any excuse is to place the decision on your shoulders as to whether or not the excuse will be accepted. Instead of that, make the employee do the thinking. For instance, with a tardy employee say, "What can we do to prevent this from happening again?" Inevitably, you'll receive some form of assurance.

That gives you an opening to say, "Great Sam, I'm glad that will cure the problem, because the next time you are tardy, I was going to have to dock your pay." You now have let Sam know that he'll be docked if he's late again. Since Sam's assured you that he won't be, he can't say much when it happens.

The basic idea is to let wholesale excuse-users know that they've used up their quota. In short, three strikes and you're out works as well in the game of excuses as it does in baseball.

TIP: Your temperament can influence the number of excuses you have to handle. If you're easygoing, people may think you're a soft touch. On the other hand, if you're hot-tempered, excuses may be made to escape your wrath.

4.16 SHOOTING DOWN PLODDERS LOOKING FOR PROMOTIONS

Wherever you work, now or in the future, it's inevitable that you'll have to finesse mediocre workers who think they should be promoted. Although you might like to say, "Produce or shut up," it's not quite that simple.

Q: There's got to be something I can do about workers who aren't qualified to be promoted, but incessantly complain that they should be. I've faced this dilemma in every supervisory position I've ever had.

A: Since most organizations are essentially pyramids, with the greatest number of people at the bottom, and with fewer folks at each level going toward the top, this will always be a problem. Therefore, your objective should be twofold, (1) make certain that everyone has an equal opportunity to be promoted, and (2) minimize the grumbling of those who will never make it, which includes not only those lacking the skills, but also workers with bad attitudes and poor work habits.

You may at times be annoyed at certain employees who angle for promotions. Not infrequently, they include people whose performance is so poor they're on the verge of being fired. If nothing else, this is positive proof that we don't see ourselves as others view us. However, that knowledge doesn't bring any solace when you're being pestered about promotions.

What can you do? Several things including answering the "When am I getting promoted?" question in the manner discussed in Sec. 3.7 on loaded questions. Beyond that, you should make every effort to upgrade the skills of your people to the point where they become promotable. This not only means telling them at performance evaluation time what they need to do for improvement, but also continually working with them throughout the year.

Despite your best efforts in this regard, there will be workers who just can't hack it, and/or don't even try. There are some folks who if you lit a fire under them would just sit there until you put it out. However, there can be hope for employees with marginal capabilities, even when they may not have the talent to get promoted to the next level in the normal progression within the company.

If they display skills better suited to other areas, work with them in seeking a possible job transfer. Or if they express interest in other fields, encourage them to pursue career goals on their own. If they quit to do this, you have the satisfaction of knowing you helped someone to see where their future was brighter. Even in the absence of a charitable motive, you will still benefit. Don't forget, you're losing a plodder, not a star.

Finally, with hard-core harassers who won't take "No" for an answer, and insist that they're being treated unfairly, tell it like it is. That is, diplomatically suggest that if they think someone else's grass is greener, perhaps they should look for another lawn to mow – which translates to another job with another supervisor to listen to their laments.

5

The Do's and Don'ts of Dishing Out Discipline

The one aspect of supervision that will test both your patience and your managerial skills is discipline. It's nice to heave a sigh of relief and think, "I haven't had a serious discipline problem in ages." Although major disciplinary actions pop-up only periodically, they're both time consuming and nerve racking. Therefore, it pays to be prepared to deal with them when they do occur.

Even more relevant on a day-to-day basis are the preventive measures you can use to prevent minor irritants from developing into major disasters. Something as insignificant as tardiness can become a major problem if it's not nipped in the bud. Unauthorized absence is another area of concern for supervisors. These along with drinking, drug use, and just plain lazy workers are all prevalent headaches that you as a supervisor must confront head-on.

The following sections discuss how to handle the realities of disciplinary problems both large and small. Beyond that, it's important to consider how best to counsel employees when they make the inevitable errors that can turn both your day and disposition from pleasant to sour. As good a place as any to begin is by looking at the need to correct mistakes in a positive rather than a negative way.

5.1 THE MYTH OF CONSTRUCTIVE CRITICISM

No one likes to be criticized, but there's a general belief that it's acceptable if it's "constructive criticism." That raises the question of constructive to whom? And who makes that judgment?

Q: What is constructive criticism? I've never liked being criticized, and furthermore, I've never considered it to be constructive. Don't get me wrong. I've received helpful suggestions, as well as good advice, but never under the guise of criticism.

A: So-called "constructive criticism" is frequently used as self-justification for giving criticism. The old bromide, "I'm just telling you this for your own good," is about as effective as telling someone to bang their head against a wall to cure a toothache. That's because even when criticism achieves the desired result, it can leave behind feelings of anger and resentment. How would you react if you were on the receiving end of comments such as these?

1. "There's only one way to do that, and I've told you that ten times." (But never showed the worker once.)
2. "I'm not being critical, but the fact is you're going too slow." (Another process is slowing the employee down.)
3. "It's not the machine's fault we're getting rejects." (It is, but the supervisor didn't check it out.)
4. "I don't care how they did it at Unger Underwear. That's not the way we do it here." (The supervisor doesn't care that the other method is more efficient, and/or explain why it can't be used.)

The whole theory behind constructive criticism is that it's proper because it's correcting something that's wrong. The problem is that it often has a negative impact on the worker. Furthermore, it's sometimes used without establishing the real cause of a problem. Simply put, criticism isn't constructive just because someone puts that label on it. Dressing up an angry rebuff to a worker in the cloak of constructive criticism is about as effective as a hairpiece that doesn't fit. Both cover up the problem without actually solving it.

5.2 THE FOUR KEYS TO EFFECTIVE CRITICISM

When an employee does something wrong there's a need to prevent a repetition of the mistake. That is, unless it was insignificant and/ or the occasional error that's to be expected. This means you have to communicate with the worker, so that the worker understands what went wrong, and how to correct it. Yet, just criticizing the employee for the failure isn't necessarily productive. In fact, it can make matters worse. Therefore, you have a far greater chance of success if you use a positive rather than a negative approach.

Q: This morning I said to an employee, "I've told you five times in the last three weeks that you can't operate that machine with one hand." She looked at me like I was crazy and replied, "No, you didn't." I'm continually telling people the same thing time and time again. Are they dense or am I missing something?

A: One reason supervisors are frequently frustrated is the inability of a worker to understand and/or positively respond to constructive criticism. A major reason is the very fact that it is just that – criticism. A natural reaction of anyone would be "Who needs this aggravation?"

The effective way around this dilemma is to correct employees by using positive tactics rather than being critical. It's easy to think, "Hey, how many times do I have to tell these people the same thing?" It's readily understandable that you can easily get angry about seemingly careless mistakes that are repeated time and time again. However, as you may have experienced for yourself, criticism in the traditional sense doesn't always work too well.

Therefore, you may find that you have far greater success by using techniques that avoid criticism, but still manage to convey the fact that an adjustment needs to be made in some aspect of the employee's performance. One way to do this is to use a four-P's strategy consisting of being positive, persistent, patient, and practical. The basics of this plan are as follows:

1. Be positive. Always correct mistakes from a positive angle and with language that doesn't indicate criticism.

Positive: "John, the best way to do that operation is with a one, two, three motion. Here, let me show you."

Negative: "When the heck are you going to learn to do that right?"

In essence, showing a worker the correct way to perform a task, and discussing any problems the worker might have, is more effective than raking the person over the coals. Why? Because there's less likelihood that people will hide their mistakes, slow down their production to get it right, or not do the work at all if they can figure out how to avoid tasks that arouse your anger.

2. Be persistent. It may take two or three times – perhaps more – for some people to absorb what you want and how you want it done. This is to be expected, so don't give up after one try.
3. Be patient. Never let anger overwhelm your ability to get your point across. There's no denying that frustration can set in as you struggle to convince a worker that a job has to be done a certain way. However, patience will allow you to persevere, while anger won't.
4. Be practical. Every employee is different, so don't establish excessive performance standards based on your best worker. You will have to work more closely with some people to get them up to an acceptable level of performance. Inevitably, you may even find that a few workers just aren't cut out for the job. Most of all, don't practice perfectionism. No one is perfect and mistakes will be made. Therefore, accept them as such and don't stress yourself out over it.

5.3 TO DISCIPLINE OR NOT TO DISCPLINE: CONSISTENCY COUNTS

One of the most undesirable tasks a supervisor must perform is to dispense discipline. It may not be pleasant, but at times it's necessary. Avoiding the issue will more often than not just make matters worse.

Q: It's pretty unnerving to think about taking disciplinary action. Frankly, I'm not the type of person who handles angry confrontations very well. Is there a way to train myself to handle these events without being a nervous wreck?

A: It's easy to work yourself into an emotional turmoil when you're considering disciplinary action. One or more of the following thoughts may go through your mind:

- What will the employee's reaction be?
- Will the face-to-face encounter get out of hand?
- Will I make a fool of myself?
- Can I control my temper if verbally attacked?
- How will other workers react when they hear the news?
- Am I making the right decision?
- If I wait to take action, will the employee straighten out?
- Can I make my point without taking formal disciplinary measures?

First of all, it's entirely proper to have concerns such as those listed. After all, a disciplinary action is a serious matter. In fact, only an unthinking fool would dish out discipline as casually as handing out noise-makers on New Year's Eve. However, you can only dwell on it for so long before recognizing that disciplinary action is both proper and necessary. Usually, supervisors mull over these decisions a lot longer than is justified.

Furthermore, there can be other consequences when a decision is postponed for too long. For instance, if you condone tardiness for an extended period of time, it sends a signal that you accept this practice. This can then lead to lateness by people who ordinarily would observe the rules.

The same is true for extended lunch hours, absenteeism, or any other form of work avoidance. All of which means that delaying action makes it harder for you to enforce discipline when you finally make a move. Therefore, if you decide that you must take disciplinary action, keep the following ideas in mind:

1. Follow the rules. Be sure you stick to the proper procedure as set forth in company rules for disciplinary action. Coordinate with both your boss and personnel people versed in the proper procedures before you move ahead. This is of even greater consequence if you're dealing with a union member.

2. Follow a predetermined game plan. Decide beforehand what action is appropriate. Then, tell the employee why you're taking the action, what it means, its impact, and what the employee has to do to improve.

3. Be decisive. Do your decision making before you initiate disciplinary measures. It's very important not to waffle in your discussions with the employee, and thereby change your mind about taking the action. Once you do that, your supervisory authority will be seriously undermined throughout your department.

4. Avoid nervousness. It's easier said than done, but remember that you're the boss and therefore you hold the upper hand. It may help if you list possible objections the worker might have before you meet with the employee. This gives you the opportunity to think about how you will handle any denials that are made.

5. Be calm. Maintain your composure even if an employee reacts angrily. Losing your temper lessens your ability to think clearly. One easy way to keep calm is to take your time in responding to anything the employee says.

6. Hold the course. Don't let the worker switch a disciplinary discussion to some other topic, or ramble on about meaningless justifications for the work violation.

Q: One aspect of disciplinary actions that bothers me is how other people in my department will respond when I discipline someone. Will this destroy the teamwork that I've worked so hard to develop?

A: As long as you're consistent in applying discipline, it shouldn't have any long-lasting effect on the unit as a whole. It's possible that one or two people who are close friends of the culprit will be more guarded in their relations with you for a short period of time. However, eventually that sort of behavior should fade.

Any supervisor who is fair with employees isn't going to experience a lot of hostility as the result of taking a necessary disciplinary action. That is, of course, unless there's an existing problem over which you have no control, such as bad company/union relations. Even here, the action is still proper, and it shouldn't be avoided solely because it might worsen matters.

The bottom line is that you have run your department irrespective of influences beyond your control. Not acting when you should can lead to greater difficulties than addressing the issue, including a loss of respect for your authority. Therefore, when disciplinary action needs to be taken, do it and be done with it. Then forget about it. After all, you weren't the one causing the trouble.

Q: When do I get to the point where I know disciplinary action is necessary?

A: When do you get to the point where you decide that you're spending too much money and had better give your credit cards a rest? There comes a time in both instances where you instinctively know that enough is enough. If you're continually correcting an employee's errant behavior and it doesn't improve, sooner or later you'll conclude that you're tilting at windmills.

NOTE: Occasionally, you'll have someone working for you who will stretch your patience to the limit, and only after you take formal disciplinary action will they fall into line. Let's face it. An employee who wants or needs a paycheck has to do some serious soul-searching when they receive a disciplinary reprimand. All in all, when you know that you've done what you can to informally cure a personal problem, then that's the time to recognize that formal disciplinary measures are needed.

5.4 HOW TO DISCIPLINE WITHOUT DISASTER

One of the dangers in doling out discipline is that the action will backfire. The objective of discipline – short of dismissal – is to get employees to correct some aspect of their behavior and/or performance. The chances of success are greatly reduced if the action isn't handled properly.

Q: It's one thing to discipline subordinates, but to my way of thinking a ticked-off worker isn't going to work any harder than he has to. What I want to know is how can you discipline people without having after effects that are worse than a New Year's Eve hangover?

A: Let's look at some of the typical problems that affect disciplinary actions. One of the most common faults that aggravate an already bad situation is the failure to act promptly. It's easy to be reluctant to take quick action, and instead nourish the notion that the problem will go away.

Unfortunately, that's about as likely as snow in San Diego. Why? Because supervisors don't usually contemplate taking disciplinary action until events have seriously deteriorated. By that point, it's a foregone conclusion that something has to be done.

The hesitancy in taking any action merely reflects the human tendency to avoid unpleasantness. However, delay generally makes matters more difficult. Often the actual confrontation isn't as bad as one's mind might imagine. Therefore, it's important to act promptly on disciplinary matters.

Actually, in most cases, the groundwork should have been laid a long time before any formal disciplinary procedure is initiated. This means sitting down with an errant worker as soon as things start to get out of hand. It should be done with an open attitude in an earnest effort to reach the root of the problem.

After all, the employee was presumably selected for a job with the company as the best qualified candidate for the position at the time. Any mistakes are often mutually shared and shouldn't be dealt with by an attitude of, "You're screwing up and if you don't improve you're going to be fired."

There are as many reasons why people have problems at work as there are people. With a new hire, it may just be that they were improperly trained --- or in some instances not trained at all. Or perhaps they're experiencing personal problems which are creeping over into their work.

A boss who shows a willingness to sit down, discuss, and what's most often overlooked – listen – can turn a problem around long before it gets to the disciplinary stage. This effort can result in greater future productivity by a worker who appreciates that someone took the time to sort things out.

To sum up, if you're supervising people who aren't performing well, take the time to sit down and hold a forthright discussion with them about, (1) what the problem is, (2) what the employee has to do to improve, and (3) what you will do to assist them in this regard. This type of intervention helps to stave off the need for disciplinary measures.

Obviously, there are many personnel problems which will require the assistance of others within the company. For example, you can't get assistance for an employee's drinking problem if the company doesn't have a policy for dealing with alcoholism. Suffice it to say, in many instances what you as a supervisor can do is limited by the organization's philosophy.

Supportive companies foster supportive managers, while rigid rules tend to encourage inflexible supervisors. If you're working for a company that isn't very supportive, take heed. The chances are that if you ever get into a personal bind, you'll be treated the same way you're being told to treat subordinates.

Telling someone to shape-up doesn't have to be done with an implied "or else" attached to it. The classic "three strikes and you're out" practice, consisting of a verbal warning, written warning, and a firing, often ignores one thing. The company is calling the pitches and that doesn't give the employee much of a chance to bat his way back into the ballgame. A very real need exists to try and rehabilitate problem people, and this is especially true if the offender has worked for the company for an extended period of time.

5.5 THE NEED FOR SELF-CONTROL IN DISCIPLINARY ACTIONS

The key ingredient when you take disciplinary measures is to remain in control of events as they unfold. How you conduct yourself can be as critical as the action you take.

Q: It's almost impossible to anticipate the response of employees when you actually sit down with them for a disciplinary session. This makes it pretty difficult to maintain self-control. Is there any way to anticipate employee reactions so I can be better prepared to deal with them?

A: People can't be programmed, so it's impossible to predict a worker's response in a one-on-one disciplinary meeting. Nevertheless, there are several general patterns of conduct, one or more of which an employee may use to defend himself. These include

- *Comparisons.* "Joe's always late too, so why are you docking my pay?"
- *Innocent Victim.* "Hey, I only took a long lunch and had a few drinks because I was with the guys from data processing. I wasn't driving, so I had no way to get back to work. I didn't know that department took two-hour lunches."
- *Partial Truths.* It's unfair not to pay me. That's the first time this year I've taken a day off without calling you." (It's only January and the guy took six unauthorized days last year.)
- *Phony Justification.* "I didn't pinch her. I was just standing in the elevator and she backed into my hand."

- *Alibi.* "The other people are lying. I wasn't in the Loser's Lounge and Grille during working hours. Just ask my brother, the bartender."
- *Discrimination.* "You're just picking on me because I'm a union member from a wealthy family."
- *Blaming You.* "It's your fault for not explaining what those, 'DANGER EXPLOSIVES – NO SMOKING ALLOWED' signs meant."
- *Anger.* "You're a no-good @#$%^&*."
- *Threats.* "I'm going to file a grievance . . . tell the plant manager about you. . . call my Congressman. . .sue…"

In keeping with the severity of the disciplinary action and the temperament of the worker, any variation of the above responses may occur. However, don't let the worker steer you off course. You both know what went wrong and why the action is being taken. Stick to the topic, be as brief as possible, and keep your emotions under control.

TIP: Obviously, a disciplinary session should be held in private with only you and the employee present. Under certain circumstances, where the infraction is serious, a personnel representative and/or your boss should also attend. When you're dealing with a union member, the shop steward or other union official may be there in accordance with the provisions of the union agreement.

In any event, hold the meeting in a conference room or other neutral site. Why not your office? Because it's more difficult to leave if the worker goes into a long harangue. In a conference room, you can just get up and walk out.

5.6 PRESERVING GOODWILL AFTER AN UNPLEASANT INCIDENT

Despite the best of intentions, events will take place where tempers flare. The worst consequence of these encounters is lingering resentment and anger. Therefore, it's necessary to put these incidents in the past as quickly as possible.

Q: Occasionally, there's a blowup between myself and one of my people. My concern is getting things back on track after this happens.

A: Naturally, both the nature of the dispute and the personalities of the parties involved – both yours and the employees – are determining factors in how quickly a spat is forgotten. A few folks never forget, while others fight and forgive quicker than a passing breeze on a hot summer night.

So personalities play a large role in how you go about clearing the air after an unpleasant encounter with a worker. However, as the boss, it's you who should take the initiative to get relations back on course. That's dictated by the nature of your position as a supervisor.

Many times workers won't take the first step simply because they're on the defensive. They probably wish an incident never took place, but nevertheless don't want to refresh your memory by bringing it up – even to apologize. In fact, they may even be worried about being shown the door to the street.

From a more practical standpoint, an unhappy worker isn't likely to go that extra yard for you when you most need a productive worker. Therefore, self-interest as a supervisor dictates that you're well advised to try to heal open wounds.

By the way, what we're talking about here are the run-of-the-mill encounters where emotions get a little out of hand in the heat of the workday. Since these occasions arise even with the most even-tempered individuals, let's look at some easy methods for cooling-off these conflicts.

- A worker storms off in a huff and avoids you for the rest of the day. Go out of your way the next morning to greet the person pleasantly. This sends a simple signal that there's no ill-will.
- You're having a bad day and needlessly yell at an employee. Apologize quietly when you calm down.
- You have a heated discussion with a worker who is complaining about too heavy a workload. When you both cool-off, sit down and calmly work the problem out.

All of this isn't to say that whenever voices are raised, you then have to rush into a cubicle to think about a "kiss and make up" routine. There are times when you don't want to give any indication that you're trying to smooth things over. With some folks, you might want them to know that you, "said what you meant" and "meant what you said."

5.7 MONITORING ABSENTEEISM FOR MAXIMUM RESULTS

Most employees are out of work a day here and a day there because of illness or personal business. For the most part, only a few workers seriously abuse company policy on absenteeism, and it's these people that you have to keep tabs on.

Q: One of my subordinates is consistently absent on Mondays and Fridays. It's obvious that he's just taking long weekends. Yet he calls in sick and has the necessary time on the books. This puts me in a bind as to what I can do about this. Any ideas?

A: One major annoyance for many supervisors is trying to solve a problem such as this when the worker has technically followed company policy on absences. It's one thing to identify who abuses leave policy, but it's quite another to pin them down.

Some workers take days off without considering the image it creates in a boss's mind. The most common practice of this nature are Monday and Friday absences. Everyone likes long weekends, and there's a natural tendency to assume that's exactly what people did, whether they're sick or not. Frankly, a sharp worker who wants to skip work to go shopping, or engage in some other leisure activity, would be better off doing it in the middle of the week. It's less suspicious, and the stores aren't as crowded.

It's a difficult job as a supervisor to monitor absenteeism without a company policy that aids in this regard. To a large extent there's little you can do if a worker calls in sick and has leave time available.

Over the course of a year, the people who abuse sick leave aren't hard to identify. Once you're convinced that a subordinate is just taking advantage of leave policy, it's good practice to let it be known that you aren't happy about it. However, you can't arbitrarily accuse people of not being ill without proof to the contrary. Be that as it may, there are a variety of methods you can use to send a subtle message.

1. Be solicitous. "How's that sprained ankle, Hank? I hope it's getting better." Naturally, you have a genuine concern for the people in your department, and do inquire when people are ill. However, sometimes a supervisor gets careless in this respect, especially with workers who appear to be faking it. This can lead to an unconscious assumption that since the worker wasn't really sick, why ask how they feel. Avoid this temptation, since it's proper to be solicitous about those folks who were genuinely ill. When it comes to goof-offs, inquiring about their health keeps them guessing, while ignoring them plays into their hands.

2. Send sick people home. Some folks journey into work with high fevers and other assorted ailments in a misplaced sense of dedication. You and others think, "That fool should be home, not coming in here to give everyone else the flu." So when you have employees come into work when they're sick, send them home. It shows a genuine concern for the welfare of those who work for you.

3. It also deals effectively with people who are just saving up sick time for sunny summer days, when they call up with an assortment of invented ailments. Therefore, sending them home when they should be there, will use their sick leave for its intended purpose. This also counters the tactics of poor performers on the job, who attempt to cover up ineptness with a questionable display of perfect attendance at any cost – which includes sharing their germs with you.

4. Don't get frustrated. If a worker takes advantage of leave policy, don't stew about it. On the other hand, don't play "generous George" when these folks want a favor that's within your discretion to grant or deny. For example,

when they're late, dock them the time instead of ignoring it. There are lots of ways to casually reap retribution for excessive absence and opportunities will abound, since it's generally the same people who abuse leave that are consistently late and/or using an excuse to try and leave early.

5. Keep accurate records. The first and foremost requirement when it comes to controlling absenteeism is to keep adequate records so you know who is out, when they're out, and why. In a busy environment, it's easy to get careless about this. If you do, you're just encouraging people who abuse leave – and if there's one thing they don't need, it's encouragement.

5.8 HOW TO MINIMIZE "MENTAL HEALTH" DAYS

No one is a robot that can perform at peak efficiency day after day at work. People get sick, sometimes are overtired, and occasionally get depressed. For many people a break from the work routine calls for taking a mental health day off. Or perhaps their personal chores have built up and need doing, so they just call in sick.

Q: Everyone in our company gets ten sick days a year. Aside from people with actual illnesses, I know my people use this time for a "mental health" day here and there. What – if anything – can or should be done about this?

A: Most supervisors don't place any particular emphasis on someone taking an occasional sick day. After all, everyone gets ill. However, sympathy often travels on a train that goes only as far as the self-interest station. Which means that a boss who is put on the spot because someone is unexpectedly absent isn't going to be happy. Some bosses are less flexible in this regard than others. However, assuming there's no rampant abuse of this practice, it's best to just ignore it.

Your ability to minimize these types of absences is pretty much controlled by company policy. Some companies pay workers for unused sick days which to some extent reduces absenteeism. Therefore, other than monitoring absenteeism as discussed in the previous section, there's little else that can be done in a specific way.

However, if you have a good working relationship with your subordinates and morale is generally high, this in itself can reduce absences. In this type of atmosphere, merely saying something such as, "We've got a big week ahead with that Ryan job," will send a message that you need everyone at work. If there's good rapport within the department, they'll show up when you need them the most.

5.9 WHY RIGID POLICY ISN'T THE ANSWER TO ABSENTEEISM

You definitely want to keep a handle on those employees who have little respect for working hours, and will go to great lengths to justify time off. But these folks don't represent the majority of workers who make an earnest effort to adhere to the rules. Furthermore, the personal circumstances of loyal workers often justify being flexible in applying the rules on absenteeism.

Q: Some of my subordinates have trouble getting in on time and also need time off to attend to personal matters. These people are good employees, but meeting their needs puts me in conflict with formal company policy on attendance. How flexible can I be?

A: When you add up the number of families where both spouses work, and add in single parents, you have a large chuck of the work force. These people often find it difficult to juggle parenting and job responsibilities. As a result, they may be late for work and/or need time off to attend to their offspring.

Obviously, the primary burden is on the employee – regardless of their circumstances – to follow the rules governing working hours. On the other hand, total rigidity in enforcing the rules doesn't make sense. Some companies have flex-time and liberal leave-granting privileges which alleviate this problem. If you're lucky enough to work for one of these businesses, this minimizes difficulties in this area.

A much broader range of companies have standard hours of work, either by choice or necessity. In many of these companies, there's a tacit recognition of the problems of working parents, and it's left to the supervisor's discretion as to how time-off for emergencies and/ or tardiness will be handled.

The practical way to treat requests for time off and/or adjustments in starting time is to be as flexible as possible in meeting the needs of your people. Of course, your ability to do so will be influenced by the constraints of the person's job. For instance, someone starting fifteen minutes later, and making it up on the other end, isn't a problem in some jobs, while it is with others. All you can really do is weigh each request on its merits, taking into consideration company policy, the job itself, and the employee's needs. (See Sec. 11.7 for more on employee's problems.)

Q: It makes sense to be flexible on time and attendance as some of my people have to drop kids off at school and/or have long commutes. But this presents a question of fairness from another angle. For example, what about folks who are never late and/or ask for time off?

A: This is a quandary that's not as hard to overcome as you might suspect. You can avoid any resentment of preferential treatment by discussing with your department how you intend to deal with requests for exceptions to time and attendance policy. Let's look at how this can be done in a group meeting.

You: "Everyone know what the working hours are, and what the policy is on time off. If anyone has an emergency that gives them a problem in this area, I'll discuss it with them on an individual basis. I'll try to be flexible, since we all run into problems now and then, but I want you people to understand that this is a business, and it can't be run with everyone setting their own hours. That means you have a responsibility to resolve any difficulties so that you're here when you're supposed to be."

Dot: "My boy starts school next week. That means if I drop him off at school, I'll be fifteen minutes late in the morning. Can I make it up on the other end?"

You: "Well Dot, you're still got a week to find some other solution. If you need more time, it's ok to make it up at night, but only on a temporary basis. I expect you to work out some other solution within the next couple of weeks."

Dot: "What's the chances of the company adopting flex-time where starting and quitting times can vary?"

You: "The company looked into it and it just wouldn't work for our business."

Peg: "I drop my daughter off at a day care center a couple of miles from here. Is it all right for me to drop over there a couple of times a week during lunch?"

You: "That's your business and if you're a few minutes late in getting back, I won't say anything, but that doesn't mean two hour lunch breaks a couple of times a week."

Sam: "What happens if you have to take your kid to the doctor? My son goes to a specialist who has nine-to-five hours. Do I get charged for taking a couple of hours off or can I make it up?

You: "It's easy to make up fifteen minutes or even a half-hour at the end of the day. However, when you start talking two or three hours, then you'll have to take leave. That raises another point. If any of you may have future problems that might require time off, plan your leave so that you'll have the time. Otherwise, you'll be on leave without pay."

Joe: Don't get me wrong. I mean I know it's tough juggling kids and work, but I don't have children and I'm in here every day before eight o'clock. It just seems unfair."

You: "Look, let's get it straight. I'm talking about being flexible for short periods of time. This applies to everyone no matter what your circumstances are. If you've got a problem, we'll try to work it out, but that doesn't mean I'm giving people time off to go to the racetrack."

Sue: "Hey, the boss is right. I don't have kids either, but last year I got to leave a half-hour early for a week to pick up my husband when his car was in the shop. Sooner or later everyone has problems of some kind. I've got no gripe as long as everyone carries their load."

Joe: "Yeh, you're right. I'm not objecting. I just wanted to mention the fact. After all, the boss is being fair."

NOTE: It may seem easier to go by the book and use no discretion in applying time and attendance policy. That way you aren't faced with sorting out real problems from shallow excuses. However, the end result will be unhappy workers who won't be as productive as they could be.

Furthermore, good workers will look for jobs elsewhere with companies that have more flexible arrangements. Therefore, the hard choice you face is being adaptable to keep good people on the job, or going by the book and attending farewell parties for your best people.

5.10 SURE-FIRE SOLUTIONS TO TARDINESS PROBLEMS

Workers can nickel and dime you to death when it comes to tardiness. Just when you think you have it under control, it pops-up again. Therefore, it's useful to develop a strategy to keep it under control.

Q: Every day someone else is late. When I finally get irritated enough to get my group together and talk about tardiness the problem goes away – for about two weeks. Then it's back to people being late. How can I get this under control?

A: For starters, if you're flexible about working out solutions when people have real problems as discussed in the preceding section, then there's no legitimate reason for people to be constantly late. Often, tardiness develops when a supervisor is lax about enforcement. Even when you hold periodic meetings to discuss the need for workers to arrive on time, that alone isn't a cure because if you don't follow-up by taking action, workers won't take you seriously. Therefore, if you have people ignoring the starting bell, try some combination of the following tactics to cure the culprits.

- Let people know they're late. You deserve an explanation.
- Dock the pay of people who don't get the message.
- Insist the time be make up on the other end, and make sure it is. Don't leave this as an open-ended offer. Get the time made up that day.
- If feasible, give undesirable tasks to late arrivals.
- Hold early morning meetings without announcing them in advance. If people don't know when you'll call the group together, they'll be more cautious about coming in late.

5.11 HOW TO POLISH UP "DIAMOND IN THE ROUGH" WORKERS

Many workers have the potential to be more productive, but for one reason or another never seem to perform up to expectations. It's natural enough for you to conclude that they don't have what it takes. Yet a little bit of encouragement and guidance can pay big dividends in improving the performance of some of these folks.

Q: I've got a couple of young guys working for me who don't have very good work habits. At times they excel, but on other occasions they just don't seem to care at all. Is there a way to make them consistently productive?

A: The first hurdle to overcome in boosting the productivity of people with bad work habits is to recognize the problem for what it is. It's easy to assume that everyone knows there are certain norms to be followed in the workplace.

Yet, many people enter the work force without having learned such fundamentals as observing work hours and following directions. Often these employees are quickly categorized as lazy or incompetent, when in reality they haven't mastered how to accept responsibility.

When you experience this sort of difficulty with younger workers, take the time to work on improving their weaknesses. Encouragement along with persistent, but patient, supervision, can yield good results. Not every worker will respond the same way, so you may have to adopt a trial and error process to find out what works best for each individual.

TIP: Sometimes a good worker's production slacks off suddenly. This may be because of personal problems which are affecting the employee's work. Divorce and family illness are two fairly common examples. In most cases, by just being supportive – without intruding in the person's affairs – you can ride these events out and the employee's performance will pick up again within a short period of time.

Q: An employee in my section is a good worker, but shuns any form of responsibility. She has the potential to do more, but she lacks confidence in her ability, and falters under pressure. Can anything be done to overcome this?

A: Some folks respond well to pressure, while others don't. One way to boost the confidence of an employee who doesn't work well under deadlines is to remove the pressure. Let's look at an example of how this can be done.

Background

Kim is an office clerk for a building supply firm. She was recently transferred to this job from a cashier position. One of her duties is to mail out customer invoices. A few days after starting her new job, the following conversation takes place with Claire, the office manager who is Kim's immediate supervisor.

Claire:	"Have you mailed yesterday's billings yet, Kim?"
Kim:	"I haven't gotten to them yet. Look at this pile of other stuff. I really don't like to work under pressure."
Claire:	"Relax Kim, don't worry about it. Let's go through this pile together. (She sits down and starts sorting through a four-inch stack of papers.) Most of this paperwork is general filing which can be done anytime. In the future,

do the billings first. The other paperwork can be done anytime."

Claire's Strategy

Claire recognizes that Kim is panic-stricken at the sight of so much paperwork. She also know that most of it is insignificant and can be done anytime. The important aspect of Kim's job is to get the billings out, so Claire wisely starts to hold the routine paperwork and just feed Kim the billings. By doing this, Claire hopes to reduce Kim's anxiety and feeling of hopelessness.

The Outcome

Over a relatively short period of time, Kim masters doing the billings with ease. Claire gradually gives her more of the routine paperwork, and at the same time continues to emphasize that the billings are to be done first. As time goes on, Kim becomes an excellent worker in terms of both quality and quantity. She even performs admirably under pressure without even realizing it.

New jobs, or changes in existing positions, often appear more formidable than they actually are. Claire recognized this, but instead of just reassuring Kim, she held back routine filing that normally would have landed in Kim's basket.

Claire instinctively knew that even though she told Kim not worry about the other paperwork, Kim would indeed do just that. After all, a new employee often thinks – even when reassured otherwise – that all the work they're given is equally important. This can lead to anxiety about their ability to do the job, or even worse, numerous errors as the result of trying to do everything at once.

Although individual circumstances will vary, it's important to be cautious about creating an unnecessary perception of pressure in a worker's mind, at least until they've experienced enough to recognize the realities of the workload. You may also find with some workers, that by feeding them work in small chunks, they'll do far more than if given the same quantity of work all at once.

CAUTION: There's a flip side to assigning work to people in small bites so they don't feel pressured. Some individuals thrive on being busy, and work better when they're faced with a heavy workload. It's important, therefore, to distinguish between the ability of people to handle pressure when making work assignments. This comes with knowing the traits of the people who work for you. However, with new employees you're generally better off by being cautious with work assignments until you can gauge exactly what they can handle.

5.12 LIGHTING A FIRE UNDER LAZY WORKERS

Some folks are fast but careless, while others are slow but sure. Yet nothing can wear you down faster than trying to motivate people who are just plain lazy.

Q: It gets my goat that I spend the bulk of my time trying to keep a couple of people moving. They only work when I'm standing over them. Am I wasting my time?

A: It's nice to think that firing a lazy worker will solve these problems. However, companies spend significant sums to hire and train new employees. In addition, there's always the possibility that a replacement might be even worse, so it pays to get them moving on the job, rather than just giving up in despair.

Frankly, the best way to manage lazy workers is to stay on top of them. Tell them to get with it, and tell 'em again. It's easy to take the path of least resistance and let these people do their work at a snail's pace, but that's playing right into their hands. Looking at the bright side, the extra time you spend prodding plodders is offset by the minimal supervision your good workers require.

There are a couple of reasons workers may appear to be lazy when they're not, and it's wise to make sure these aren't the basis for people not producing. One possibility is that a worker is simply bored. If that's the problem, see if you can add some duties and/or change assignments to provide a little motivation.

A second reason for people slowing down may be some problem of which you're not aware. This is especially true when an adequate worker starts to show a decline in output. Since practically anything could be the cause, sit down with the worker and see if you can pinpoint what's wrong.

5.13 SOLVING THE MYSTERIES OF LIARS

Liars are generally more of a nuisance than anything else. However, their potential for causing trouble can increase significantly if you're not careful about separating fact from fiction when they swing into action.

Q: Is there a way to identify habitual liars, other than discovering this trait after the fact?

A: It's a mistake to second-guess someone's intentions. You have to start by assuming that people are telling you the truth until it's proven otherwise. The more active you are in promoting open and honest communication with subordinates, the less likely are the chances that you'll be suckered by a sneak. Conversely, the more supervisors distance themselves from subordinates, the greater is the ability of a liar to operate successfully.

Q: I've got a couple of people who seem to lie about certain subjects, but are generally honest about everything else. Does this make sense?

A: It's a risky business to try and place people's traits in neat little boxes. However, from the standpoint of work, there are a couple of categories that cover most of the hassles you'll experience with liars. These are as follows:

- The backstabber. Tells lies to damage co-workers' reputations. ("I don't know how Ted gets to work on time. He's drunk every night.")

- The cover-up artist. Lies to avoid the blame for doing something wrong and/or not doing it at all. ("I didn't finish the filing because of the fire drill.")
- The favor seeker. Tells stories to impress you. ("Do you know Sal, the VP of Manufacturing? He's my next door neighbor.") Actually, Sal lives four miles away and doesn't even know this guy works for the same company.

The shorthand method of dealing with these types is to ignore a backstabber's gossip, pin cover-up artists down with the facts, and avoid the pandering of favor seekers.

5.14 DEALING DIRECTLY WITH DRINKING AND DRUGS

It's easy to deny that an employee is having a problem with alcohol or drugs. After all, if families have difficulty in confronting this issue, should you be expected to intervene? The answer is that denial, whether it's by the user, family, or worker's boss, only allows the problem to continue and worsen. To claim that drinking and drug use don't affect worker performance is nothing more than a means of avoiding the reality of the situation.

Q: I'm just the supervisor. Why should I have to get involved with people's personal problems?

A: When it comes to alcohol and other forms of drug use, it's not hard to think, "Why should I have to deal with this? It's a personal problem." That it is, but it's also a work problem when drinking and drug use take place at work, and/or affect the employee's job performance. Allowing it to go unchecked can only contribute to it becoming more common.

How drinking and drug problems are dealt with is largely dictated by whether or not the company has some form of employee assistance program in place. If there is one, then employees should be referred to the program at the first sign of a problem. Some companies don't have on-site arrangements, but instead use outside sources where employees can be referred.

If there is no procedure in place for dealing with these problems, then you're pretty much limited to following the disciplinary route. But whatever company policy may be, the important element from your position as a supervisor is to act promptly.

There's no question that it's not easy to confront employees with the facts, but on the brighter side, an employee may well take heed when the alternatives are either seeking help or losing a job.

WARNING: How these cases are handled on an individual basis hinge upon a particular set of facts peculiar to the particular circumstances. Before taking any action, consult with both your own boss, human resources people, and of course, employee counselors if the company has them. This is a sensitive area in which legal implications could arise, so it's important to seek prior advice and not use a "shoot from the hip" approach.

5.15 PUTTING THE LID ON LONG AND LIQUID LUNCHES

Lunch time drinking is virtually a tradition with a few workers, and an occasional event with others. However, where it's a practice it should be discouraged, and where it's not, preventive measures should be taken to keep it in check.

Q: Friday is payday and it's unwritten company policy that workers are allowed extra time at lunch to cash their checks. As a result, about one-third of my crew return sloshed, a couple never come back, and the drunks keep the sober few from getting their work done. I'm leery about cracking down since it's a company-wide problem. Any suggestions?

A: The best starting place to resolve this is by having a talk with your boss. Explain the problem in detail, since upper level managers aren't always aware of these problems unless they get feedback from first-level managers. Perhaps your boss will decide that since this can of worms isn't confined to your department, other managers should be involved. Hopefully, a directive of some sort will ultimately be issued.

It's reasonable to expect that such a mandate will state to employees that continued abuse of the extended lunch hour on paydays will result in the privilege being revoked. No matter how this is done procedurally, you will then have the necessary management support to make enforcement stick.

However, whether or not top management gets involved, you should take essentially the same action. Call a group meeting and let everyone know that, (1) the extended lunch hour to cash checks is a privilege that will be revoked if it's abused, (2) the time is granted to cash checks, not lap up liquor at lounges, (3) anyone returning drunk will be sent home, and (4) those not back by a set time will have their pay docked.

Doing this not only puts people on notice that existing practices won't be tolerated, but it also brings peer pressure from other employees on the worst offenders. Apart from this, you should take separate steps with any workers who don't even bother to return. They should be talked to individually and warned that formal disciplinary measures will be taken the next time they fail to return to work.

Q: I've got a couple of lunch lizards who slither off to every farewell luncheon in the company. They couldn't possibly know that many people. It's obvious that they just use these events as an excuse to spend a couple hours drinking instead of working. How can I end this?

A: Tell your people that time-off for farewell luncheons will only apply to people within the department. If you get a lot of static, tell people they can use vacation time or personal leave if they choose to.

TIP: If you happen to have a high turnover rate within your department, and farewell luncheons are numerous enough to be a nuisance, schedule them after work. It's a simple tactic that avoids the headaches associated with having them at noontime.

6

The Performance Generators: Pay, Promotions, Praise

Molding a group of employees with diverse backgrounds and abilities into a productive unit is a daunting task. As a supervisor, this job is further complicated by corporate policies on pay, promotions, and training, over which you have little control. Despite these constraints, it's possible to produce solid results at the supervisory level.

This can be achieved through the effective use of basic practices that influence performance. These include everything from praise to performance evaluations, from building trust to planning training needs, all the way down to simple steps such as sincerity in employee relations. The following topics explore how to do this irrespective of any roadblocks in your path.

6.1 POSITIVE WAYS TO REWARD PERFORMANCE

As a superior, you are often limited in what you can do to reward performance. Company policy, a boss's opposition, budgetary constraints, and other factors are all potential obstacles. Nevertheless, it's necessary to reward outstanding performance by workers in ways both large and small.

Q: My boss says that pay raises should always be within a narrow range with everyone getting about the same percentage. This frustrates me, since I believe that employees who put forth extra effort should get larger raises than people who just do enough to get by. Am I wrong?

A: You're right, but you obviously have a selling job to do with your boss. Surprisingly enough, your boss's attitude isn't unusual. Although pay raises based on merit are the avowed policy of most businesses, it's not always done that way in practice.

There are a couple of reasons for this. The first one is nothing more than a reluctance to put forth the effort to justify a pay increase that's higher than average. Frequently, particularly in larger companies, there's an abundance of paperwork that has to be completed to justify any pay raise that exceeds predetermined limits. This tends to discourage raises that deviate from the norm.

A second reason is the unsubstantiated fear that giving higher raises to some workers will arouse resentment among those not qualifying for above average increases in pay. There's a hidden hope that everyone will be satisfied if they all get essentially the same raise. What happens instead is that the best workers are the unhappy ones. Their attitude becomes simply, "Why should I work hard only to get the same raise as a goof-off?"

What can you as a supervisor do when your boss has this sort of reluctance toward rewarding workers based on their performance? The best tactic is to be well prepared when you make your pitch. Bring along backup that shows how the worker has outperformed others. You may find that you don't initially succeed, but keep trying. Persistence alone sometimes wins over a reluctant boss who ultimately thinks, "Well, if Joe keeps going to bat like this, the employee must deserve the raise."

TIP: A great convincer when you seek approval of a large raise for a worker is to show the boss that some high-priority project was successful because of the efforts of the worker you're not pushing for a pay raise. Of course, that's not always possible, but it happens enough to keep this strategy in the back of your mind.

Q: I don't have any flexibility to reward workers with above average pay raises. Everyone get increases within a narrow range. Are there other ways to reward performance?

A: Even when you're in a position where merit pay increases based on performance aren't used – even though it's stated policy – there are other forms of recognition you can use to reward performance. Although the possibilities will vary according to circumstances, a short list includes

- giving preferred assignments to your best workers.
- delegating more responsibility to workers who excel.
- pushing your best people for promotions within and/or outside your department.
- complimenting people on tasks that are performed well.
- being more flexible about time and attendance policy with employees who exceed expectations.

In essence, even when pay and promotional considerations are too restrictive to motivate performance, you can at least partially overcome this handicap by practices that show you recognize and appreciate the job people are doing.

6.2 HOW TO WORK AROUND RIGID JOB DESCRIPTIONS

One of the most difficult tasks is to maintain productivity in the face of rigid job descriptions. Sometimes these are company originated, but simply don't relate to the realities of the job. Perhaps they weren't drawn-up correctly, and/or they're simply outdated. In other instances, they are the end product of union negotiated work rules which restrict your efforts to effectively manage your department.

Q: It's much easier to run my department if I can make assignments without people objecting that, "It's not my job." How can I work around this attitude?

A: A good working relationship within a department will encourage the kind of cooperation you need for people to do jobs that aren't normally their responsibility. However, this is an atmosphere that's developed over a period of time as workers learn to know and respect your judgment as a supervisor. Even then, you may have one or two people who resist any request to help out in other areas.

From a more immediate standpoint, it's useful to tell employees the benefits of being able to perform a variety of jobs. These include improving their chances for future advancement, as well as greater job security. In this regard, it helps to emphasize that an employee skilled at performing a wide variety of duties is a more valuable worker to the company. (See Sec. 6.6 for more on the advantages of cross-training.)

Perhaps the most effective tool for preventing a "That's not my job," atmosphere is to practice a "team" concept within your group. Where practicable, rotate assignments, and when this isn't feasible, regularly have people fill-in for absent workers. If employees are frequently asked to help out – no matter what the task – this develops into an expectation. On the other hand, if workers are rarely asked to do other duties, they tend to treat such a request as an exception to what's expected of them, and that in itself leads to resistance.

Q: I've got a union to deal with, and that makes it tricky to get people to do non assigned jobs. It's hampering productivity, so I have to do something about it. The question is, "What can I do?"

A: Union or no union, the job has to be done and any outright refusal is grounds for disciplinary action. Admittedly, you don't want a union grievance filed every five minutes. Therefore, try to work within the confines of the union contract as far as work rules are concerned.

Despite the obvious constraints you have to work around when your people are unionized, even here it's not impossible to get cooperation when you need it. If the workers and the shop steward (their union representative) know you to be fair, they'll bend the rules to help you out once in a while. Obviously, that doesn't mean trying to run roughshod over people. However, if you earnestly try to maintain a good working relationship with union members, they'll tend to overlook the contract provisions to help you out.

TIP: Take the time to read and understand employee job descriptions and union contract work rules. Many disagreements arise because of a simple lack of understanding. Then emotions take over and trouble ensues, when knowing the facts could have avoided an angry confrontation.

GOOD TECHNIQUE: Understanding the job descriptions of your group has other advantages. For example, if you have a good worker you would like to promote to a higher classification, you can do this by demonstrating that the employee is performing significant duties that aren't presently listed in the job description. Get it rewritten to include the additional duties, and that will give you justification to support a higher pay level for the person. Once you do this successfully, it sends a signal to workers that taking on other tasks may lead to a heftier paycheck.

6.3 AVOIDING THE PITFALLS OF PERFORMANCE EVALUATIONS

One of the duties you may detest is giving performance evaluations. It's not an easy job and frequently the only guidance you receive when doing your first evaluation is, "Go by the previous one." Yet, despite a cavalier attitude by your boss when you seek counsel, the employee on the receiving end of an evaluation has a large stake in the outcome. That means you better have answers for what can sometimes be hardball questions from your subordinates.

Q: Skipping all of the highfalutin theory and jargon, what should I accomplish when I give an employee a performance evaluation?

A: It's easier said than done, but you should let them know what they did well, or not so well, during the past year – or whatever time period the evaluation covers. In addition, you should discuss any training the employee requires, and attempt to resolve any problems the worker may have. Sounds simple, but you know it isn't because, (1) it's not easy to go eyeball to eyeball and tell someone where they're deficient, and (2) it's even less likely that they'll agree with you.

Q: Any ideas on how best to tell a worker what he did poorly?

A: Give good news before bad news. That may sound trivial, but it's not and here's why. If you first go over what the employee has done well, that will put him in a good frame of mind. That makes it more likely that he'll be less hostile when you point out his weaknesses. The flip side of the coin is that if you start off by being critical the person won't even be listening by the time you say, "But here's where you did a bang-up job." By that point, the only bang-up job the worker is contemplating may be your facial features after an encounter with a grizzly bear.

Incidentally, don't just switch from good points to bad ones like flicking an on/off switch. Ease into the negative aspects and do it with the focus on curing – not criticizing. For example:

Supervisor:	"Clara, you've really done well in all of the areas we've talked about. Got any thoughts on that?"
Clara Klutz:	"No."
Supervisor:	"Good, well let's talk about training possibilities. Training always looks good in your personnel file. I'd like to schedule you for a word processing course. It will update you in the new technology."
Clara:	"Great."

NOTE: Actually, Clara is slow and needs to pick up her word processing speed. The course she's scheduled for will help her do that. Talking about the new technology aspect of the course emphasizes the positive and doesn't put Clara on the defensive. For comparison, let's look at the wrong way to do this.

Supervisor:	"I'm scheduling you for a word processing course that will help you pick up your speed."
Clara:	"What's wrong with my speed?"
Supervisor:	"It's a little slow."
Clara:	"The documents I work on are more difficult than anyone else's."
Supervisor:	"How so?"
Clara:	"Rambles on and on and farther and farther from the facts.

Clara, in this latter case, has the supervisor on the defensive, and the only way out of it may be to state unpleasant details that demonstrate that Clara on a word processor is slower than Sammy the Snail. Clara isn't likely to be realistic about her performance and the entire discussion will end with bad feelings on both sides.

All in all, no matter what the particulars of poor performance are, take pains to put as positive a spin as is possible on the subject.

Q: I'm confused about how to rate my people when I do performance evaluations. How should this be done?"

A: There are several different formats for performance evaluations, but in general don't get bogged down in rating people one against the other.

Evaluate each person on an objective basis against the criteria. There are a couple of hidden obstacles to avoid. The first is not to rate everyone against your best worker. There are a couple of reasons that make this a bad practice. Length of time on the job is one, and the other is the complexity of the workload, which may vary from worker to worker making comparisons unfair.

Another trap to avoid is the tendency to rate an employee on all factors based on one outstanding trait the individual may have. For instance, if you have a person who works very fast, it may be alluring to overlook the employee's habit of being late for work and/or below average in attention to quality.

POINTER: The most important aspect of performance evaluations is to be thoroughly prepared before you start. Assemble all of the facts beforehand, and sit down by yourself and think through what the worker has or hasn't done well. It's very helpful to keep a file throughout the year where you can deposit notes about the minor successes or failures of each employee. Otherwise, when you go to sit down and put everything together, you may discover that your memory isn't quite as good as you thought.

6.4 HOW TO SIMPLIFY ON-THE-JOB TRAINING

Whether it's new equipment, revised procedures, or just a novice employee, on-the-job training can be a nuisance. It's even more frustrating when you're trying to juggle training with the need to keep pace with a heavy workload.

Q: I'm in a Catch-22 box. My people need training on new machines, and my boss says, "Train them!" while at the same time he tells me that production quotas have increased. I can't do both.

A: Try an overtime approach. Use the increased production goals to justify your overtime request. Then take time during the day for on-the-job training. Train as many of your group at once as is possible. That way, general knowledge and helpful hints are more apt to be passed around.

The reason for having the training during working hours is so everyone will participate. If you have voluntary overtime, some people won't stay. Scheduling mandatory overtime for training is also unsatisfactory, because workers who didn't want to be there would be less than willing learners, which would make the exercise self-defeating.

You may be thinking that this isn't a very cost-effective way to schedule training. However, any training that brings workers quickly up to speed more than pays for itself over a short period of time. By the way, this is the very argument to use with your boss if your overtime request is challenged.

Q: Every time I get a new worker it's "catch as catch can" in terms of training. I simply can't spare anyone to train the person. I'm sure others have the same problem, and I wonder if there's any solution?

A: This is a frequent cause of concern that is heightened by a desire to get the new person working as soon as possible. This can result in a crash course on the basics of the job, and then leaving the employee on his own. The end result can be a string of endless errors.

When you're caught with little slack time, it may be preferable to ease the employee along with simple assignments that can be performed with a minimum of supervision. You can even assign minor jobs that aren't related to the reason for hiring the employee. However, it's beneficial to explain this so that the newcomer understands what you're doing.

Another obvious technique is to have the new hire observe others until someone is free to conduct hands-on training.

CAUTION: It's important to get new hires trained as quickly as possible. Although that objective may be temporarily sidetracked by workload, it's necessary not to prolong the process. In other words, don't continually postpone training for extended periods. If a heavy workload is forecast for the foreseeable future, you may have to sacrifice someone's productivity to have them train the new employee.

6.5 WHY YOUR BEST WORKER SHOULDN'T TRAIN PEOPLE

It may seem logical to assign new employees to your best worker so that they'll learn the job from an expert and also have a good role model to follow. Yet, there are several reasons why this may not be a good idea.

Q: My best worker complains constantly about training new people. You can give this person all the work in the world and never a word is said. However, the minute you assign this guy a trainee, the groaning starts. What am I doing wrong?

A: There are a number of reasons why this employee may not be suited to train people. There's a common misconception that the perfect person to train a new hire is the most productive worker in the department. After all, what better way to learn than from the best? However, this notion overlooks several considerations, the most important of which is that your best producer may not be the best trainer.

Often, employees who excel at their work may not have the right temperament to train people Their communication skills may be poor, patience might be lacking, or they might resent being slowed down in their work.

The flip side of the coin is the effect they may have on a novice. A trainee can easily lose confidence when watching an expert on the job. It's easy for them to think, "I'll never be able to perform at that pace." This thought process could result in a new hire quitting after losing all incentive to learn the job. At the least, the trainee may take longer to get up to speed, because instead of learning the ropes, he races ahead trying to keep pace with the expert. This leads to errors and poor quality work. The trainee may eventually overcome these obstacles, but it could take longer than if a better choice of mentors had been made.

Q: What should I look for in terms of the "best" person to train new people.

A: Actually, the best approach may be to use a combination of people. Folks have different strengths and weaknesses and these traits carry down to the shop floor or office. One worker may be slow but sure, rarely making errors. At the other extreme is someone who churns the work out, but on occasion gives quality short shrift.

Furthermore, people have different ways of performing the same job. So by assigning a new hire to a number of people a more balanced approach to doing the job may be taught. The ultimate aim is for the trainee to be able to pick up the best tips from several sources.

A secondary advantage is that the novice gets to know more people and consequently gets absorbed into the social side of the group at a faster pace. This incidentally isn't an inconsequential matter, since a person is apt to feel more at ease and will ask more questions when they know someone. If a new employee is assigned to one person for any length of time, it can take longer for them to be accepted as part of the team.

At any rate, whether or not one or more people are assigned to train a new worker, there are crucial qualities to look for when picking a trainer. These are as follows:

1. Patience. Learning anything is tough at first and it's essential that any instructor be a patient person who has the ability to repeat instructions and accept the errors of a novice.

2. Temperament. A good general disposition is a valuable asset in a trainer. Someone with a good disposition relaxes those around him and a nervous novice can appreciate a genial guide.

3. Communication skills. A trainer needs to be able to both show and explain the intricacies of the job. Needless to say, someone whose conversation is limited to a grunt at lunch isn't a candidate to teach anyone anything.

4. Work ethic. You may have good workers who are also prone to complain a lot. That may not bother you, but be sure to assign training duties to people who genuinely like both their job and the company. New people take everything at face value until they learn otherwise, so it doesn't make sense for them to be discouraged by griping – even if it is harmless.

6.6 THE NEGLECTED PAYOFF IN CROSS-TRAINING EMPLOYEES

One of the most neglected aspects of employee training involves teaching workers how to do other jobs within the department. Yet, it's a technique that offers benefits to both employers and workers. A great part of the undertaking is no more complicated than taking the initiative to start such a program.

Q: What are the advantages of cross-training people in other jobs?

A: • You have someone trained to fill in for absent workers.
  • Trained people are available to meet workload peaks when they have idle time on their own job.
  • It encourages teamwork as workers get to know the details of other people's jobs.
  • Training new employees is easier when your workers are multi-skilled.

- Employees have a wider range of promotional opportunities when they can do a variety of jobs.
- You eliminate the "expert" excuse. The one that goes, "Gee, I don't know how to do that. Joe's the expert."

Q: How do I convince workers that cross-training will benefit them personally?

A: By appealing to their self-interest in terms of job security and promotional possibilities. Here's an example.

Background

Phil is a supervisor in one of the regional distribution centers of a national retail chain. He wants to train Jose to track back orders for out-of-stock merchandise.

Phil:	"Hey Jose, I'd like to show you how to track back orders so you can fill in for Phyllis when she goes on vacation."
Jose:	"Not me. I hate paperwork. Can't you get someone else Phil?"
Phil:	"Jose, you're one of my best workers which is why I want you to learn the job."
Jose:	"What good does it do me to learn how to push paper?"
Phil:	"Tracking orders pays more than filling orders. That means when a back order position opens up, you'll be already qualified to fill the spot."
Jose:	"Yea, but I don't know if I want to do that full time."
Phil:	"Well even if you don't, the only way to find out for sure is to give it a try. Even if you didn't want to do it full time, the experience is good to have."
Jose:	"How come?"
Phil:	"Hey, let's face it. The more jobs you can do around here, the more valuable you are to the company. If layoffs ever take place, who will they keep? Those who can do the most jobs, that's who."
Jose:	"OK, I'll give it a shot."

Q: What I don't like is having my people cross-train in other departments. The next thing I'll know is that all of my people are putting in bids to work someplace else.

A: Actually, the opposite holds true. The better the supervisor you are, the more likely it is that people will want to work for you.

Frankly, an interdepartmental cross-training program benefits everyone. After all, you may be supervising a department that offers little in the way of advancement. If your people have opportunities to learn other jobs within the company, it will motivate them to perform better in their present job.

This type of cross-training also gives you a pool of trained workers to draw upon from other departments if your group's workload is subject to wide fluctuations. This lessens the need for short-term hiring and layoffs which are always a disruptive influence.

6.7 BASIC SKILLS: GETTING EMPLOYEES TO HELP THEMSELVES

Many companies offer extensive training opportunities for workers in job-related subjects. A few also basic skills training in subjects such as English and math. However, for the most part, it's left up to workers to seek help in these areas. Even here though, it's useful to offer encouragement and advice in an effort to assist workers in upgrading their skills.

Q: A lot of the new people being hired are lacking in the basic fundamentals necessary to do the job. This is causing a lot of unnecessary errors. What can I do to help people in my group who need basic skills training?

A: It might be helpful to discuss this subject with your boss. Supervisors bringing this problem to management's attention may encourage the company to offer remedial programs. Try networking on this subject with other supervisors, since collective complaints will have more of an impact.

On a more personal level, encourage workers to pursue courses on their own. It's also useful to coordinate with the company's training specialists to find out where easily accessible schools offering these courses are located. This is especially true if you have workers who are new to the area and/or have a limited command of English.

What do you accomplish by doing this? Other than the personal satisfaction of helping people to improve themselves, you also get workers started toward improving their skills. You may be pleasantly surprised as to how quickly this takes place.

6.8 AVOIDING THE WORLD'S WORST TRAINING BLUNDER

There are few people who would question the need for a highly trained work force. With the continuing introduction of new technology on both the factory floor and in the office, training needs are – or should be – a constant concern.

However, there are times when training takes a back seat to other priorities. This is often a short-sighted maneuver, and cancelling training that's already scheduled is the worst mistake of all. Not only does it send a general message to employees that training isn't important, but it has an even greater impact on the individuals whose training has been scuttled.

Q: On more than one occasion, training scheduled for people in my department has been cancelled by staff people without even discussing it with me. I wind up listening to complaints from the workers affected. What, if anything, can be done about this?

A: There are actually two problems here. The first one is that staff specialists should operate through supervisors – not around them. As you may have had the misfortune to experience, some staff people get carried away in the performance of their duties. This may result in their ignoring the chain of command – some thoughtlessly and others not so. In any event, let staffers that do this know that it's unacceptable to you. If it continues, take it up with your boss so it can be straightened out on a higher level.

The second problem in the question concerns the cancellation of the training. This creates real headaches when it happens, so make your feelings known to your boss. Unfortunately, some companies don't take training very seriously, and it tends to be the first casualty when cost-cutting measures takes place. From a practical standpoint, all you can do is fight the good fight when it comes to getting training for your department.

6.9 FIGHTING AND WINNING THE TRAINING BUDGET BATTLE

In some organizations, first-level supervisors prepare the training budget for their department. In others, supervisors are just asked for general input about their department's training needs. Though still fewer in number, there are even organizations where supervisors aren't even consulted about training, which certainly doesn't say much for the concept of participative management. Whatever the process may be within your own company, training budgets shouldn't be given short shrift.

Q: Every year when I submit a training budget, my boss butchers it. It's costing my department a lot of training which is badly needed. How can I better defend my budget?

A: You may be the victim of a boss who isn't a very big advocate of training. Whether or not that's true, there are certain basics that you can follow to support your training requests. These include:

1. Be as specific as possible. Identify courses, dates, and employees to be scheduled for the training.
2. Pinpoint why the training is needed. This is the most crucial element in supporting a training request. Generalities won't win the battle here. What you must do is relate the training to improving the person's productivity, eliminating errors, or other factors that distinctly highlight the advantage to the company that will be gained from the training.

3. Use a "the heavens are falling" clincher in your presentation. It's easy to think that if you identify the advantages of the training, then that should be sufficient justification. Sadly, training is a topic that everyone tacitly supports, but when crunch time arrives its importance is quickly forgotten. When budget cuts are implemented, many managers forget about everything else and aim their red pencil at training, and for some bosses, training is nothing more than a security blanket to protect other budgetary items. That way, when cuts are called for, everything else goes untouched and training gets lopped off.

So to buttress your training requests, try to include the negative impact that will result if the training isn't completed. For example, "...if technicians aren't trained to use the new test equipment, then product returns and recalls will significantly increase..." Where possible, quantify these arguments with estimates. It's amazing how convincing numbers are, even when they're nothing more than pie-in-the-sky estimates.

POINTER: Having a "the heavens are falling" argument in your training request can reap dividends down the road. When training is cut from a budget, it's soon forgotten. Six months later, the same manager who wielded the axe may berate you about poor productivity. It's handy then to be able to say, "That's what I told you would happen if we didn't train these people."

Q: Should I overload my budget 10% to 20% in anticipation of it being cut?

A: Padding budget requests is an age-old game that's played wherever budgets are prepared. However, aside from the issues of ethics and honesty, there are other pitfalls in padding a budget request. When careful scrutiny of a budget reveals padding, it destroys the credibility of the preparer. In essence, nothing becomes believable. Anyone who develops this sort of reputation will have a tough time selling anything to anyone. The upshot is that legitimate requests are shot down because of a lack of believability.

Rather than resort to this sort of fiction, you're better off beefing-up your justification in defense of what you propose. If you establish a reputation for preparing supportable budgets that are easy to defend, budget cutters will look elsewhere for easier fish to fry.

That's not to say that you shouldn't include contingency amounts in budget requests. For instance, if you reasonably expect that two new employees will be hired for your department in the coming year, include an estimate for any training they may need. The best method to follow in preparing your budget request is to take the time to prepare a detailed estimate for everything you think you'll need, and then be prepared to defend that position.

6.10 THE NEED FOR GIVING COMPLIMENTS

One of the most overlooked tools in keeping people productive is no more complicated than a simple compliment. It's natural to think that pay and promotions are all that matter to workers, but that overlooks the fact that pay raises and promotions don't come very often. On a day-to-day basis the employee that's doing a good job likes to hear about it.

Q: I've got a worker who never fails to respond to a compliment with a sarcastic remark. Should I just skip the compliments when he does a good job?

A: No, even though it's not easy to be nice when you're dealing with a wise guy. Actually, this person may just not know how to handle compliments and this is his way of reacting. Even if the person is just a jerk, express your appreciation. Remember, you're complimenting him on his work – not his personality.

Q: I'm not a very outgoing person and I don't find it easy to give compliments. What can I do about this?

A: Just be yourself. Don't forget that folks who work for you know that you're a reserved type of person. Even though your compliments aren't as frequent, those you do give will have a greater impact.

REMINDER: Don't forget to praise people outside your department for a job well done. The cooperation of a wide range of people is necessary for success. And a word of "thanks" now and again will keep the cooperation coming. One good way to do this when you have received exceptional assistance is to let the person's boss know how helpful the employee was. That also pleases the worker's boss who can then bask in the reflected glow of the subordinate's performance.

6.11 CONQUERING THE DEADLY SIN OF INSINCERITY

Whether it's something as simple as complimenting a job well done, or as demanding as backing up an employee in a dispute outside the department, sincerity can establish you as a leader. On the other hand, supervisors who don't go to bat for their workers are destined to reap the unhappy backlash from disillusioned employees.

Q: Roland – another supervisor – told one of my workers that I was complaining about the worker's attitude. Roland is a good friend and I often discuss things with him, but not on the expectation that they'll be repeated.

A: First of all, remember that if you don't want something repeated to others, don't tell anyone about it. Once employees hear from someone else that you have been talking about them, they'll no longer trust you. It's admittedly reassuring to have a friend at work with whom you can talk over your respective problems. However, the risks can outweigh the rewards if negative comments get repeated.

In fact, what you discuss doesn't even have to be negative. For instance, suppose you discuss with another supervisor the fact that you put employee "X" in for a 10% pay raise. That gets back to the worker, but in the meantime your request is denied and the employee only gets a 5% raise. It's not your fault that management rejected the raise, but now you have a resentful worker whose hopes for more money have been shattered. Therefore, it's smart to be careful about discussing the pros and cons of your subordinates with others, except in the course of official business. It can only come back to haunt you.

Q: One of my workers was threatened with being written up by another manager for allegedly swearing at him. The two have never gotten along and everyone knows it. I think this manager just goes out of his way to make life hard for my worker. How should this be handled?

A: If possible, limit the need for your employee to deal with this manager, since this is probably just a personality clash. Nevertheless, the manager may be taking advantage of his position to belittle your subordinate.

If there's no simple way to avoid contact between these two people, then it's prudent for you to talk with the manager. Be casual about the matter, but see what he has to say. Then suggest that any further difficulties be referred to you. A typical conversation might go something like this.

You:	"Ollie, I heard rumbles that you and Joe are having difficulties. Is there anything to it?"
Ollie:	"Yeh, where did you get that guy?" He's got no respect for authority. If he gives me any more lip, I'll have him fired."
You:	"I don't understand. What did he do? He always seems pretty good-natured."
Ollie:	"I told him to do something and he said, 'Don't act self-important with me, I don't work for you."
You:	"What did you ask him to do?"
Ollie:	"I don't remember, but I do know that he gave me some cheap guff."
You:	"Look, he might have just been having a bad day. If you need help in the future, see me."

From the conversation it's pretty obvious that Ollie just likes to throw his weight around. It would be prudent to sit down and explain what's happening to your boss. That way, knowing the facts before another incident occurs, your boss will be informed when Ollie gets there first with a lopsided version of the event.

NOTE: It's by no means unusual for you to have to step in when problems occur with other departments. Always get the facts and remain calm, but back your people when it's called for. Not only does this serve you well within your own group, but it also establishes you as a no-nonsense boss who won't let his people be pushed around. Letting this be known, in and of itself, will cut down on these encounters. People in other departments will recognize that if they give one of your workers a hard time, it won't end there.

6.12 WHY "HOW YOU SAY IT" RELIEVES BAD NEWS

It's always an unenviable chore to have to convey bad news, either to your department as a whole, or to a single worker. Yet, it's inevitable that everything from layoffs to pay freezes, to telling someone they didn't get the promotion, have to be dealt with. Although it's always an unpleasant duty, approaching it properly can minimize the damage.

Q: I really hate pay reviews, and always put them off until the last possible moment. To say the least, they're not fun to do. No matter what kind of a raise people get, it never seems to meet their expectations. Are there foolproof ways to handle this chore?

A: Nothing is foolproof and pay reviews can't be transformed into a fun thing to do. Nevertheless, there are methods you can use to make them more matter of fact. A good place to start is by looking at guidelines that can be followed to either eliminate problems and/ or deal with them when they arise.

1. Never procrastinate and let pay reviews slide beyond their due date. If an employee is scheduled for a pay raise on February 1, that employee has every right to expect that the review and paperwork will be completed by that date. All too often, reviews are delayed based on the justification that the raise will be retroactive. That doesn't

cut it with workers who are looking for a pay raise when it's due – not when someone gets to it.

2. Keep your own log of review dates so you know when pay reviews are scheduled. If the paperwork originates in the personnel department or elsewhere, follow-up with these folks well before the scheduled date. Doing this will give you sufficient time to do a review and get the necessary approvals on time.

3. Don't tie an employee's performance appraisal into his pay raise. Do the performance appraisal without discussing pay raises. Then, if a raise is forthcoming, process it without discussing the specifics with the employee. There are several reasons for this.

- Pay raises aren't a negotiated item to be bargained with every worker.

- The raise you propose may be disapproved at another level.

- Telling the employee beforehand what their raise will be is an open invitation for the employee to argue for a higher raise.

4. Familiarize yourself with the going market rate for the jobs your workers have. This sort of information is valuable when and if employees complain to you about the size of their raise. Don't overlook comparable fringe benefits when you do this. Although employees aren't often aware of it, the cost of fringe benefits are a part of compensation.

In other words, jobs in your company may pay slightly less than elsewhere, but excellent fringe benefits may offset this. Job security is also a factor, so if your company has a stable work force this can also be pointed out to someone griping about one's paycheck.

Q: What's the best way to respond when a worker complains about his or her pay raise?

A: Listen and let them vent their steam. That alone relieves some of the tension. Always remain calm and don't let an employee put you on the defensive. If the person is being fairly paid, then they don't have a legitimate complaint.

Often, workers complain about their pay because they have an overinflated idea of what the going rate is for someone with their experience in that type of job. That's why it's important for you to know the facts and figures about what jobs pay elsewhere in the area. Knowing this, you can often effectively counter the employee's argument with ease. Let's look at an example.

Background. Sarah, an assembly line worker in a light manufacturing facility, storms into the office of Carol, her immediate supervisor.

Discussion.

Sarah:	"Carol, how come I got such a measly raise. I work hard, and this is all I'm worth?"
Carol:	"Sit down Sarah and relax. Let's talk about it and see what your problem is."
Sarah:	"I'm getting a $20 a week raise and that's before deductions. My friend over at Out-of-Line Manufacturing Company does the same kind of work as me and just got a $30 raise.
Carol:	"First of all, Sarah, I don't know anything about your friend, but I do know that our pay is competitive with other companies in the area. I also know that our fringe benefits are much better."
Sarah:	"My friend gets two weeks' vacation, just like me."
Carol:	"That may be true, but vacation time is just one factor. We also have health, dental, life and disability insurance, a child care facility, tuition assistance, and several other benefits."
Sarah:	"I can't eat fringe benefits."
Carol:	(Smiling at Sarah's comment says,) "That's true Sarah, but all of those things cost money if you have to pay for them out of your own pocket. I think if you take some

time and think about it, you'll find that all-in-all this is a good place to work."

Sarah: "I know I could get more money somewhere else."

Carol: "That may be true Sarah, but don't overlook anything. After all, this company hasn't had a layoff in ten years. You may find some jobs that pay a high hourly wage and have a layoff once a year. That's no fun as you know. Weren't you laid off from your last job two years ago before you started working for us?"

Sarah: "Yes I was and I see what you're saying, but it's tough to make ends meet."

Carol: "I sure agree with you on that. It's hard for everyone these days."

NOTE: Obviously, every pay raise complaint will differ in some respect, but the way Carol handled the problem has several common themes that you can successfully adopt. These are

- Let the employee blow off steam.
- Don't get drawn into comparison debates. (Everyone claims the grass is greener elsewhere.)
- Refuse to discuss other employees' raises. This is a deadly trap and counter it quickly by saying, "We're discussing your raise, not anyone else's."
- Know your facts so you can easily dispute phony claims.

Q: Are there any standard practices to follow when you have to tell your department about unpleasant topics such as reorganizations?

A: No matter what the topic, get all of the facts you can before talking to your people. Tell them what you know, answer their questions if you can, and get answers to questions raised that you can't respond to on the spot. Most of all, be forthright with your people. No one wants to hear bad news, but it's more acceptable when they know you're leveling with them. (Also see Sec. 4.1 on dealing with complaints about company policy.)

6.13 SAYING "NO" WHEN IT'S NECESSARY – THE RIGHT WAY

Saying "No!" to anyone is seldom easy. However, learning to do it the right way can make your job a lot easier. The trick is to avoid an abrupt "No!" whenever possible. It's almost always better to say something such as, "Let me look into that and get back to you," or "Let's sit down and talk about it."

People aren't as put-off by refusal if they feel you're giving serious consideration to their request, along with stating valid reasons as to why it can't be granted. This technique is less likely to provoke thoughts such as, "My boss just doesn't like me," or even worse, heated discussions which place you on the defensive.

Q: How can you turn down promotion requests from subordinates without bitter feelings developing?

A: The more emotion laden a topic, the harder it is to deal with. Nothing is a hotter topic with employees than promotions, with the possible exception of pay raises. There's a school of thought that would have you believe that money isn't important in terms of job satisfaction. Sure, money isn't everything, but it's a lot easier to cope with the dreams and dilemmas of life, such as health problems, a kid's college tuition, or perhaps a fantasy trip to Tahiti, if you have a bulging bank balance. All of which means that, "Yes folks, Sally is serious when she asks for a promotion." Therefore, an abrupt "No!" isn't the way to deal with this sort of problem.

On the other hand, don't postpone a response too long. Give it a day or two, then sit down with Sally, discuss why she wants a promotion, and openly and honestly tell her why it isn't in the cards at the present time.

However, don't stop there. Explain what she has to do to improve her prospects, how you will help her to do this, and most important, what she can expect in return when she accomplishes her part of the bargain.

Being upfront, and holding out promise for the future, can lessen the negative aspects of a "No!" not only with promotion requests, but also in most other circumstances. Just make sure that you follow through with your promises, and of course, don't follow through with your promises, and of course, don't make promises that you can't deliver. Although it's preferable in most instances to avoid an abrupt "No!" don't confuse this with indecision. Sometimes answers have to be "No!" in plain vanilla, with no hot fudge sauce to sweeten the refusal.

Q: I'm always having to say "No!" to something or other. After a while I start to wonder if I'm being too negative in my replies. Are there better substitutes for conveying a "No!" message which will let people down easier?"

A: How you give a "No!" answer is pretty much controlled by the nature of the request. Although it's proper to be as considerate as possible when turning down a request, it's equally important not to get hung-up over having to do so. There are many instances that don't require a great deal of explanation. For example:

1. **Mid-day absence.** "Can I take a long lunch to pick up my new car?" "Sorry Fred, I can't spare you today. We're too busy."
2. **Unscheduled vacation day.** "I'd like to take Friday off, if it's okay with you?" "Sorry, can't do it this Friday Ann. We've already got three people on scheduled vacations. How about next week?"
3. **Equipment request.** "Can you get me some portable racks? The stationary ones don't give us as much flexibility." "Gee Jack, that's a good idea, but it has to be budgeted. We'll have to wait six months until we do the next budget request."

NOTE: The requests that shouldn't be dispensed of so quickly are generally those that are of major significance, and which you would probably grant if it were possible to do so. For instance, perhaps an employee deserves a promotion, but there's no immediate opening. In short, if you know it's important to the employee, and basically agree that the request is reasonable, take the time to explain why it can't be honored at the moment.

6.14 BEING UPFRONT WITH WORKERS ABOUT POCKETBOOK ISSUES

If there is one major source of instant conflict with subordinates, it's their paycheck. Despite the potential for controversy, there's no substitute for being upfront and honest about their pay.

Q: A new boss has taken over the manufacturing department. I supervise five people in shipping and report directly to him. His first edict to me was, "No more overtime." My people have been working overtime regularly for the past two years and count on this money. How do I break the bad news?

A: Lay it on the line and then duck. Assuming shipments remain the same – and that your people haven't been bagging it – this may be only temporary. If so, sooner or later overtime will have to résumé and/or additional people will have to be hired. Your first job is to give your people the news. Get everyone together at once, so everyone hears the bad news at the same time. That way, nothing gets misinterpreted, and you save answering the same questions several times. Spell it out something like this.

John:	(the supervisor) "I called you together to give you some news. Effective immediately there will be no more overtime."
Jim:	"How come?"
John:	"Instructions from Perry Pinchot."
Jim:	"How long will this be for?"
John:	"Until further notice."
Fred:	"What does that mean? How are the shipments going to get out? You know we don't dog it during the day."
John:	"We'll just have to do the best we can. I told Pinchot there was no way we could keep up without overtime."

Arthur: "Heck John, you know we count on that overtime money. I'll have to get a second job."

John: "I know it's tough Arthur, but we'll all have to do the best we can."

John: (After another ten minutes of complaining and griping.) "Look, we can sit around here all day and complain, but I can't change things. Let's just settle down and get to work. We'll just have to see what happens."

Fred: "Hey, this may not be so bad after all. There's no way we can keep up with shipments, so OT will have to résumé soon. In the meantime, we get a couple of weekends to enjoy ourselves."

John: "You may be right Fred, but I don't want anyone to count on it. Let's get back to work."

NOTE: Notice that although John, the supervisor, was honest about what took place, he avoided criticizing his boss. Even though he knew the boss was wrong, he kept it to himself. There is nothing to be gained and much to be lost if a supervisor is critical of upper management in front of subordinates.

Although overtime was the topic here, any number of pocketbook issues can arise that aren't good news for the work force. However, no matter what the specifics are, give out the facts, control your temper, and don't be critical of anyone. Remember, you're only the messenger, so any anger on the part of your workers isn't directed at you personally.

6.15 BASIC PRACTICES THAT BUILD TRUST WITH EMPLOYEES

Over the long haul, a good supervisory relationship with subordinates is built on a foundation of trust. Not only do you wield tremendous power over employees, but you are also the source of their answers on subjects large and small. Much can be said about how to motivate people, but in the final analysis, if there's one quality that stands out, it's trust.

Employees may not always agree with what you're doing, but they'll be far more accommodating if there's a bond of trust. To develop this type of working relationship isn't easy, and it can't be done overnight, but it's worth the extra effort in the long run – for both you and those you supervise.

Q: What are the keys to building a solid working relationship with subordinates?

A: Building a productive relationship with those who work for you is a difficult endeavor. It develops slowly based on daily interactions. There's no instant formula for success, and no buzzer sounds to let you know you've achieved your goal, and much like a well-kept car, it requires constant maintenance. Following is a list of general guidelines that can help you in this regard:

- Always be courteous – even when you're under pressure and nothing seems to be going right.
- Show confidence in employees by giving them responsibility.
- Don't panic or act unsure of yourself in front of subordinates. They expect you to be in charge.
- Don't berate or belittle people when they make mistakes.
- Fight for your employees. If you don't, who will?
- Be yourself. Don't try to project a personality that isn't you.
- Be consistent, but not inflexible. Employees should know what to expect from you on a day-to-day basis. Nevertheless, when necessary, adjust to events that are unusual.
- Expect the unexpected. No one likes unpleasant surprises, but they'll happen anyway, therefore, don't let them throw you off balance.
- Show your appreciation for a job well done.
- Don't expect miracles. Mistakes should be accepted and corrected – not criticized.
- Don't take the job too seriously. Do your best, but remember that the job is only one aspect of your life.

7

The In's and Out's of Hiring and Firing

One of the most distasteful jobs any supervisor has to face is firing someone. Luckily, it's not an everyday event, but because of the serious nature of this most unpleasant of duties, it's sensible to be prepared beforehand.

A more pleasant – yet time-consuming – task is hiring additional help. To some extent, the care you take in hiring is linked to how often you'll be faced with firing. In fact, careful selection of new employees is the key to minimizing many of the miseries of a supervisory role. The better the selection process, the less likely it is that you'll have discipline, morale, motivation, and productivity problems.

Unfortunately, despite its importance, hiring can be haphazard on occasion. Part of the problem is that little or no instruction on interviewing techniques is given to supervisory personnel. You're left to wing it on your own – and to live with the consequences.

This is true even though you're often at the mercy of a screening process that sends you less than stellar candidates to choose from. Even before you get to that point, you may be forced to fight a seemingly endless battle just to justify the need to hire.

All in all, hiring and firing are crucial components for success as a supervisor. Let's look at the factors that can help make hiring more fruitful and firing more remote.

7.1 BASIC INTERVIEWING TECHNIQUES THAT WORK

Interviewing job candidates is a supervisory responsibility that's often considered to be a relatively minor duty. Consequently, interviewing techniques receive little or no attention. Yet, the end result of the interviewing process is a new hire that you have to work with for the indefinite future.

And even though good interviewing methods can't guarantee success, poor practices aren't much better than picking a name out of a hat. As a result, it's worthwhile to look at some easy-to-use interviewing strategies that will boost your success rate in hiring good workers.

Q: Two or three times a year I have to interview applicants to fill vacancies in my department. To put it bluntly, I haven't the foggiest idea of how to proceed. No one ever told me how to interview anyone, and I don't do it often enough to figure it out for myself.

A: The elements of a successful interview aren't difficult to master. The trick is in executing them properly. The fundamentals are as follows:

- Start interviews with general conversation to make applicants feel comfortable.
- Avoid mentioning any subjects that are prohibited by law. Basically, stick to job-related questions. If you're not sure of what you can't ask, coordinate with the human resources department before beginning interviews.
- Ask questions that key on the applicant's prior experience and how it relates to the open position.
- Let applicants do most of the talking, or else you won't learn anything about their backgrounds. Only ask questions when people start to wander far afield.
- Skip trick questions that attempt to trip people up. This technique can alienate candidates you might want to hire. After all, if they're smart enough to finesse loaded

questions, they're also bright enough to look for a job where the boss isn't laying land mines.

- Describe the job that's open, and answer any questions the applicant raises.
- Take the time to conduct a detailed interview. It's tempting to rush through interviews when you're busy, but remember, a bad selection will make you even busier after they're hired.

7.2 WHAT TO TELL AN APPLICANT ABOUT THE JOB

Where you work is undoubtedly neither heaven nor hell. Yet, it's common to leave job applicants with the impression that it's indeed one or the other. This happens when interviewers either overemphasize the benefits of the job, or else convince candidates that the pace is so hectic there isn't time for lunch. Avoid these extremes, since what you say to job applicants influences whether or not they accept a job offer, as well as what they expect in the future if they are hired.

Q: Whenever I'm scheduled to interview someone, my boss reminds me to plug how great the company is to work for. He's always in a hurry to fill vacancies, and wants to hire the first person through the door, even though their IQ may be lower than their shoe size. Just how positive should I be about the company in general and the job in particular?

A: Your boss's attitude is no problem for him. After all, you're the one who will have to work with the new hire. It's certainly important to inform a candidate about both the company and the job. However, in doing this, be as factual as possible.

If you unfairly sell the applicant on the benefits of the job, you'll end up with an unhappy worker. This often happens in the eagerness to convince a "perfect" choice to accept a job offer.

In this regard, keep two thoughts in mind. In the first place, you're essentially the buyer, not the seller. Let candidates show you why they should be hired, instead of you convincing them to take the job.

Furthermore, there is no "perfect" applicant. For most jobs, there are a number of people who could fill the position quite adequately.

As opposed to overselling the job, the other extreme is an approach that frightens people off. Sometimes, there's an inclination during interviews to dramatize how difficult a job is and/or how much work it involves. If that's true, that's fine, but don't make the job appear to be harder than it is. This can result from a desire to hire someone who is hard working and diligent. This leads to assuming that only a good worker will take a position if it sounds like the job requires working at a frenzied pace. However, if you're too convincing, the only applicants that will want the job may be those whose elevator doesn't travel all the way to the top.

Q: Given that the two extremes, of either emphasizing "great job," or "hectic hassle" aren't a well-considered approach, what specifically should you tell job applicants?

A: In general give them

- a broad overview of the company
- details of the job
- direct answers to their questions
- a brief synopsis of fringe benefits. (The more that's covered in company brochures, the less you have to explain.)

In principle, what you want to convey to each job applicant is an honest appraisal of the job, the company, what you expect from them, and what they can expect in return. Remember, applicants are expected to be forthright about their qualifications, so you should strive for the same objective when describing what the job has to offer. That way, no one will be deceived and the new employer/employee relationship will get off on the right foot.

7.3 THE ONE THING YOU SHOULD NEVER SAY TO A JOB SEEKER

It's easy to get carried away when discussing a job possibility with an applicant – especially one that you would like to hire. However, don't make future promises that the candidate may view as a commitment, even though you're only coaching them in terms of possibilities. The most significant issue to avoid is a promise of future promotions and/or pay raises. If they never come to pass, a productive worker will quickly sour.

Q: Job seekers often ask me questions about advancement opportunities, and I'm not sure of how to respond.

A: You certainly don't want to make commitments, or even infer that promotions and/or pay raises are inevitable. On the other hand, you don't want to leave the impression that they're impossible to achieve. The goal is to provide generalized information that offers hope, without sending signals of a future commitment. Let's look at an example of how this can be done through the techniques used by Dan, a supervisor of computer programmers for a software firm.

Applicant: "What are the opportunities for advancement?"
Dan: "I may be partial about this, but in general, opportunities here are good. However, as you know, that depends upon many factors."
Applicant: "Such as?"
Dan: "First of all, the performance of the individual on the job."
Applicant: "Let's assume I do a bang-up job, as I'm sure I will."
Dan: "I want to be honest with your and it's certainly reasonable to assume that if you perform well, the future will be bright. But that's down the road and to be realistic, I can't foresee the future. Other things can influence advancement opportunities."
Applicant: "What do you mean?"
Dan: "For example, the future growth of the company and the performance of the economy. Obviously, future growth

will influence the number of higher level positions that open up."

Applicant: "How's the company doing?"

Dan: "Over the past five years we've averaged 20% year-to-year growth in sales. I have fifteen people working for me. Three years ago when I started as a programmer here, there were only seven people in the department."

Applicant: "Sounds good."

NOTE: Notice that Dan mentions the growth of the company, as well as the fact that he started as a programmer and now supervises fifteen people. That, in a casual way, tells the applicant that future opportunities are good. Yet, Dan doesn't make any statements that could be construed as a commitment. That's the best method for handling these types of questions. In brief, even though individual circumstances will vary, always be, (1) matter-of-fact, (2) honest, and (3) noncommittal.

POINTER: It's worth noting that salary specifics shouldn't be discussed during initial interviews. If a job seeker raises the question, simply respond that, "It's negotiable." If someone tries to pin you down, counter by asking them what their salary requirement is.

It's far better for your personnel people to make salary offers. They have the expertise to handle these matters, and it also keeps you out of the negotiation loop. This is worthwhile, since if salary becomes a sticking point, you won't be stuck in the position of haggling with a future subordinate.

Q: I'm a first-line supervisor in a retail operation, and the people working for me are in dead-end jobs. What can I tell applicants about future opportunities when there aren't any?

A: Emphasize the positive aspects of the position such as valuable experience and/or a good working environment. This isn't something to be overly concerned about. There are many entry level positions that aren't necessarily springboards to success. There are also many job seekers who aren't looking for career advancement. They may only seek to supplement their income, or want the job because of flexible hours, a convenient location, or some other personal factor. Most folks know before they start to look, that a dead-end job is just that.

7.4 THE BEST QUESTION TO ASK ANY JOB CANDIDATE

Among the typical questions asked of job seekers are, (1) Why do you want to leave your present job? and, (2) Why are you interested in working for this company? Frequently, if the first question is answered satisfactorily, the second one is never raised, and that's a mistake.

Q: Whenever I ask job applicants whey they want to leave their present job, the answer is invariably, "For better opportunities." It's important for me to know their reasons for leaving, but a generalized answer like that tells me nothing. Is there a better way to deal with this topic?

A: The best question to ask is a follow-on to the, "Why do you want to leave your present job," query, and that is to ask applicants why they want to work for your company. The answer to this question can be very revealing.

For one thing, it tells you whether or not the applicant knows anything about the company. An affirmative answer may indicate that the person really wants the open job, and isn't just interviewing to see where the best job offer comes from.

But the biggest advantage of asking this question is that it doesn't readily allow for a packaged answer. It forces applicants to think, which means they may reveal more about themselves and their background. This can give you a better idea of whether or not someone will be happy in the available job. And that, in the final analysis is what it's all about.

7.5 GUIDELINES FOR HIRING THE BEST PERSON

Reviewing job applications and holding interviews are a critical part of the selection process. However, squeezing this work in while keeping your department running smoothly can be rough. Even so, it's necessary to select a worker who not only is qualified, but is also a good "fit" for the vacancy and will adjust well to both the job and other employees.

Q: My problem starts long before interviews. The simple truth is that I always get a lousy bunch of applications when there's a vacancy. What can be done about this?

A: This often results from a failure to adequately pinpoint the requirements of the job before soliciting applications. Often, there's a penchant to blame a weak group of job candidates on the personnel people responsible for soliciting candidates.

This isn't fair, since personnel staffers can't know the qualifications for every position in the company. They can only base their search on the requirements furnished to them by the hiring department. For this reason, one of the imperatives for success in hiring starts with clearly and concisely specifying what you're looking for in terms of education and experience.

Frequently, it's assumed that the same qualifications used in the past still apply. However, that ignores the fact that the original requirement may have been written poorly, and/or the job may have changed significantly over time. Therefore, your first duty in filling a vacancy is to make sure that the exact qualifications and type of experience you're looking for are furnished to whoever is responsible for soliciting applicants. If necessary, sit down with these staffers and go over the requirements they are going to use.

In doing this, stay away from extremes. Making the qualifications too broad will result in a flood of applications from the folks not qualified to fill the position. The other extreme is being too rigid in the standards you set, so only a handful of applications result. Your best bet is to be realistic. Simply put, if you're shopping for an entry level technician, don't advertise for a rocket scientist.

Q: I've given up on what to expect when I hire new workers. I specify what I want and I always hire someone whose application fits that bill and without fail, it turns out later that they don't know what they're doing. What is going wrong here?

A: It may be that you're not asking the right questions during the interview. There are a couple of actions you can take to improve your chances of success.

To start with, be careful of the sequence you use when discussing applicant's experience and your job requirements. If you start out by telling them about the job, you're setting yourself up, because sharp applicants will then discuss their background in exactly those terms.

Instead, let candidates discuss their experience first, so they don't know your objectives. When necessary, ask all the questions you need to get direct replies, rather than generalities. For instance, if someone is telling you about their experience with test equipment, ask what kind of equipment. In short, find out if their experience is specifically what you're looking for, or only generally related.

Q: I seem to get qualified people, but a few of them have been social misfits and don't get along well with other employees. This has created problems and I'd like to know how to steer clear of this in the future.

A: One element that can be missed when interviewing is appraising the personality of the candidate. Obviously, you want to hire someone who can do the job. Nevertheless, you – and your subordinates – will be working together on a daily basis with the person you hire. If you want to maximize teamwork within your group, be sure you feel comfortable about the candidate.

Even though it's not possible to pinpoint someone's personality in a relatively short interview, don't ignore your instincts. If two candidates are competitive in terms of qualifications, go with the one your instincts tell you will adapt more quickly to a new work environment.

TIP: Interviewing job seekers is a relatively rare event for most supervisors. Therefore, you may not have had much interviewing experience. If that's so, it might be helpful to rank the candidates you intend to interview based on their applications.

Then, schedule interviews starting with the least likely choice and ending up with the best possibility. This will give you a chance to sharpen your interview skills, so that you feel comfortable in interviewing when you get to the better candidates. Admittedly, the rankings may change after interviews are held, but this technique can be of some help in being better prepared to interview what – at least on paper – appears to be the better candidates.

7.6 BASIC TRAINING FOR NEW EMPLOYEES

Chapter 6 covered various aspects of training new hires. However, effectively integrating a nervous novice into the work force requires more than just teaching them the job.

Q: Are there certain procedures that can be followed to help new employees adjust more quickly?

A: Everyone has experienced uncertainties surrounding a new job. Of course, seeing that a trainee is taught the job properly is a primary concern of any supervisor. Yet, aside from that, it's beneficial to navigate new hires through the nonfunctional aspects of their first days and weeks at work.

In fact, doing this effectively indirectly contributes to the worker learning his job at a faster pace. The more preoccupied a new employee is with nonworking aspects of his employment, the lower will be his concentration on the job itself. There's real value in easing the anxieties of new hires. The following suggestions are useful in accomplishing this goal:

1. Let new people know that mistakes are inevitable when learning a new job.
2. Make certain that new employees learn all of the little things that go with their new surroundings. This includes when and where to eat lunch, park their cars, and all of the other minor matters that will make their transition easier.
3. Until you're certain that novices are feeling at home in their new job, meet regularly with them to discuss their concerns.
4. Go over the details of pay and fringe benefits with new workers. These topics are often covered by personnel

staffers when new employees come on board. However, the first few days on the job are a constant stream of new faces, all furnishing information of one sort or another. Consequently, it's virtually impossible to retain everything. Once employees are assigned to you, they're hesitant to seek out others for answers to their questions, therefore, it's worthwhile to go over the basics for a second time.

5. Let trainees know they should come to you with any questions they might have, but go beyond this and seek them out for brief bull sessions. New workers are often reluctant to approach the boss, and this is especially true with shy people.

6. Offer encouragement as people learn their job. This gives them assurance that they're meeting expectations.

7. Be patient. It's easy to get annoyed with what seem like simplistic questions, but remember that everything is of consequence when you're a stranger in new surroundings.

Q: One difficulty I've had in the past is with experienced workers we've hired. They have a habit of doing the job differently, which causes all kinds of problems. How can I get them to adjust to our way of doing the job?

A: This is pretty common, and it calls for diplomacy on your part, and relearning on the part of the employee. No matter what the job is, there are seemingly as many ways of doing it as there are people. That's not true of course, but there are enough differences from company to company to require adjustments by new workers. Often, experienced workers readily adapt to these changes, but sometimes it's necessary to coax them along.

The major pitfall in getting an experienced worker to change one's habits is failing to understand that this isn't always easy. After all, anyone who has done a job one way for any length of time tends to perform that function as second nature. Therefore, retain your composure if an employee doesn't adjust right away.

Sit down with the worker and explain why a task is done differently from what the employee has learned elsewhere. Emphasize the importance of the employee making the necessary adjustment without criticizing what he did in the past.

TIP: When experienced workers are hired, it's not a bad idea to think about how they do the job that differs from present methods. Some of their practices may be worth adopting.

7.7 STEERING THE NEW HIRE THROUGH UNFAMILIAR MINEFIELDS

Every company is a composite of its people, procedures, and products. To the outside observer, most businesses are pretty much alike in how they operate. Yet, for new employees – including those with years of experience elsewhere – starting a new job is like sailing in uncharted waters. They're not quite sure of what they'll find, but they hope it's smooth sailing.

And even when the products and procedures are similar to those encountered on a previous job, the people are always different. Many of the subtle contradictions of a new job are only discovered by trial and error. However, an alert supervisor can coach a new hire on the hidden pitfalls that lie in wait for an unsuspecting novice. Doing this can save both yourself and the worker a good deal of grief.

Q: Herb, who was hired for my group three weeks ago, has already had two run-ins with the supervisor of another department. It's partly my fault, since Herb shouldn't have been going to that supervisor in the first place. I'd like to tell new people who to avoid, as well as other peculiarities to watch out for. It would make life easier for them, but I don't want to sound negative to someone who has just started work.

A: The problem addresses an issue that's often forgotten when new employees are hired. That's because it's a hidden agenda that doesn't surface until a new worker experiences some sort of difficulty.

Anyone who has worked somewhere for any length of time learns that there are certain people and/or techniques that can simplify getting the job done. They learn how best to approach someone whose assistance they seek, who to contact for the best results when there are several choices, and any number of other distinctions that can make work a little less complicated.

All of this comes from the experience of working at a company for some length of time. It can't be learned elsewhere, and in fact it's almost instinctive in nature. That's precisely why it's often neglected when new people are trained.

When new employees miss out on this "inside scoop," they eventually learn the ropes as they gain experience. That isn't necessarily devastating for either them, or for you. Nevertheless, if you take the time to explain the subsurface snares that exist, it can help guide new employees through unfamiliar minefields.

For instance, there may be certain people, who for one reason or another, it's best for a new hire to avoid. Perhaps it's someone who has a running feud with your department, or maybe a person with a reputation for being a bottleneck. Whatever the reason, it's easy to refrain from being openly critical of these people by telling new employees who to see, rather than pinpointing who to avoid. Doing it this way projects a more positive image. After all, first impressions are lasting, and if recent hires are constantly cautioned about avoiding people, they may start to wonder what kind of an outfit they're working for.

7.8 CONVINCING ANYONE WHY YOU NEED MORE HELP

If there's one function of supervision that requires an aggressive attitude, it's in securing more help for your department. Having a "laid back" frame of mind can condemn you to being permanently understaffed, and constantly struggling to meet workload demands.

Q: Every time I ask for more help, all my boss does is stall. My workers are grumbling and I'm getting frustrated. What can I do to get the people I need?

A: The surest way to get more help is to prove that it's in your boss's interest, as well as your own. If the only problem a boss has is to say "No" when you ask, plead, or beg for help, that isn't likely to motivate him. However, if you can demonstrate that without more help performance will suffer – and upper management will want to know why – you then make your boss an instant partner in seeking additional manpower. Naturally, how you frame your argument is pivotal. It shouldn't be posed as a veiled threat, but rather as a detailed explanation outlining the future impact of continuing to operate with too few people.

It also makes sense to put your justification in writing, even when you're planning to talk about it over with your boss. Having facts and figures to back you up can be the clincher that gets you a "Yes" rather than a "No." Let's look at a good appeal for help after a supervisor has been previously turned down by the boss.

Background. Alan, a supervisor in a job shop operation at a large manufacturing company, was turned down three months ago when he asked Stan, his boss, to fill a long-standing vacancy in the department. The crisis is even more severe now as some of Alan's subordinates are complaining about working too much overtime to fill the void.

The Pitch for Help.

Alan:	"Stan, can I have a few minutes? I've got a real problem."
Stan:	"Sure, sit down. What's on your mind?"
Alan:	"Well, remember about three months ago we talked about getting another person for my department? Since then, I put everyone on scheduled overtime to try and fill the gap. That hasn't solved the problem, and I still need someone."
Stan:	"Darn it Alan, I'd like to help out, but you know how top management feels about additional hiring."
Alan:	"I know that, and I wouldn't be asking if it wasn't serious. Incidentally, don't forget we're talking about a vacant space, not a new slot."

Stan: "I know that, and let's face it. Once a vacancy goes unfilled for a while, everyone assumes it's not needed. And that spot's been vacant for months."

Alan: "We've survived on unlimited overtime, but now my people are all burnt out. I can't keep working them at that pace."

Stan: "Look, it's not easy, but management is intent on keeping this outfit slimmed down. I just don't know how I could justify it."

Alan: "Actually, the overtime is only partly compensating for the increase in workload. We're putting in 20% more hours with the overtime, but workload has increased 30%. And remember, we were only scheduling OT to cover for the vacant slot. I've got some figures worked up here." (Alan hands a graph to Stan.)

Stan: "Yea, I see what you mean. You've been doing a heck of a job with that group. Frankly Alan, the bottom line is that the job is getting done, and as long as that happens, we've got nothing to worry about."

Alan: "Well that just it Stan. We're headed for big trouble. If you look on page two of that workload analysis, you'll see that our backlog has increased from two weeks to five weeks. We've been falling a week behind every month. By next month, we'll be missing promised deliveries and we've got no slack, so our choice is missed deliveries or another body."

Stan: "Geez, I didn't realize it was that bad. There's no way we can miss deliveries. I'll get ground into dog food if that happens. Look, let me keep this work analysis. I'll go up to McGregor's office (Stan's boss) and get a priority hiring approval right now. Holy smoke, keep everyone working down there. In the meantime, I'll see about shifting someone from another department to help out. Keep me posted on this."

There are several observations about this scenario that have general application when making a plea for more manpower. First of all, don't be accusatory with comments such as, "If we got the help when we first needed it, we wouldn't have a problem right now." You might be right, and you may even get the help you need, but your boss won't forget your remarks.

Another point is that anytime you can show an either/or dilemma, you're more likely to be successful. In the example, Stan had two choices, (1) get help or, (2) slip deliveries. This worked for Alan, and the same type of pitch will work for you.

It's also wise to fight to get vacancies filled right away. If you don't, and the work gets done, the obvious assumption is that you didn't need the person in the first place.

In this regard, it's valuable to think about how upper management looks at requests for help. The higher up in the organization managers are, the more removed they are from the day-to-day realities of what's taking place at the working level. Budgets, sales revenues, and production figures are what those not in the trenches deal with. You may know you need help, but unless everyone in the approval process is convinced of that, you're just not going to get it. You have to make a pitch that upper management can relate to, which may mean demonstrating that without additional help, their production projections may have to be revised downward.

It admittedly takes time to prepare figures comparing workload and output, but the presentation doesn't have to be pretty – just effective. The alternative is that you'll be spinning your wheels holding things together until the roof falls in. In brief, the one formula for success in getting the people necessary to do the job, is a combination of justification and persistence. First, prove you need the help, and then keep pushing until you get it.

CAUTION: Don't challenge the impossible when you're looking for help. For example, if there's a hiring freeze, you're wasting your time in pestering the boss. Make your pitch and forget it until circumstances change. Also, don't look for help that you don't need. If you've got enough bodies, but they're not producing, you've got problems requiring attention, but asking for more help isn't the answer.

7.9 WHAT TO DO WHEN YOU'RE GIVEN DUDS YOU DIDN'T WANT

For a variety of reasons you can end up with folks working for you that you don't want, and/or don't need. This might happen when upper management decides to reorganize operations, and you're given little or no say in the matter. Or it may occur when the solution to a personality clash is to transfer the culprit to your group.

These transfers may be accompanied by a compliment to you such as, "You'll have no problem, since you're good at handling people." These kinds of compliments you can do without, especially if every bad apple gets tossed into your barrel. Whatever the circumstances, you may find yourself dealing with duds that were foisted upon you.

Q: My boss is transferring an employee into my department who had problems with his previous boss. How should I handle this?

A: To begin with, don't start off with preconceived notions about the employee. Unfortunately, bad reputations travel with workers when they're transferred internally. These reputations may, or may not, be deserved. Even if they are, there's reason for hope. It may be that a bad reputation stems from a personality conflict with a prior supervisor which won't carry over into your department. It's also possible that an employee's transfer might be an awakening fact to either succeed in your department or risk losing a job.

That said, it's sensible to start off with a clean slate when a problem employee is assigned to you. Give them the benefit of the doubt and see what happens. You may be pleasantly surprised, but if not, deal with any difficulties as you would with any other worker.

Q: I've got a guy working for me who was transferred into my department six months ago. I don't know why he wasn't canned instead of being passed off on me. That bothers me, since I want to get rid of this employee, but I'm afraid he's being kept on the payroll for reasons that I don't know about. Am I stuck with this dud?

A: Ineffective employees are transferred for several reasons, not all of which are bad. A transfer may be made to give an employee a new lease on his work life in an honest attempt to be fair. Sometimes it works out, and other times it doesn't.

Occasionally, a boss may use a transfer as a convenient way around a dilemma. For instance, a manager may have two supervisors complaining to him, one about getting rid of a dud, and the other screaming for more help. The manager may seize upon a golden opportunity to cure both hassles by transferring the dud to the supervisor who is demanding more help. This method is by no means universal, but it is done and you should be aware of the possibility that it can happen.

But whatever the reason for your being the unhappy recipient of an ineffective worker, if the employee's performance doesn't improve, dismissal may be necessary. Feel out your boss on the possibility of firing the employee, but if you get strong objections drop the idea, since it's likely that internal politics are operating to protect the incompetent.

Does that mean you're stuck? Not necessarily. Perhaps the employee is ill-suited for the type of work your department does. Your best bet – which requires a little luck and a lot of thought – is to convince your boss that this person would be better suited to another position. Of course, to make this argument fly, you have to identify a specific job that the worker could competently fill. How imaginative you are at this will partially depend upon how badly you want to get rid of the problem.

7.10 A LAST RESORT TO SALVAGE PROBLEM PEOPLE

Both you and the company have a significant investment in your subordinates. The company's concern is primarily financial, in terms of the expense of hiring and training. Yours is principally the time and effort you have expended to develop employees skilled at their jobs. For both reasons, it's only as a last resort that you want to fire someone. Therefore, it's useful to explore other alternatives when an employee isn't performing up to par.

Q: One woman who works for me has been here almost four months, but she's just not measuring up to the job. She's not a discipline problem, so I really want to avoid letting her go if that's at all possible. Any suggestions?

A: There are several choices you can consider, one or more of which might work, depending upon the type of job, and the size and scope of your company.

The first and simplest course of action is to see if there's some way you can change the existing job to bring it more in line with the employee's capabilities. Sometimes, there's one aspect of a job that a worker doesn't seem able to master. Assuming they've received adequate training to no avail, restructuring the job itself may be the solution. Take away the duty that causes the difficulty and substitute work that's more in line with the person's skills. That's not always possible, but many times, with a little bit of thought, it can be an effective remedy.

A second option is to reassign the individual to a different job, preferably within your group, but if that's not feasible, then elsewhere within the company. It's not unusual for a less than adequate worker at one job to perform quite satisfactorily when placed in a position more attuned to his or her skills.

No matter what course you follow when an employee is experiencing rough going on the job, it's necessary to supervise them more closely than would otherwise be the case. This shouldn't be done from the aspect of looking over someone's shoulder, but from the viewpoint of identifying what is causing the difficulty.

The solution may be nothing more complex than the need for additional training. Or maybe the person is just trying too hard which is causing mistakes to be made. When this happens, just talking it out with the worker often results in improvement. Of course, in the end you may find that a poor hiring decision was made and the only answer is to terminate the employee. But if you've tried everything else, then both you and the employee will be better off in finding that out sooner, rather than later.

7.11 PAVING THE PATH TO GET RID OF LOST CAUSES

Given the diverse cast of characters you have to work with, tackling the problem of terminating incompetents isn't any picnic. Seemingly sound advice such as, "Deal with a problem directly and promptly," doesn't always cut it. Although the theory may be sound, you're faced with living, breathing individuals who aren't going to clasp you to their bosom when you say, "Hey Jack, get off your butt and do some work, or I'm going to have to fire you."

Chances are that the response will be either pithy profanity or a pretense of compliance. In either event, the culprit's mindset may not change at all. Ultimately, you're going to have to proceed with a termination action.

Q: I've got an employee who probably should be let go, and my boss is urging me to do just that, but I'm having trouble biting the bullet.

A: One of the biggest headaches facing anyone with a supervisory position is getting rid of people. No matter how adept you are at managing people, there are always a few who just don't work out, and getting rid of them isn't a piece of cake.

The first hurdle to overcome is your own reluctance to recognize that an employee won't and/or can't hack it. The longer you procrastinate, the more difficult it is to make the final decision to dismiss someone. Admittedly, it's never pleasant to fire anyone, but delaying the inevitable doesn't turn it into a day at the beach.

On the other hand, don't be pushed into a hasty decision by your own boss. After all, it's easy to say, "Fire him!" when you don't have to do the dirty work.

Most folks know when they're not performing satisfactorily, although a few continue to think that they're whizzing along on their way to stardom. Try as you might, it's impossible to destroy these illusions. When you have to deal with this type, it's prudent to go strictly by the book, since they're likely to treat dismissal as a cruel injustice, which means that the firing better be well documented to prevent and/or defend a lawsuit for wrongful discharge.

Fortunately, most people know when their future is somewhere else. Here it's often possible to avoid outright firing, since the employee sees the handwriting on the wall and looks for employment elsewhere.

7.12 HOW TO FIRE WITHOUT FEAR OF REPERCUSSIONS

Preparing to fire an employee is similar to hiring an attorney to defend you in court. Both are necessary preparation for events you would rather avoid. Unfortunately, both legal advice and termination guidance are often ignored until it's too late.

It's easy to understand why too little planning is done prior to dismissing employees. After all, someone isn't hired to be fired, but even the best hiring practices aren't foolproof. Therefore, following termination rules can prevent future problems when dismissals are necessary.

Q: Are there guidelines to follow when firing an employee?

A: Actually, future problems are best avoided by what is done long before a worker is told of his termination. That means disciplinary actions should be carefully documented to build a case that will stand objective scrutiny. Of course, every company has specific policies on termination, therefore, coordinate your actions with both your boss and the personnel department. Some general factors to consider are as follows:

- Never promise job security to workers. This could later be construed as an implied contract of permanent employment. From a practical standpoint, it's not within your power to guarantee a job, so don't make useless reassurances in a moment of good cheer.
- Document every disciplinary action taken. It's good practice to send copies to both your boss and the personnel department.

- Don't procrastinate in firing decisions. If it has to be done, do it and get it over with.
- You, as a supervisor, should deliver the firing decision to the dismissed employee. It's good to have a personnel representative along so you can quickly depart and then let the staffer explain any benefits the employee is entitled to.
- Try to use an office other than your own when you notify an employee he's being let go. That lets you leave and return to work. If you use your own office, you could be trapping yourself into listening to a long harangue from an angry employee who's just become an ex-employee.
- Don't try to justify a firing to your other workers. When someone's fired, everyone knows why anyway.
- Do everything possible to maintain a normal routine after a firing.
- Don't blame yourself. Firing someone is difficult, but it's sometimes necessary.

7.13 WHY DEADWOOD DOESN'T ALWAYS GET DUMPED

One annoyance for some supervisors is the misfortune of having a deadbeat in the department who can't be dumped. This usually results from internal politics, but whatever the cause, when you have to deal with this dilemma, it's sensible to treat it with a strong dose of delicacy.

Q: There's a senior technician opening in my unit, and my boss has told me that management wants an individual from another department in the job. I'm ticked off, since I have a couple of top quality people who should get first crack at this opening. Can I fight this?

A: Sure you can fight it, but the real question is whether or not you can win. You may succeed if you stick to your guns, but the ultimate cost of victory might not justify the battle.

It's one thing to say that what's happening is wrong, but it's quite another to successfully oppose it. The hard fact of life is that everything doesn't always work out as it should. Sometimes we have to recognize a losing battle when we see it and avoid the conflict. This kind of situation is just such a case.

Putting someone not qualified into a position because of friendship, family ties, or whatever, is just one of the reasons that deadwood can thrive within a company. Transferring an employee because a boss doesn't have the courage to tell the worker to "shape up or ship out" is another way that deadwood may arrive in your group.

Transfers may also be unjustly used to shunt aside long-time employees who are perceived to be past their peak. Whatever the reason, don't ignore the internal politics of situations such as these, since you do so at your peril.

Q: What can I do about the morale in my department when an outsider I didn't want is given a job ahead of people already in the group?

A: You can expect poor morale when something like this happens, but the long-term impact should be minimal. Chances are that your subordinates know the actions wasn't of your doing. They probably also know that there wasn't much you could do about it, so after a short period of time everything should return to normal.

TIP: When someone you didn't want is dumped in your department over your objections, you may at least be able to use it to your long-term advantage. Let your boss know that you won't make waves, but imply that he owes you a favor. Down the road when the opportunity arises, cash in your chit by saying in so many words, "Remember when..."

8

Holding Your Own Outside Your Department

Although much of your time may be spent managing the daily doings of the people who work for you, part of your duties include working with people outside of your department. Success in these outside relationships can have a direct bearing, both on departmental operations, and your own career as a supervisor.

To succeed with those outside your direct supervision requires an ability to secure cooperation on the one hand, and to fight for resources on the other. You have to circumvent bottlenecks within the company that can bog your department down, and on occasion you may have to battle to defend your turf.

Finally, you need to be successful in your customer relations. Although you may not think of it as such, you do in fact have a customer. That's because your department is performing a function that in some way services one or more users of the end result.

Your customer may be no further away than the next step in the production process, or perhaps it's every employee in the company if you supervise an administrative unit. In this context, a customer is anyone dependent upon the output of your group, and it really makes no difference whether you're dealing in products or paperwork.

To be successful in these endeavors requires a combination of skills, but most of all, it demands awareness and flexibility in knowing both when and how to react to conditions as they develop. Let's look at how this can be done.

8.1 WHY COOPERATION WITH OTHERS IS A TWO-WAY STREET

Keeping everything running smoothly within your own group requires the cooperation of people in a wide range of functions throughout the company. Your ability to secure the necessary assistance has a direct bearing on your success.

Q: My boss suggested that I be more diplomatic in my dealings with other supervisors and staff people. This upsets me since I'm just trying to get my job done. I think my boss should be getting other people off their duffs instead of criticizing me.

A: Diligence is a commendable trait, but just being a hard-charger won't get the job done. When it comes to securing the cooperation of other people, several elements have to be considered.

One is the recognition of priorities – your own as well as those of other people. It's comfortable to think that what you're doing is more important than anything else. That may be true – at least as far as you are concerned. Even so, everyone you do business with may not reach the same conclusion.

Therefore, in securing the cooperation of other people, an awareness of their workload and priorities is essential. This may mean a willingness to wait your turn on occasion. By prioritizing the importance of your tasks, and not demanding an instant response every time you need assistance, people will more readily respond when you do have a rush job.

Diplomacy is also an essential ingredient in securing cooperation. In the heat of a pressure cooker kind of day it's possible to operate with a short fuse, but blowing your top at someone will at best work only once. Although keeping calm may not move mountains, it will get the job done, whereas a volcanic eruption will only destroy working relationships. This isn't to say that you won't encounter plenty of circumstances where you would be justified in exploding, but you're much better off in searching for another way to let off steam.

TIP: Unless you possess an unusual degree of patience, it's inevitable that you'll get angry on occasion. But even when it's warranted, it's a good idea to apologize after things calm down. It doesn't have to be any big deal, just something like, "Hey, Beth, I'm sorry I blew a fuse yesterday." Doing this prevents lingering resentment which can cause difficulty the next time you need to work with that person.

8.2 WHEN DOING FAVORS WILL GET FAVORS

Motivating people within the company that you don't supervise isn't a goal that is readily apparent. After all, if they're doing their job, everything you need from them to get your work done will be accomplished. If not, you can always complain to the appropriate manager to bring pressure to bear. That seems like a pretty sensible course to follow, but it falls apart under closer scrutiny.

Q: My department counts on the machine shop to do work that is critical to getting our projects completed on schedule. It's always touch and go trying to meet production goals when I have to rely on these people. How can I get a better response to my needs?

A: It's standard practice to complain to a supervisor when workers you don't manager aren't meeting requirements that affect your operations. That's a prescribed course of action, which is often both necessary and justified. However, at best it secures your place in line with everyone else in getting your work done. Sure, on occasion you may be successful in speeding the job along by pleading priority, but that doesn't fly very often. Anyone who constantly pleads priority soon has folks pegging all of their requests as routine – including the real priorities.

Complaining to someone's boss may be necessary, but it's best used as a last resort rather than standard procedure. You can obtain speedier responses to any of your requests by motivating people to respond because they want to – not because they have to. Accomplishing that isn't as impossible as you might think.

One way to succeed is to establish a track record with those whose services you use on a regular basis. Ask them to do you a small favor that doesn't require a lot of time and effort. For instance,

"Bill, could you bang this out for me? I know how busy you are, but I'm in a real bind. I'd sure appreciate it." Since the task only takes a few minutes, chances are that you'll get no argument. Do this a few times and people will become accustomed to your requests.

But don't stop there. Let their boss know how cooperative they are. When people hear that you've been praising them, your stock will rise rapidly. You're now in a perfect position to ask and receive priority attention when you have a bigger task to perform.

On a more general level, if you're responsive when people ask you for favors, it's likely that they will do the same for you in return. Of course, the folks you do favors for may not be the same people you need a favor from. Even here, a willingness to help others has carry-over value. As you know, word travels fast through the grapevine of any company. If you have a reputation for being helpful, everyone will know it, and that works to your advantage.

CAUTION: Sooner or later, you'll run into someone who considers their every task to be top priority. They'll attempt to run over you and everyone else to get their job done. Usually, their method of operation is to complain to an upper-level manager when someone doesn't drop everything to attend to their needs.

Be wary of this type of operator, since they often cause trouble. Let them know that their job will be done as soon as possible, and be ready to explain to your boss why it's not being done right away. Use factual reasons and avoid being critical of the individual. People who work in this fashion aren't pleasant to deal with. Fortunately, over time their complaints become second nature and are pretty much ignored.

8.3 USING STAFF FUNCTIONS EFFECTIVELY

No matter how large a company is, for more supervisors their world of work revolves around a relatively small group of people. First and foremost are one's subordinates and immediate boss. You can add to this number the people in other departments with whom you interact on a regular basis. It's not uncommon to be unfamiliar – even in a general way – with other functions within the company. That's to be expected, especially if you're employed by a large corporation.

Nevertheless, your success as a supervisor is influenced by your ability to use a wide range of staff functions when the need arises.

Q: I work in a manufacturing area where we get our hands dirty. As far as I'm concerned, staff people are overpaid paper shufflers.

A: This is an unfortunate – but all too prevalent – attitude that develops when a company doesn't promote a strong sense of teamwork. The fact is that every job contributes to the overall well-being of a company.

When you're running a busy department, it's easy to get annoyed by staff interruptions which mean little or nothing to you. However, that doesn't mean what they're doing isn't worthwhile. It's a two-way street when it comes to developing good relations between those with operating responsibilities and people in staff functions. As a supervisor, you can further this cause by complying with staff requests in a timely matter.

For their part, staffers should recognize that every supervisor has work priorities and sometimes an immediate response isn't possible. The bottom line in improving staff/operating relationship is nothing more complex than a little bit of friendly dialogue. This can be helped along immeasurably if staffers explain the need for information so its importance can be understood.

TIP: When you're given confusing reports to prepare for staffers, don't seek to interpret what the requester is looking for. Go back to the source and get the answers to your questions. At the same time, try to negotiate a deal to furnish readily available data in place of what's requested. This may be possible since requests for information are often broader than they need to be.

Q: What's the big advantage in learning what staff people do?

A: Pure and simple, it can make your job easier. Let's look at this point through the eyes of Ned and Nellie who are both supervisors in a paper mill. Ned wants nothing to do with staff people, while Nellie recognizes their importance and cultivates their friendship. Here's the result of what happens when they have to handle similar duties.

Ned and Nellie each need another workbench for their departments.

Ned's approach. Ned goes to his boss who tells him to fill out a requisition. Three sign-offs and five weeks later Ned gets his bench.

Nellie's approach. Nellie goes to see Mike who manages the facilities group. He tells her that there's an unused bench in building "D" and that he'll get it for her. She has it delivered to her area the next day.

The success factor. Two months ago, Mike's people were doing an equipment inventory. Ned gave him a hard time and they parted on unfriendly terms. Nellie, on the other hand, sat down with Mike, found out what he needed, and then helped his people inventory the equipment in her area. She also learned that Mike was the person to see whenever you needed a piece of equipment in a hurry.

Joe, from Ned's department, and Jerry, from Nellie's group, each complain to personnel about their supervisor being unfair. Bob, in the personnel office, handles both matters.

Bob with Ned. Bob calls Ned's boss and arranges to meet with both Ned and his boss. Ned is put on the defensive and is cautioned by his boss to be less abrupt when dealing with Joe.

Bob with Nellie. Bob calls Nellie on the phone and tells her that Jerry has complained about her. Nellie explains that Jerry is hot-tempered and is sometimes reluctant to follow directions. Bob says he'll talk to Jerry. He does, and that's the end of it.

The success factor. Ned and Nellie have both dealt with Bob in the past on personnel matters. Ned has been openly critical of the personnel office for being too slow in getting anything done.

By contract, Nellie has always worked closely with personnel and has sought their advice in the past on personnel issues. When Bob has a similar problem arise with both supervisors, he knew Nellie was cooperative so he helped her out. As for Ned, Bob put his personal philosophy to work, "Don't get mad, get even," and proceeded to put Ned on the spot with his boss.

Q: How can I get to know staff people better and use them more effectively?

A: There are several ways to do this that don't involve a lot of effort. For example, if you don't know who to contact on a particular problem, a good source of that type of information is none other than the company receptionist. It's a receptionist's job to know who people are and what they do.

Naturally, you can pick up the phone yourself and track someone down, but the larger a company is the more time-consuming that can be. When more than one person performs similar duties, the receptionist may steer you to a more obliging individual, by virtue of knowing who tends to be friendly and helpful.

In a more general way, you can get to know a wide variety of people you don't work with on a daily basis at company sponsored social events. At your next company picnic or party make an effort to meet people outside of your department. This helps you broaden your base of contacts within the company, since in business as in politics, who you know can be a big help in boosting your career along.

8.4 KEEPING OUTSIDE INFLUENCES AT BAY

You may have a boss whose constant refrain is, "Keep me posted," which is an indirect way of telling you not to go over his head to other managers. Of course, it's certainly proper for a boss to expect that he won't be constantly bypassed by those who work for him. The irony is that this observance of protocol may be ignored by your boss and other managers who barge around your department as if you didn't exist. Most of the time this is relatively harmless, but on occasion it can cause real problems.

Q: My boss continually issues directions to my people without discussing it with me. I'm pretty fed up about it, but I don't know what to do.

A: To some extent, how closely your boss interacts with your workers depends upon the type of working relationship you have with your boss. If it's relaxed, and the boss isn't really undercutting your authority, it's best to simply ignore it. However, there are circumstances where this can create confusion in the workplace.

One such case is when you've told someone to work on a particular job, and your boss comes along and countermands your instructions.

If this happens frequently the only solution is to have a talk with your boss and "tell it like it is." Explain the difficulties it creates for you in trying to manage the department. If you don't want to fire point blank on the topic, then attack it from a third party angle such as this.

You: "Boss, I'm having a problem with a couple of managers who go directly to my people with work requests. It's screwing up my operation. Got any ideas on how to handle it?

Boss: "Tell them to come to you..."

Unless your boss is a dunce, he'll get this message. However, if his light bulb doesn't blink, you may have to proceed further and tell him that he's causing the problem.

This type of difficulty is most common when a boss who used to supervise the department has been promoted. Usually, a boss will slowly drift away from this sort of hands-on involvement. If not, say something like, "Joe, I don't know quite how to say this, but my people aren't recognizing me as the supervisor because of you being their old boss. Do you think it would help if you came to me instead of going directly to them?"

Q: My boss is no problems, but other managers are always going directly to my people. What's the best way to stop this?

A: Tell your workers not to take directions from other people. Instead, have them send the people to you. However, if workers are reluctant to say "No" to upper-level managers, have your people tell you after the fact. If it's diplomatic to do so, talk to the erring manager. If not, bring the matter to your boss's attention.

8.5 PUTTING POMPOUS STAFFERS IN THEIR PLACE

As was discussed in Sec. 8.3, there is often unnecessary friction between operating groups and staff functions. In fact, you may have the misfortune to run into an obnoxious staffer or two who have their own sense of importance blown out of proportion. If that happens, there's nothing quite so rewarding as puncturing their balloon.

Q: I've got a young management type with a freshly minted college degree who thinks he's running the company. He comes down here to my department and gets everyone agitated. How can I corral this clown?

A: Assuming he's got a right to be there – if not, tell him to get lost – then the best tactic is to sit him down for a chat. Explain in no uncertain terms that your people have work to do and that his business is to be conducted without interfering with your operation. Do this in a friendly fashion – at least until you get static. Then, be as insistent as possible within the bounds of dignity.

Q: First it's time-study people, then it's personnel staffers doing job position surveys. I'm trying to get work done. How can I clamp a lid on this nonsense?

A: Every supervisor experiences some frustration from outside influences that hinder operations. For the most part, these are a necessary evil that you have to learn to live with. Nevertheless, if it gets out of hand, try to rein these people in. If they don't cooperate, tell your boss that production is being hampered by these interlopers.

Q: Are there any secrets for putting pompous people in their place in a dignified way?

A: A few ways to win this war are

- Always insist that staffers go through you before seeing anyone in your department. (See Sec. 3.13 for more on this.)
- Yes them to death, then ignore everything they say.
- Don't educate them. If they're that smart, let them figure things out for themselves.
- Never let them know they're getting under your skin. Try smiling a lot. It may not be easy, but grinding your teeth will only make your dentist happy.

8.6 RESOURCES: TRICKS FOR GETTING YOUR FAIR SHARE

You may be in a position where you find yourself stretched to the limit in getting the job done with the people and equipment assigned to your department. However, competition for additional resources can make getting your fair share a tough battle.

This is also an area where corporate infighting rears its ugly head. After all, it's not easy to be rational and objective when you're putting in long hours to survive, while other supervisors skilled at empire-building have more people than they need – at least from your perspective.

If there's a motto for success in this area, it's "the timid will toil, while fighters flourish." Therefore, if you want to keep your head above water in meeting workload demands, you better learn how to swim in shark-infested waters.

Q: I'm stretched to the limit in my group, while other departments don't seem to be overwhelmed with work. Despite this, whenever I talk to my boss about more help all he says is, "You'll have to do the best you can with what you've got."

A: The first fact you must face is that workload alone doesn't dictate whether or not you're successful in getting the people you need to do the job. Some supervisors are skilled at justifying the need for additional people, while others continue to operate understaffed departments.

The folks without manpower problems are usually well-schooled in the art of corporate infighting and empire-building. They know how to justify adding people to their department whether they're needed or not. That's not necessarily good when viewed from a cost-effectiveness standpoint. However, that's of little solace to a supervisor that doesn't have sufficient resources to operate effectively.

Sure, top management may realize sooner or later that overall productivity isn't what it should be. The problem is that cutbacks may then be implemented on an across-the-board basis. The end result is that departments that were already thinly staffed are squeezed even further, while top-heavy groups lose folks they didn't need anyway.

Obviously, cutbacks shouldn't be made in this fashion and alert managers know where the fat is within an organization. However, in many instances, the empire-builders win out, since they're not only skilled at getting help, but are equally adept at protecting their turf when times are tough. Therefore, if you're not holding your own in terms of resources, and upper-level management simply responds to those who plead their case best, you better learn how to live with the lions.

Q: Where I work the squeaky wheel theory determines who gets help. The only way I can get my fair share of resources is to play this game. Are there guidelines that can be used to get additional help when I need it?

A: Using one, or a combination of the following practices, will boost your chances for success in the battle for resources.

1. **Plead your track record.** This is a sure-fire tactic to support your need for additional help. Try to document the output of your group over a period of time. The longer the period, the better, but this involves a trade-off in terms of how long it will take you to compile the information.

    In doing this, relate people to production. What you want to show is average output per worker in comparison with your current and projected workload. For example, if each worker has been averaging ten widgets per week, and production requirements are increasing by twenty widgets a week, then you need two more people. Obviously, the details will depend upon the type of work your unit does, but the objective is to show that additional people are needed to meet increased workload demands.

    Although in some positions it's not quite as simple to relate output to people, it can be done. For instance, a supervisor of a human resources department might use an increase in total company employees as a baseline for this kind of argument. It may require some thought if you supervise an operation whose duties aren't easily quantifiable, but it can be done in most cases.

CAUTION: You may have several different options for presenting output per worker. For instance, if you supervise a purchasing function, you could conceivably use either number of purchase orders, or total value of orders processed, as the basis for seeking more help. Needless to say, when alternatives such as these are possible, use the one that works in your favor.

2. **Use a benefit analysis.** If you can pinpoint precisely how the company can save money by incurring the additional costs of hiring another worker you're home free. However, this is an area that requires hard facts to prove the point. A handy spin-off to this approach is to show how new equipment will save the expense of hiring additional help. For example, a more powerful computer that will speed-up document processing may negate the need for another clerk.

3. **Problem elimination.** When you want to requisition a new piece of equipment with a hefty price tag, it's much easier to sell the idea when you can show that the equipment will eliminate an existing problem. It's doubly effective if this is a problem in which your boss has expressed an interest.

4. **Nibbling at the corners.** Sometimes the best way to get what you want is to settle for something less. As an example, if you've been unsuccessful in persuading management that you need another full-time employee, try to get them to settle for a part-time worker. Then, after the employee is on board for a while, work at getting the slot upgraded to a full-time position. The same approach works for new equipment needs. A large outlay for ten word processors might be rejected, while buying one at a time might not meet with resistance.

SUGGESTION: When you're looking for resources, you may find yourself stopped short by a boss reminding you that he's seen your people idle on several occasions. This happens often in operations that have sharp peaks and valleys in their workload. Therefore, it's smart when things are slow to keep people busy with other chores, because a manager walking through your department may not realize – or care about – the fluctuations that occur.

TIP: Always make a case for any resources you need even though the circumstances are such that there's little hope for success. That's because if you've had requests turned down in the past, should times turn tough for the company, you've got a defensive position to protect against cutbacks in your department. The argument goes, "Hey, I've been short for one person for six months. You can't cut my group." It may not work, but you're in a far better position if you can at least make the argument.

8.7 WHEN AND HOW TO PROTECT YOUR PEOPLE

The fastest way a supervisor can lose the respect of subordinates is to leave them high and dry when they're being blamed for something they may or may not have done – or failed to do when they should have.

Q: A manager came into my office and complained that one of my people didn't complete an assignment on time. I accepted the responsibility by saying that I had given her something else to do that interfered with completing the other job on time. Was it wrong to do this?

A: No, but anytime assertions such as this are made, try to respond with, "I'll look into it and get back to you." That gives you a chance to assemble the facts to find out where any fault lies. Sometimes, when people are put on the spot they look for a scapegoat for their own failures. When that happens, it's common for the person on the bottom of the totem pole to be blamed.

It's important for a supervisor to act as a buffer between his or her own employees and other departments. It's equally necessary for work to be channeled through the supervisor. Otherwise, conflicting assignments can result in someone being shortchanged which results in a complaint.

The bottom line is that it's your department and you should accept responsibility for any errors or failures that occur. Obviously, corrective action should be taken with the employee, but that's an internal affair.

WARNING: A cardinal rule of leadership is not to accept at face value an assertion of an employee error just because it's made by a higher level employee. It's important to defend your workers when they're right, even when it means sticking your neck out. It pays dividends with your own workers, and you may find that it earns you respect well beyond the confines of your own department.

8.8 HOW TO OUTSMART YOUR ENEMIES

If competition is the spice of life, then you had better stock up on antacids, because guerrilla warfare at work is the inevitable consequence of supervisors competing for promotions and resources. Although competition may be good for the football field, or even in the corporate race for the customer's dollar, it's self-destructive in the internal struggle for positions of power within a company. The reason is basic enough. If everyone is expending their energy in competing for career advancement, then they're not working in harmony to further the company's ability to prosper in the marketplace.

From a personal standpoint, you may find yourself looked upon as a foe by supervisors who place their own goals ahead of teamwork. One of the tactics used by such individuals is to knock you when you're not looking. Therefore, it's worth considering how you can defend yourself against attempts to belittle your accomplishments.

Q: One of the other supervisors reporting to my boss is a back-stabber who is trying to make me look bad. I know this because the boss's secretary has heard the guy do it. The boss is retiring next year and I know this jerk is angling for the job. I want to put a stop to his back-stabbing, but I'm not quite sure what to do.

A: When you have this kind of dilemma, your first impulse may be to react in anger. That's usually fruitless, since the culprit will just deny everything and you'll end up looking foolish. Furthermore, this may lead the boss to conclude that you're not able to handle issues with tact and diplomacy. The right place to begin with this sort of difficulty is to calmly explore your options.

Your response will be dictated, not only by the actions of the person who is doing the damage, but also a wide range of other influences. For example, consider the personality of your boss. Is he likely to resent accusations made by a backbiter, and to view the negative remarks as a shallow attempt to curry favor at your expense?

Or conversely, is he unlikely to figure out the culprit's motive. In addition, what's his opinion of you and your peer on a comparative basis? Going beyond your boss, how are you and your competitor thought of by others throughout the company? These aren't simple questions to answer, but with a little soul-searching you should be able to reach a reasonable conclusion as to your relative standing in the eyes of others.

Nevertheless, even if you decide that the other supervisor is a well-known – but not well-liked – backstabber, you can never go wrong by overestimating the gullibility of people when it comes to gossip. In any event, it behooves you to counter the negative picture your competitor is trying to create. Depending upon the particular circumstances of your own situation, here are some do's and don'ts to keep in mind.

- Don't corner the other supervisor with a, "Hey, Billy, if you keep talking about me behind my back, I'm going to clean your clock."
- Don't place your boss in the position of becoming a referee by starting a contest of nasty job-related accusations with your opponent.
- Cater to your boss's quirks. If your boss places a great deal of emphasis on particular facets of the job, give him what he wants – even when it's not the simplest way to do it.
- Be friendly and businesslike with your opponent. Don't let him know that you realize what he's up to.

- If you're well-liked by a manager at your boss's level –
  who also gets along well with your boss – confide in him.
  This is an around-the-loop method of letting your boss
  know about the problem.
- Work well with other managers. They give you a power
  base above and beyond your own boss.
- When your foe screws-up on the job, make sure it gets
  back to the boss without pointing the finger at yourself.
- Cultivate friendships with your foe's workers. They can
  be a solid source of information.
- Play on your opponent's weaknesses. For example, if he
  arrives late every morning, make sure you're on time.
- Play to your strengths. If for instance, you're good at
  written reports and the other person isn't, try to dream
  up a couple of new reports that might appeal to the boss.
  This makes you look good by comparison.

NOTE: Some of the above suggestions aren't made with the
fine art of fair play in mind. The fact of the matter is that lies and
distortions about you can stick if you don't react. Therefore, if
someone is trying to nail you unfairly, remaining above the fray
may be admirable – but unsuccessful.

8.9 BATTLING WITH BOTTLENECKS IN OTHER DEPARTMENTS

Generally, necessary assistance from other departments is given as a
matter of course – although perhaps grudgingly at times. However,
you can run into bottlenecks whose sole aim in life seems to be making
your job difficult. If there's any solace in this, it's that everyone must
learn to overcome these hurdles sooner or later.

*Q: The data processing department furnishes information
which I need to prepare a weekly report. It's a constant struggle to
get these inputs on time, and on more than one occasion my report
has been late because of this. I've begged, pleaded, and cajoled, all
to no avail. What next?*

A: The obvious answer is to apply pressure through a higher level manager. This means going to the DP department head's boss, either yourself, or through your boss. Although sometimes necessary, this can evolve into a regular event whenever you need information.

Actually, the best cure for this type of problem is prevention. With unerring failure, whenever a new requirement is imposed and folks are asked how long it will take, they underestimate. Few people take the time to study what's required, and fewer still add in a fudge factor to compensate for unexpected delays that may occur.

This results from a combination of failing to think things through, as well as an "impress the boss" syndrome. But it ignores the fact that the boss expects a realistic answer, rather than eternal optimism. After all, if the completion estimate isn't satisfactory, the boss will inquire as to what can be done to shorten it. So try to practice factoring in contingencies such as bottlenecks in other departments whenever you're faced with estimating completion dates for new requirements.

It's also helpful when inputs are regularly required from other groups to pin them down on deadlines. Either get a commitment in writing, or schedule a meeting where everyone involved will have to commit to a schedule. Take minutes of the meeting and distribute them to refresh memories at a later date should instant amnesia strike.

Incidentally, it's a good idea to establish due dates from other departments that are before the actual time that you need something. This is an excellent tactic to master the inevitable procrastination that occurs. For instance, if someone knows you need input for a report you must complete by Friday afternoon, they'll probably wait until Friday morning to compile their contribution.

TIP: If you have only limited success when applying pressure to get input from a recurring bottleneck, try rescheduling whatever has to be done without the bottleneck knowing it. For example, arrange to push back report dates, but keep the same deadline for the bottleneck. Naturally, this isn't always feasible, but it's a simple solution that can save you a lot of grief.

8.10 TEN WAYS TO COPE WITH CUSTOMER COMPLAINTS

You may deal with customers in the traditional sense of the word. On the other hand, your customer may be the next unit on the assembly line. Whatever you job is, whoever is dependent upon the output of your department is a customer in a general way. Also, that includes everyone's boss, since their job is dependent – at least in part – on you doing your job. Let's look at some common methods of handling complaints from a customer satisfaction viewpoint.

1. Always apologize for anything that goes wrong. It's isn't that the other party is necessarily right. It's that everything goes more smoothly when they at least thing they are.

2. Always listen without interruption, even when you're getting yelled at. The other person's anger is like a release valve. By letting them blow off steam, they'll cool down and be more cooperative when it comes time to discuss what's going to be done to resolve the problem.

3. Sometimes people get so angry that they don't clearly state what the problem is. Make sure you know what the specific complaint is before you reply.

4. There are times when people complain about something other than the actual problem. If you think that's happening, engage in conversation to get to the heart of the matter. For example, "Incidentally Martha, is there anything else I can do to help out?"

5. Skip excuses. No one believes them, and they can just make people madder.

6. When action is required to resolve a complaint, make sure it's taken as soon as possible.

7. If there's more than one way to handle a complaint, offer the alternatives. One of them may be more satisfactory than another to the complaining party.

8. Don't disregard minor complaints, since if they're not resolved they can escalate into major ones.

9. Always do what you can to have the person doing the complaining leave with a good attitude about you and your department.
10. Never place the blame on your subordinates. If they goofed, take it up with them later.

8.11 DEFENDING YOUR DEPARTMENT IN A CRISIS – REAL OR IMAGINED

There may come a time when serious misfortune descends upon your department. It may be in the form of personnel cutbacks or perhaps a planned reorganization which will reduce or eliminate your unit. Whatever the circumstances, these events can seriously test your survival skills.

Q: There are rumors in the air that my section will be merged into another group. If that happens, I'll still retain my supervisory position, but I'll be reporting to a new boss. How hard should I fight this move?

A: There are many reasons for internal reorganizations – some highly practical and others less so. Obviously, you should make your feelings known about any proposed change, but the flip side of the coin is knowing when to quit trying to save the status quo.

Anytime you get wind of a possible change that will affect your department, try to find out as much as possible early on. The best time to turn proposed changes around is before they get off the ground. Assemble all of the facts you can to justify keeping things as they are. Even if you're only dealing with rumors, it's best to be prepared. Otherwise – as often happens – you're stuck scrambling to defend against a change after a final decision has been made. And that, in most cases, is an exercise in futility.

However, even when it appears that you can justify the existence of your department from a practical standpoint, don't neglect the internal politics of a proposed change. If those with clout in the organization favor the change, you'll just be swimming against the tide to buck it. Therefore, even though your position may be correct, don't waste time defending it.

In general, when these situations arise, make your position known, but once a decision is made, accept it and support it. When you're dealing with top management, know how to win sometimes means knowing when to quit opposing decisions you dislike.

9

Overcoming Obstacles to Productivity

As a supervisor your performance is judged on many elements, but if there's one overriding component, it's the productivity of your unit. Yet, to maintain a high level of productivity it's necessary to constantly overcome a number of obstacles that are strewn in your path. These include everything from poor morale to union problems.

Countering these difficulties requires the use of a wide range of people-handling skills. At any given time you may be called upon to be a motivator, arbitrator, or negotiator. So getting your people to function as a top producing team isn't easy, but it can be done. This chapter explores how to surmount many of the obstacles that stand in the way of greater productivity.

9.1 WHY SELF-INTEREST IS THE KEY TO PRODUCTIVITY

When it comes to getting your subordinates to give that little bit of extra effort that will improve productivity, self-interest can't be ignored. Most people will do their job because of many influences spanning everything from personal pride to paychecks. However, anytime you can show employees that doing a little more work is in their own best interest, they're more likely to put forth the extra effort that means increases in productivity.

Q: I don't have the foggiest idea of how to show workers that it's in their best interests to work harder than they have to. How can that be done?

A: The foundation for convincing workers that hard work pays, lies in rewarding those who produce the best. The most obvious reward you have to bestow is money. Those folks who excel should be the ones rewarded with the best pay raises and promotional opportunities.

Obviously, there are limits to what you as a supervisor can do in this regard. However, to the extent that you can financially reward people for their efforts, by all means do so. Equally important, let it be known that this is your policy so subordinates know that their efforts won't be in vain.

NOTE: If your company has a profit-sharing plan, you have a sound basis for preaching productivity gains as a pocketbook issue. In fact, a substantive profit-sharing plan can act as a motivator in and of itself. However, be sure to continually emphasize the link between productivity and profit-sharing. If this isn't communicated effectively to workers, they aren't likely to see the correlation between working harder and the dollars and cents payback that results.

Monetary rewards, of course, are limited in their effect on a day-to-day basis. Furthermore, you may be working in a company that doesn't offer many financial incentives that reward initiative. Therefore, let's look at other self-interest arguments that can be used to further productivity.

- Appreciation. People seek praise. If you acknowledge extra effort, a worker will respond favorably.
- Discipline avoidance. You can make it in the employee's self-interest to improve performance by offering to postpone disciplinary action if performance picks up.
- Peer pressure. Let workers know that those not performing up to par are penalizing other employees. Emphasizing this puts laggards under pressure from fellow employees.

- Carrot and stick tactics. Give preferred assignments and extra privileges to those who produce, while reserving the "dirty" jobs for sluggish performers.

9.2 HOW TO SELL IDEAS TO ANYONE

Often, productivity gains are linked to changes that are made to increase efficiency. At the same time, employees get comfortable with familiar ways of doing their work. Consequently, they have to be sold on making changes or they won't fully cooperate in the implementation of new ideas. Furthermore, you have to sell ideas to your boss and others within the company, so coming up with a great idea doesn't get you anywhere until it's accepted by those affected.

Q: Every time I suggest something that will improve operations, I get shot down. If it's not employee resistance, then it's my boss's veto of my ideas. I need help selling my suggestions.

A: Nothing turns off enthusiasm faster than consistently watching ideas get shot down, either by active objectors, and/or passive resisters. The main reason that ideas aren't accepted – assuming they're practical to start with – is that little thought is given to the selling effort involved. To a large extent that means identifying and countering potential objections. Let's look at several steps that can be taken to successful pitch ideas.

1. Is the idea feasible? The simpler an idea is to understand, the easier it is to implement, and the greater the tangible benefits, the easier it should be to sell the idea to others.
2. Be your own critic. Evaluate your idea to decide who must be convinced in order for it to be adopted. The larger the number of people involved, the greater is the opportunity for opposition.
3. Outline the approval process. Identify who will play a role in approving and implementing your idea. Often, changes are made with the concurrence of a boss, only to later discover substantial opposition from unforeseen

sources such as upper management, other departments, and/or subordinates.

4. Counter objectives before they are raised. Figure out the likely protests that people will make. Then, whether you're presenting the idea in person or in writing, raise these potential objections yourself and rebut them. By doing this, you not only have countered complaints before they can be raised. But you're also demonstrated that you did your homework before proposing the idea.

TIP: It's sometimes easy to be seduced by the appeal of ignoring problems in the hope that they won't be noticed. However, this tactic is both deceptive and foolhardy. It also makes it more difficult to deflect criticism. Instead of suppressing opposition, support may be lost. After all, neutral observers may assume that you didn't think the idea through, or else you would have addressed the problem in your presentation.

5. Solicit supporters. Before you formally present an idea, sound out potential supporters beforehand. That adds weight to your argument for adoption of the idea.

6. Neutralize the opposition. You may be able to lessen opposition by incorporating the suggestions of others with your idea. This is especially true if people in positions of power support your idea.

7. Make a good presentation. Whenever possible, present your idea in person rather than in writing. It makes it easier to counter objections, and there's a greater reluctance for someone to say "No" when they have to do it face-to-face.

Obviously, the amount of planning you do before presenting ideas will depend upon the magnitude of the suggestion as well as the level of approval required. However, even simple suggestions should be well thought out, since if you lose credibility in presenting minor changes you may not have the believability it takes to pitch and win the big ones.

9.3 CONQUERING FACILITY AND SUPPLY FIASCOS

Beyond getting the necessary resources you need to keep your department functioning (see Sec. 8.6), there are a host of minor work area irritants that can ruin your average day. Although each separate incident may be relatively trivial, on a cumulative basis they can be burdensome.

Q: It may not sound like a big deal, but my people drive me nuts complaining about nit-picking details such as the coffee area we have in the department, the vending machines, and a dozen other things. Can I do anything to control this?

A: As you know, it's often the petty working environment issues that can cause more gripes than anything else. A representative list of these types of complaints might include the following:

- It's too hot (or cold) in here."
- "Someone didn't make the coffee in the morning."
- "The vending machine swallowed my morning."
- "No one cleaned the refrigerator."
- "If we work Saturday, will the cafeteria be open?"
- "The parking lot is always full." (Often followed by a statement such as, "That's why I'm late.")
- "The pay phone doesn't work."

The important aspect of these complaints is their impact on productivity. When people are griping, they're not working. That alone makes it necessary to do what you can to resolve these pesky problems.

Many of the working environment issues that employees grumble about can be quickly resolved by a phone call to facility or maintenance people, and/or a common sense solution of your own. The one overriding consideration in any of these instances is to do something right away that indicates you take the complaint seriously.

It's tempting to chalk this type of bellyaching off as nit-picking and either ignore it, or tell the person to stop squawking about nothing. But this tends to magnify the grumbling with a further loss of productive time. The irony is that sometimes people are satisfied by just getting a response that indicates you'll do something about the problem – even when in fact little can be done.

9.4 MAKING LITTLE THINGS COUNT AS MOTIVATORS

Motivation and levitation (rising or floating in the air) are both easy to define, but equally difficult to accomplish. Stripped of theory and jargon, motivation is simply "How do you make Harriet work harder?"

For starters, perhaps Harriet is happy as things stand, and doesn't want to work harder. Or, if that's not true, then certainly Harriet would rather be happier without working harder. All of which means that to make Harriet – or anyone else – work harder you have to make it worth her while.

Q: In terms of specifics, what can I do as a supervisor to motivate my subordinates?

A: The quid-pro-quo requirement of giving something to get something in terms of motivating workers consists of monetary rewards such as higher pay, performance bonuses, and profit sharing. It also includes a wide array of other motivators such as a good working environment, adequate training, and the right fringe benefits; which, for example, may mean child-care centers rather than company picnics.

However, these rewards are to a large extent beyond your control as a supervisor. Therefore, from your perspective, motivating employees means relying on the little things that can make a difference. Among these are the following:

- Be positive yourself. Enthusiasm is contagious and if you're positive about work this attitude can carry over to your group.
- Show an interest in subordinates as people – not just as workers. The guy or gal who has you labeled as an SOB

may not be swayed by a birthday card – but then again, little gestures can tilt the scales in your favor.

- Solicit employee suggestions as to how to do the job better. People respond positively when they have some degree of control over what they're doing.
- Recognize that there's no single solution to motivational problems. Motivating people is an on-going endeavor, so avoid "quick fixes."
- Establish mutual trust so subordinates feel free to discuss matters with you.

In the final analysis, despite all of your efforts, it's difficult to motivate your subordinates unless a company policy is in place that rewards achievement. Nevertheless, your own efforts can improve group efficiency to some extent with or without company backing.

9.5 WHY SUGGESTION SYSTEMS DON'T WORK

Many companies have formal suggestion systems that encourage workers to submit ideas that can improve productivity and/or reduce costs. As a supervisor, this can be a useful tool if the system itself is sound. If not, its value is limited.

Q: We have a suggestion system in place, but even though I encourage workers to submit ideas, the response is poor. Is it me or the system that's at fault?

A: About all you can do is let your people know about the suggestion system, and urge them to submit ideas for possible adoption. Unfortunately, there are inherent weaknesses in many suggestion systems that discourage participation. First and foremost, they require written presentations and lot of folks don't like to write. They either feel ill at ease in trying to put their thoughts down on paper, or simply don't possess adequate writing skills.

Other factors that tend to discourage the use of suggestion systems include a lengthy review process, inadequate financial rewards, and a lack of commitment on the part of top management.

Needless to say, if your company has a system with these weaknesses there's little you can do to overcome it on your own. If you have a good system, encourage and assist workers in taking advantage of it. Otherwise, don't put a lot of effort into it, since your energies can be better utilized in other areas.

9.6 SEVEN SIMPLE STEPS TO IMPROVE PRODUCTIVITY

The following steps provide a general framework for improving productivity within any type of operating environment. However, it's important to remember that although it sounds simple enough in theory, successful implementation is an on-going battle.

1. Have workers participate in problem solving. If your company doesn't have "quality circles" which encourage employee participation in decision making, start your own informal group. Anything you can do to make your subordinates feel like partners within the department can help productivity.

2. Pay attention to details, since minor adjustments can increase productivity over the long haul. Look for ways to combine work steps, simplify jobs, and eliminate or reduce obstacles such as excessive paperwork.

3. Don't use production goals to pit one worker against another. Strive for teamwork – not individual competition.

4. Don't concentrate on automation, and other technical improvements, to the exclusion of the human element. Remember to use the motivational techniques listed in Sec. 9.4.

5. Cross-train your people to do other jobs to the extent possible within the constraints of company policy and/or union contracts. (See Sec. 6.6 on cross-training).

6. Approach productivity from a dual angle. Look both for new ideas, as well as existing bottlenecks that may be hampering productivity.

7. Sell the advantages of productivity gains to subordinates. Whenever possible, relate productivity to financial

rewards, job security, and/or just making tasks easier for an employee to do.

9.7 THE ABC'S OF NEGOTIATING TO GET WHAT YOU WANT

Although it's not always thought of as such, the chances are that you're conducting some sort of informal negotiations on a regular basis. You might be bargaining with a union steward, dickering with another supervisor about some aspect of work, or performing any number of other tasks that require give and take. Actually, anytime you're trying to reach an agreement with someone else, informal negotiations are taking place. Therefore, by practicing some basic fundamentals you can easily increase your negotiating skills.

Q: I've heard people say you should always negotiate from a "position of strength." What does that mean?

A: Briefly, it refers to the fact that you should avoid bargaining with someone when they have a clear advantage. For example, a company that desperately needs business may be forced to accept a lower price for their product – at least if the other company is aware of their plight. However, relative strengths and weaknesses aren't always what they appear to be on the surface. Therefore, it's not always wise to give someone a "take it or leave it" offer on the assumption that they have little other choice, because they may just say "No."

No matter what you're bargaining for, always perform a "what if" analysis of alternatives before you start bargaining. Decide what course of action you'll take if you're not successful, since having other options available lessens the temptation to accept a bad deal.

Q: Whenever I try to reach agreement with another supervisor, he always tells me he has to check with his boss. Then he comes back and tells me he can't supply the items I want when I need them, and he can't supply the items I want when I need them, and he then offers another later date as an alternative. Is he yanking my chain?

A: Anytime someone says, "I'll have to check with…," one of three things is possible. The person doesn't have authority to make a decision, is just stalling to evaluate your offer, or is using this ploy as a wedge to get a better deal. Always establish whether or not someone has the power to make an arrangement with you and you'll avoid these types of problems.

Q: I deal with outside vendors on a regular basis, and I've noticed that some of them get angry every time I'm trying to reach a reasonable agreement.

A: Sometimes, experienced negotiators attempt to frustrate you into making a mistake by trying to get you angry. Keep your emotions under control, as losing one's temper can cause errors that turn a good deal into a not-so-good bargain.

9.8 TEN NEGOTIATION TACTICS YOU CAN LEARN TODAY

1. Always prepare your negotiating position before you talk to the other party. What are you seeking to achieve and what will they offer you in return?
2. Put yourself in the other person's position and think about what they want and what they're likely to settle for.
3. Establish a fallback position and decide what concessions you can make to reach an agreement.
4. Brief everyone who will be participating in negotiation meetings, so no one says the wrong thing.
5. If possible, arrange meetings in your office or other location of your choosing. This gives you a "home court" advantage.
6. Never negotiate with someone who doesn't have the authority to reach an agreement.
7. Always keep your emotions in check during negotiations.

8. Suggest a break for coffee or lunch if things aren't going your way. This will give you time to rethink your strategy.
9. Confirm all agreements in writing as soon as possible.
10. If you can't reach agreement and discussions break off, leave it up to the other party to contact you.

9.9 COUNTERING THE "THAT'S NOT MY JOB" COMPLEX

Teamwork is essential for maximum productivity which means you have to defeat the "That's not my job," argument used by employees when you ask them to perform tasks other than their assigned jobs. General techniques for accomplishing this were discussed in Sec. 6.2, while cross-training was covered in Sec. 6.6. Whether it's union work rules, or individual attitudes, you'll have people who are reluctant to pitch in elsewhere when it's needed. Let's look at how you can conquer this resistance in face-to-face confrontations.

Q: Most of my workers are pretty cooperative and recognize the importance of teamwork, but a couple of people always give me arguments. What can I do about this?

A: Despite everything you do to convince subordinates that doing other jobs can benefit them personally, you'll always have one or two people who don't see the light. When this happens, state calmly that their job isn't what they say it is, but instead is what you assign them to do. Let's look at a variety of replies that one supervisor – let's call her Evelyn – uses with Henry, the human excuse machine.

Evelyn:	"Henry, help Ralph out down in shipping today."
Henry:	"Why me?"
Evelyn:	"You're the only person I can spare."
Henry:	"I don't know what to do down there."
Evelyn:	"See Ralph. He'll show you what to do."
Henry:	"I've got my own work to do."
Evelyn:	"I've already asked Marilyn to cover for you."
Henry:	"I've got a bad back. I can't do any heavy lifting."

Evelyn:	"The physical requirements for your job are the same as the shipping department's. In any event, you'll be counting, not lifting."
Henry:	"I was hired as a production worker, not a shipping clerk."
Evelyn:	"Your job description also says, 'All other duties as assigned'."
Henry:	"You always send me instead of other people."
Evelyn:	"I rotate everyone and it's your turn."
Henry:	"This assignment isn't in the bargaining agreement."
Evelyn:	"Paragraph 3.8 of the agreement says, …temporary assignments outside the employee's department are not to exceed eight consecutive working hours at one time, or forty hours per year…"

NOTE: The long and the short of it, when subordinates object to doing other jobs, is that you're the boss. If you face continuing opposition from workers who don't want to help out willingly, tell them point blank to, "Just do it!" It's certainly preferable to receive cooperation, rather than resorting to threatened disciplinary action. Nevertheless, it's foolish to assume that you won't have cases where disciplinary action – or the threat of it – are necessary.

9.10 CONVERTING ATTITUDES FROM "CAN'T DO" TO "CAN DO"

There are many reasons why people don't do their jobs in a satisfactory manner. Although a few folks may just be goof-offs with little hope of salvation, most workers will do a credible job if they're trained properly and treated with respect. Therefore, it's necessary to pinpoint the cause of poor performance before you take steps to improve a worker's productivity.

Q: From my experience as a supervisor, I find that a lot of workers don't ask questions when they don't know what to do. As a result, they guess and do the job wrong. Why don't they just ask how to do something?

A: At some point or another, everyone has probably been told, "If you have any questions, just ask." That sounds sensible, but what happens? In the first place, if someone doesn't realize they're doing something the wrong way, there's nothing to ask about.

Employees often muddle through as best they can for another reason. No one wants to appear stupid by asking too many questions, while simultaneously they want to impress their boss. The result is that questions don't get asked, and the little gimmicks that make every job simpler are never learned – or are at best absorbed through trial and error over a long period of time.

You can minimize these problems by making sure that everyone has been sufficiently trained, and by encouraging employee feedback on a regular basis.

Besides inadequate training, other factors can prevent workers from doing their jobs properly. These can range from inadequate equipment to bottlenecks presented by other people within the organization.

The heart of the matter is finding out what's preventing someone from doing the job to the best of one's ability. All too often, the determination is made that a worker just can't hack it, with only a perfunctory attempt made to see if something else might be responsible for the person's poor performance.

9.11 THE RIGHT WAY TO EMPHASIZE QUALITY

Increasing output per worker is a fruitless exercise if an adequate level of quality isn't maintained. Therefore, it's necessary to be on the alert for quality slippage when management pressure and/or work backlog is placing emphasis on output.

Q: Top management at my company seems to alternate between demanding greater output and criticizing quality control. How can I resolve these competing demands?

A: Increasing output per worker should only be accomplished while simultaneously meeting whatever quality standards apply to your particular unit. Naturally, how quality is measured will vary according to the product or service produced by your department.

As a supervisor, one major irritant is keeping quality levels up when you're under pressure from the boss to get the work out. As you know, under these conditions something has to give. More often than not, it's quality, especially in functions where a decrease in quality only shows up further down the road in time. This is particularly true in clerical and other functions where quality isn't subject to the refined quality control techniques in place within manufacturing operations.

When you're faced with quantity/quality trade-offs, use a dual approach to contain the problem. First of all, make it clear to subordinates that quality isn't to be sacrificed in order to meet production goals. In addition, make your boss aware that increasing production without compensating factors such as overtime and/or more help will impact quality. If the response is simply, "Don't worry about it," then don't, since it's obvious that production goals are paramount in the eyes of top management.

Frankly over the long haul you're limited in your efforts to sustain quality work if you don't have a corporate environment that focuses on the issue and is supportive of your efforts.

9.12 CUTTING DOWN ON EMPLOYEE DOWNTIME

A really serious productivity buster is the unauthorized employee downtime that occurs when workers aren't performing their jobs. This can take many forms with the most common being socializing, conducting personal business at work, extended coffee breaks, and long lunch hours. Although no supervisor wants to – or can effectively – monitor every move a worker makes, it's necessary to take action that will keep downtime to a minimum.

Q: Keeping my people occupied instead of gossiping, making personal phone calls, and doing everything but their work is frustrating. I don't want to be too restrictive, but enough is enough. How can I control this?

A: Controlling employee downtime requires both awareness and consistency. It's easy enough to identify and take the necessary corrective action to curb obvious instances of workers loafing instead of working. It's considerably more difficult to control minor repetitive abuses such as prolonged conversations around the water cooler, or a few minutes extra take for lunch. Yet, these seemingly insignificant actions consume a large chunk of unproductive time over the course of a year.

Controlling downtime of this sort requires alertness, so that you can let people know that they're taking advantage of the situation. That sounds simple, but as you know, it's impossible to constantly monitor people and still get your other work done. However, take the time to let people know that you take abuse of working hours seriously. Otherwise, workers may assume that you condone their actions, and when that kind of attitude becomes ingrained, it's much harder to eventually get people back on the proper track.

TIP: The holiday season from Thanksgiving through New Year's is a particularly trying time to keep productivity levels up. It's a traditional period for mirth, merriment, and downtime, and although you don't want to act like Scrooge, business must go on. Therefore, during this period it's wise to supervise a little more aggressively than you normally would.

Follow-up on things more closely and maximize your visibility, since being seen can work as well or better than being heard. Therefore, merely making your presence known can keep the wheels turning.

As far as granting time off from work during holiday periods, try to be as flexible as possible, but emphasize that it's a one-shot deal. That way, you avoid creating a precedent for succeeding years. Actually, the best tactic is to tie-in time off with getting the workload completed.

9.13 THE WRONG WAY TO DEAL WITH UNION PROBLEMS

If workers are unionized, then you have an additional element to cope with in managing your department. Even though unions can influence worker attitudes and resist changes that increase productivity, cooperation – not conflict – is the proper path to follow.

Q: There's a great deal of animosity between management and labor within our company. It seems like the union fights every minor change tooth and nail. I'd like to have better relations, but it just doesn't seem possible.

A: Even when you work in an environment where labor relations aren't the best, you can still improve your own relationship with union members by following a few basic principles.

1. Read the collective bargaining agreement carefully. Provisions of the contract are constantly being interpreted throughout the term of the agreement. The more detailed your knowledge of the contract is, the greater will be your ability to interpret it in your favor.
2. Always control your emotions, even when you're being baited. A cool head will allow you to prevail, even when the deck is stacked against you.
3. Don't be confrontational in your dealings with the union. Treat it as a business relationship – which it is – and not like a mud wrestling contest.

Obviously, there will be times when reason doesn't work, and the union steward insists that you aren't complying with the contract. When differences can't be reconciled, insist that the work be done and document the record to support disciplinary actions and/or defend grievances.

NOTE: Although unions are often considered to be an impediment to productivity, they can also be a positive force. This is especially true when they bring problems the company may not have been aware of to the surface.

9.14 HOW TO AVOID UNION-RELATED DIFFICULTIES

Using certain practices on a regular basis can help to reduce union-related problems. These techniques include:

• Use the union steward as a conduit to channel information to workers. For example, when rumors are flying, ask the union steward to help dispel them.

- When a grievance doesn't make sense, don't accept it at face value. The actual problem may be something other than what the worker is claiming.
- Use trade-offs whenever possible. Give in on one dispute to get what you want on another.
- Changes in work procedures generally require union support. Build this support gradually by developing a reputation for fairness.
- Demonstrate a willingness to listen to union concerns even though you don't agree with them.

9.15 THE KEY TO COUNTERING UNION HARDLINERS

No matter how diplomatic you are in your attitude toward the union, there may be union members who insist on viewing you as an adversary in matters large and small.

Q: I have to work with a union steward who is totally unreasonable. This attitude carries over to a couple of subordinates who always seem to be looking for an excuse to file a grievance. How can I handle these hardnoses?

A: You are, of necessity, influenced in your relationship with union members by the overall union /company attitude toward one another. If there's a spirit of cooperation, then that makes your job easier. Conversely, if the company and union are constantly at odds, this philosophy filters down to the troops in the trenches. Nevertheless, whatever the overall relations are, there are certain fundamentals you can follow.

First of all, it's beneficial to recognize that worker loyalty is of vital concern to unions. Therefore, some union members may construe any attempt at cooperation to be undermining worker loyalty to the union. That, in itself, can cause a hardline attitude by an unenlightened union steward.

There are two techniques that can be used to counteract hardliners who make your job difficult. The first is to establish rapport with your workers through your daily actions. Being both fair and friendly on a consistent basis will counter the hostile attitude of a handful of hardliners, and put you in a reasonable working relationship with the bulk of your subordinates.

Second, on a more specific level, you can tone down combative individuals by neutralizing their ability to impress peers with a hard-nosed stance. To do this, when employees and/or a steward start to argue issues in front of the group, don't respond. Instead, move the discussion to your office or some other private location. This removes the opportunity to impress peers, and in fact you may find a total change in attitude when the conversation becomes private.

9.16 MANAGING GRIEVANCES AND GRIPES

Union or no union, every supervisor has to tackle grievances and gripes. Although in a union environment there may be a more formal grievance procedure, complaints are no less significant in a nonunion atmosphere.

Q: I get a few grievances along with a lot of petty griping. Is there anything I can do about this?

A: Actually, it's not wise to discourage grievances from being aired, since they perform two useful purposes, (1) they bring problems to the surface, and (2) they provide a release valve for tensions that can build up in the workplace. Therefore, it's far better to let your people know that you want to hear about their difficulties. The trick, of course, is to resolve the minor problems before they become major ones.

Although grievances can take many forms, there are a couple of essential elements involved in resolving most complaints. These are (a) to do something that satisfies the worker's complaint, or (b) to convince the worker that the desired action can't be taken.

Individual circumstances will dictate how this is done, but let's look at how Sam, a first-line supervisor, handles a grievance when Larry, a subordinate, complains about a job reassignment.

Larry: "Sam, I've worked on press #1 for over a year. It's not fair to reassign me to press #5."

Sam: "Larry, you're the most reliable worker I have. Press #5 is a little trickier to operate and I need an experienced hand on it."

Larry: "There are other experienced people around here besides me."

Sam: "Not with your know-how Larry."

Larry: "Well, I'm going to talk with Hank (the shop steward) about this."

Sam: "That's all right with me Larry, but I have the right to move you."

Fifteen minutes later, Hank, the shop steward, enters Sam's office.

Hank: "What the heck are you doing Sam? You're violating the contract, and you've got Larry all bent out of shape."

Sam: "Come on Hank. You know the contract says I can reassign people to the same or similar work within the department."

Hank: "Screw the contract. Larry isn't happy and we may just take this all the way to arbitration. You only preach the contract when it's in your favor."

Sam: "Settle down Hank. You know I'm always fair. Level with me Hank. There's more to this than I know about."

Hank: "OK, off-the-record. Larry and Smitty (a co-worker) hate each other's guts. They have for years. If Larry gets press #5, he'll be working beside Smitty. There's no end to the problems that that will create."

Sam: "I didn't know that. Look Hank, I'll move McGuire to press #4 beside Larry on press #5 and put Smitty in McGuire's spot. That puts them fifty yards apart."

Hank: "I knew you'd see it my way, Sam."

Sam: "You owe me one, Hank. Why don't you let Larry know that you worked it out with me. Then, send him in and I'll make it official."

Hank: "OK buddy."

Naturally, every problem won't work out as simply as this one. Yet, there are several valuable lessons to be learned from how Sam coped with this complaint.

- Sam knew the details of the contract before he made the reassignment.
- Sam listened to both Larry and Hank even though he didn't have to. By doing so, he learned that there was an underlying reason for Larry not wanting the reassignment.
- He let Hank take the credit for solving the problem. This helps him to keep a good rapport with the steward.
- By switching people around as he did, Sam prevented a great deal of future grief that might have resulted from Larry and Smitty working side-by-side.
- Sam let Hank think that Sam did him a favor, which gives Sam a bargaining chip for use in a future dispute.

9.17 SIX WAYS TO RUIN MORALE WITHOUT REALLY TRYING

One of the contributors to poor productivity is low morale. Yet, frequently it goes undetected, while the search goes on for other factors that may be causing the problem. Even when it's recognized that morale is low, it's not an easy job to turn it around.

Q: Although none of my people have told me directly, I sense that morale is pretty low. My workers also seem to project an "us versus them" attitude, with the "us" being the workers and "them" being supervisors and other managers. Can I do anything about this?

A: People are often reluctant to complain to the boss. Instead, they gripe to family, friends, and coworkers. That's why it's essential to have open and honest communications with your people. That in itself keeps you tuned-in to problems that may be lurking beneath the surface.

As far as "us versus them" attitudes, they're often triggered by employee resentment over what is perceived to be preferential treatment for managers. Such items as executive perks feed the "us versus them" attitudes of lower level workers. To some extent, this is a problem beyond your control. However, from a supervisory standpoint, there are several measures you can take to avoid contributing to morale problems. These include the following:

1. Think through the impact on your subordinates of any decision that you make. "Think before you act" is a no-frills solution that prevents morale wrecking solutions.
2. Establish credibility with your subordinates. It's fair treatment in person – not in an employment manual – that counts with workers.
3. Be consistent in your actions and don't play favorites.
4. Practice what you preach. Set a good example in terms of being at work on time and observing other rules and regulations.
5. Do performance appraisals and pay reviews on time. Nothing upsets workers more than letting these deadlines pass without taking action.

6. Discipline workers in private and praise them in public.

Neglecting the above practices can place you in the unenviable position of ruining morale without even trying.

9.18 MAINTAINING MORALE WHEN TIMES ARE TOUGH

One of the hardest chores for any company is to maintain morale during tough times. The problem is compounded for supervisors when workers seek information which may not always be forthcoming from top management.

Q: My company has experienced a downtown in business which has resulted in layoffs and other cost-cutting measures. Needless to say, morale is bad and getting worse. What can I do?

A: When hard times descend upon a business, the tough task of being a supervisor becomes even harder. Top management, applies pressure to keep production flowing smoothly, while unhappy subordinates want to know what's coming next. Your job is eased somewhat if top management has a policy of keeping everyone informed. But even under the best of circumstances, there are only a limited number of actions you can take to bolster morale.

First and foremost, is to project a positive "business as usual" demeanor on a daily basis. When workers see that their boss isn't worried, that alone can boost their confidence.

Secondly, make every effort to keep your people informed about events that will impact them such as layoffs, wage freezes, and the like. Get as much information as possible from your boss. In addition, learn what you can from other contacts throughout the company.

It's also useful to squelch rumors as quickly as possible. To do this, hold regular "damage control" meetings with your people. No matter how little information you have to pass along, meeting with subordinates in itself helps to relieve the tension.

9.19 WHY YOU'RE THE CRUCIAL LINK IN IMPROVING PRODUCTIVITY

Although improving productivity is a constant concern of top management, the key to productivity gains rests with the person you see in the mirror every morning – namely yourself. That's because all of the technology in the world is of little use if workers aren't trained and motivated to use it effectively.

Furthermore, automation and state-of-the-art equipment are available for any business to use. Therefore, from a competitive standpoint, it's a dedicated and efficient work force that spells the difference between a company being a winner or an also-ran. That alone makes every supervisor a crucial link in achieving productivity gains.

Q: Top management where I work always talks about automating this or that to achieve greater productivity. Yet, little is done to improve the performance of the work force. Is this a successful strategy?

A: There's a lot of glamour and glitz associated with automation which may partially explain why some executives view it as a panacea for poor productivity. Furthermore, it's also something which – at least on paper – offers the possibility of yielding significant benefits.

A problem arises only when managers fail to realize that the people who operate the machinery are an equally essential force for improving productivity. When this is generally recognized – and some companies are better at it than others – then you, as a supervisor, will receive the support you need to properly train and motivate your people. The bottom line when it comes to productivity isn't the machinery – it's the people operating it.

9.20 THE PITFALLS OF PUSHING THE PANIC BUTTON

You may have the misfortune to work in a pressure cooker atmosphere where your boss, or other managers, are constantly pushing the panic button. Sometimes this results from the nature of the job where urgent deadlines are the rule rather than the exception. In other instances, it may be caused by a boss with a penchant for creating turmoil. And yet another – not uncommon – reason is simply because the company itself operates in a disorganized manner. Whatever the cause, for your sake, as well as your subordinates, it pays to avoid being sucked into "no-win" situations.

Q: My boss always tries to pawn off "rush" jobs on my unit. It's frequently a "no-win" scenario, since the deadlines are impossible to meet. What can I do about this?

A: Obviously, if push comes to shove, you can't refuse to take on an assignment. However, short of that happening, you have to weigh the pros and cons before deciding whether to willingly accept the assignment or to try and beg off. To do this, ask yourself these questions.

• Should your group be the one to do the job?

- What impact will it have on normal workload?
- What will be the reaction of your workers?
- Is it a political plus or minus to accept the assignment?

Q: My boss thinks everything is urgent, and he's constantly running around asking, "When will that be done?" He makes me nervous doing this, but I don't know what to do.

A: An anxious boss can have you spinning your wheels if you're not careful. But don't take it personally, since a boss who rants and raves often just isn't a good communicator.

It also helps if you develop a "worst case" scenario when you have so-called "urgent" assignments. Ask yourself, "What could happen if this deadline isn't met?" You may find yourself surprised at the answer, which much of the time is usually, "Not much."

In any event, it's essential to keep your composure for the following reasons:

1. It enables you to think clearly about how best to do the job.
2. Remaining calm lets you weed out the true emergencies from the false alarms.
3. Your subordinates will lose confidence in you if they sense that you have lost control of the situation.
4. Keeping a cool head avoids putting your people in a pressure cooker environment which causes mistakes and puts workers on edge.
5. Pushing the panic button encourages people to take short cuts which cause errors.

10

Bearing Up Under Your Boss

Just as you have a considerable amount of control over the success or failure of subordinates, your boss holds similar power over your own destiny. That presents a real challenge, since for the most part you can't choose a boss, so you're stuck with what you get; "for better" if you handle it right, or "for worse" if you don't.

Frequently, folks grumble and moan about their boss, all too often forgetting that the key to success is learning how to manage a boss, much as you strive to manage your subordinates – although from a different perspective.

A good place to start is by evaluating your boss in terms of his or her strengths and weaknesses, and how you can relate to these in a positive fashion. In any event, before you begin a quick and nasty mental appraisal of your own superior, remember that your boss may not be as bad as you think – only different from you in terms of personality and operating methods.

There are also other angles to consider in terms of a boss. For example, what's the appropriate course to take when you get a new boss? And last but not least, with a boss – old or new – how can you best get your talents recognized and rewarded? None of these facets of managing a boss are easy to achieve. However, like any close relationship, you can thrive and prosper if you work at it.

10.1 POINTERS ON PRODUCING UNDER PRESSURE

If there's one trait that impresses a boss – or anyone else – it's someone who responds well under pressure. Crunch time performers are impressive, be it on the battlefield, or under the gun in the world

of work. Still, a constant stream of pressure-packed days can be overwhelming, unless you recognize your limitations and learn how to handle the strain.

Q: My boss overloads me with work, but I don't know what to do about it.

A: There are two main methods you can use to grapple with an overload of work. One is to learn how to fend off your boss, while the other is improving how you manage your workload. The following pointers can aid you in the latter regard:

- Concentrate the resources of your department on priority assignments and put less important tasks on the back burner.
- Delegate as much as possible. Don't try to do everything yourself. Learn to let go and trust your subordinates to accept responsibility.
- Don't put self-imposed pressures on yourself. Everyone works best when they're relaxed and well-rested.
- Anticipate and plan ahead whenever possible. Start known projects before they're actually assigned.
- Don't procrastinate. Seemingly impossible jobs become less daunting the further along you are at working on them.
- Eliminate other chores when possible. See Sec. 2.17 on skipping meetings and Sec. 2.18 on eliminating written memos.

As far as avoiding assignments in the first place, let's look at how you can counterattack when your boss is overloading you with work. Some handy tactics include

1. *Pleading poverty.* "I'm short two people this week." "One of my machines is down." "Joe's on vacation." "Marvin's out sick.
2. *Pawning it off elsewhere.* "The machines in Kate's group are more suitable for this type of job."

3. *Trading-off work.* "The only way I can handle this job is if you move the Bishop order somewhere else."

NOTE: Another twist is to get your boss to push back completion dates on other work that you have. Be careful here though, especially if you have a boss who tends to forget about agreements.

4. *Standing tall.* "You know I'm cooperative, but my people are overworked." "This is the fourth time in a row that my group has been given a rush job. Can't we share the wealth?

TIP: If you think your unit gets the lion's share of rush jobs, keep notes to prove it when you argue this point with the boss.

10.2 THE IMPORTANCE OF ESTABLISHING PRIORITIES

It's bad enough to have a boss who overloads you with work, but there's nothing worse – outside of being fired – than getting stuck with "can't win" projects that interfere with your regular duties. These range from tasks that are impossible to complete within the assigned deadline to exercises that are doomed to failure from the start. For example, perhaps your boss gives you a job to do simply because top management wants it done, even though you both know it isn't feasible.

Whatever the reasons, these kinds of tasks can do nothing but cause headaches. At the least, you waste time that could be better spent on other work, and at the worst, you may be blamed for not doing a job which couldn't be completed under any conditions.

Q: My section always ends up getting the dirty jobs to do. How can I avoid these assignments?

A: Your primary weapon should always be a ready response that indicates you're busy working on high priority tasks. This will frequently lead your boss to seek another victim for the dirty work. Naturally, you're not always going to be working on something that can't wait, so you have to learn to attach importance to whatever you're currently doing.

Even inconsequential work can be used for this purpose if you attach a presumed priority to it. For instance, every job has routine and/or boring elements that no one likes to do. Accumulate this work as a safety valve – the bigger the pile the better – and immediately respond to, "Are you busy?" with, "Are you kidding? Look at this mess I'm trying to catch up on." Usually, this is sufficient to ward off unwanted tasks.

HINT: Assuming that pleading, pouting, and logic all fail, and you're stuck with a can of worms, the golden rule of survival is to cover yourself with concurrences. Get as many people from other departments involved as you can. Then, when the inevitable failure occurs, the blame can be spread like fertilizer. Hopefully, the bulk will fall on someone else's turf.

10.3 WHY YOU SHOULD PIN DOWN YOUR RESPONSIBILITIES

You may have discovered a peculiar phenomenon which is, the more work you do, the more you get to do. If your boss delegates assignments haphazardly, then your desk may be the landing pad for more work than you can handle. If you don't pin your responsibilities down, you may well get stuck with duties that aren't and/or shouldn't be placed upon your shoulders.

Q: My boss dumps everything on me, but I just don't know how to say "No."

A: Being able to level with your boss isn't something that can be accomplished overnight. It's a slow process to build your boss's confidence in your ability to be both reliable and trustworthy. A basic step in this direction is to avoid the gossip circuit at work. You're judged by the company you keep, and if you hang around with gossips, you'll be pegged as one yourself.

Another point is to be open and honest in answering your boss's questions. Sometimes it's easy to avoid calling attention to trouble spots in jobs you're working on. However, if you don't level with your boss, and problems pop up later, the conclusion will be drawn that either you don't know what you're doing, or you were try to sneak something by the boss. Since no one likes an underhanded subordinate, leveling with your boss is a convincing trust builder.

Once you're satisfied that you have the confidence of your boss, the bottom line is to talk over your concerns. There's no substitute for honesty in this area. Say something like, "Boss, I can't put my finger on it, but it seems like I'm getting more than my fair share of the work." You may be surprised to learn that your boss is sympathetic to your plight. That's because it's difficult for a boss to know your capacity for work unless you tell him.

10.4 THE BEST TACTIC FOR BARGAINING WITH YOUR BOSS

Although it's easy to conveniently pigeonhole bosses into categories – good, bad, hot-tempered, -- they don't always fit the mold, either all of the time, or even infrequently. Even though there are occasions when you may think otherwise, bosses are human just like everyone else. After all, you're a boss yourself.

They have their likes and dislikes, as well as their good days and bad days. They also have prejudices, play favorites, and last but not least, have a boss of their own to contend with. So it's crucial to learn how to manage your boss.

Q: How do you manage a boss? That's confusing to me.

A: Basically, you play to your boss's strengths and weaknesses. To start with, every company has rules, some more than others. Although on paper those rules appear to be pretty straightforward, it's the implementation that dictates what happens on a day-to-day basis. The interpreter of those rules, as they apply to you, is your boss.

If you work for a boss who goes by the book, then your success depends upon adhering to the rules as he interprets them. For example, someone who is habitually griping about everything loses credibility over a period of time. When they finally have a legitimate complaint, it isn't likely to get a fair hearing, since it's treated as just another routine gripe.

On the other hand, if you develop a reputation for being cooperative, you'll be listened to when you have a grievance to air. Incidentally, little things can make a big difference when you're trying to get your boss to do something for you. One such minor detail is timing. Avoid making a pitch to your boss when he's in a bad mood, and instead approach him when he's upbeat. That sounds simplistic, but it's sensible advice that's often overlooked.

Your ratio of "Yes" to "No" answers will increase significantly if you try to anticipate your boss's moods. But that doesn't mean you have to try and analyze his every action. A little common sense and direct observation will do nicely. It's commonly recommended – and generally sound advice – not to approach your boss with an, "I've got a little problem," early on Monday morning or late Friday afternoon. And don't tie a boss up just before lunch, because a growling stomach may erupt into a growling boss.

Where most folks fail in their relationship with a boss is by not recognizing that the boss's personality is different from their own. For instance, if a boss likes everything in writing, then that's the way to go, even though you personally find that to be picky or inefficient. All in all, making a boss look good is a fail-safe way to put yourself in a good bargaining position when you want something from your boss.

NOTE: Sometimes people worry about the boss stealing their thunder and getting the recognition for their own achievements. Don't dwell on this, since even if you're carrying the load for an incompetent boss, everyone knows who the power is behind the throne.

10.5 A GOOD WAY TO GET COMMITMENTS FROM YOUR BOSS

Getting commitments from your boss not only depends upon how good a working relationship you have, but also on whether or not your boss is a decisive sort of individual.

Q: My boss is an expert at the "brush-off." Whenever I try to get any sort of commitment out of him, he gives me the old, "We'll talk about it later." The trouble is that "later" never gets here. What can I do?

A: Short of getting another job, you have to force the issue when you have a boss who consistently avoids making decisions. Let's look at how Agnes corners her boss Paul, who is known for this trait.

Agnes:	"Paul, I need this requisition signed-off for personnel to start the hiring process for that vacancy I have."
Paul:	"Let's talk about that later Agnes."
Agnes:	"I need to have it down to personnel today so they can place a "Help Wanted" ad in next Sunday's paper."
Paul:	"Just leave it on my desk. I'll get to it later."
Agnes:	"I need it by 10:00 A.M."
Paul:	"No sweat. Just put it in my box."

At 10:20 A.M., Agnes returns to Paul's office.

Agnes:	"Paul, is that requisition signed?"
Paul:	"Gee Agnes, I haven't gotten to it yet."
Agnes:	"Well Peggy in personnel called looking for it. Incidentally, Mr. Trumbell (Paul's boss) was asking me if I was going to make my production quota for the quarter. I told him that it wasn't likely unless we filled the vacancy I have within the next two weeks."
Paul:	"Oh yeh. What did he say then?"
Agnes:	"He asked me what the delay was."
Paul:	"What did you tell him?"
Agnes:	"Oh, no problem, I said there wasn't any and that you were signing-off this morning so I could hand-carry the request to personnel. He just said, "Great!"
Paul:	"Well, we better get it down there. Let me sign that right now."

Although it's not generally recommended to put your boss on the spot, if you have an indecisive boss, the best method for getting action is to present them with an alternative that's worse than taking the action you seek. And that's precisely what Agnes did here.

TIP: Don't automatically assume that your boss is indecisive just because you get a "Wally the Waffler" response such as, "I don't know...What do you think?" A boss who does this isn't necessarily indecisive. He may instead just respect your judgment and/or know that you are better able to make a decision on the subject under discussion.

10.6 HOW TO PROFIT WHEN YOUR BOSS SAYS "NO"

Obviously, for a wide variety of reasons, your boss won't agree with you on everything. Still, even a "turn-down" can be used to your advantage.

Q: My boss never says "Yes" to anything the first time around. I'm used to that, but what I don't like is having to start all over from scratch the next time I pitch the same proposal. Is there a way around this?

A: One method is to shoot for a future commitment when you get a "No" answer. For example, say something such as, "Can we order this equipment the beginning of the fiscal year, so it's in next year's budget?"

The key to this tactic is to give your boss a reason that makes it easy to say "Yes." For instance, in the above example, the selling point was that the equipment would be funded out of next year's budget.

TIP: Don't be timid when you get a future commitment. When the time rolls around, proceed on the assumption that what you're doing was pre-approved. If your boss's memory has failed, pull out the note from your file that shows it was discussed earlier. Otherwise, if you didn't write a memo to yourself for future reference, you may find yourself back at the starting gate.

10.7 THE FINE ART OF BYPASSING YOUR BOSS

In the ordinary course of events, it's improper to deliberately bypass your boss except for unusual conditions dictated by necessity. Even so, you may have a boss so totally indecisive that it's impossible to operate through normal channels.

Q: My boss is just coasting toward retirement and won't make a decision on anything. I don't like working around him, but it's necessary to get the job done. How can I do this without getting myself in trouble?

A: The best time to work around your boss is when he isn't in. So when your boss is out, put everything else on the back burner and concentrate on tasks that would ordinarily require your boss's approval.

Unfortunately, this kind of opportunity doesn't present itself that often. That means you'll have to learn how to outmaneuver your boss on a regular basis. As a general rule, see your boss's boss (or whoever else you would secure approval from) when your boss is off somewhere at a meeting, lunch, or hovering over someone else.

The best excuse for doing this is always an urgent task that requires immediate resolution. To be successful at bypassing your boss, it's also necessary to build good rapport with the managers you'll be dealing with.

CAUTION: Never belittle your boss to other managers. They're savvy enough to know why you're circumventing the chain of command without you filling them in on the specifics. In those instances where someone asks, "Why didn't Joe (your boss) approve this?" make an excuse such as "It's a priority and he's at a meeting."

Q: Suppose my boss notices that I'm bypassing him and brings it up. What do I say?

A: Be casual and ready with an excuse. Try some of the following:

Boss: "Fred, I didn't see the defects report."

You:	"Mr. Arsenault (his boss) was looking for it and you were at a meeting, so I gave it to him directly."
Boss:	"Where's the monthly production report? I don't remember signing-off."
You:	"I sent it to Mr. Arsenault last Friday. You were out that day."
Boss:	"Fred, I'm not sure I'm seeing everything I should before it leaves the department."
You:	"Gee boss, the only time I go direct to someone else is when you're not around."
Boss:	"Fred, you're not keeping me posted as much as you should."
You:	"Sorry boss, but I know how busy you are, and I don't like to bother you with the nickel and dime stuff."

Obviously, how successful you are at bypassing your boss depends to a large degree on whether or not the boss takes issue with your operating procedure. If it gets to the point where he's insistent on seeing everything, then for the most part you'll have to comply.

WARNING: If you find it virtually impossible to circumvent a bottleneck boss, and problems develop because he holds things up, make sure he isn't using you as the scapegoat. Casually let people know that what they are looking for was completed by you and given to your boss. Do this without being vindictive. The purpose isn't to knock your boss, but rather to protect yourself from unjustified blame because of the boss's procrastination.

10.8 THE RIGHT WAY TO TOOT YOUR OWN HORN

Folks aren't particularly fond of pushy people who self-promote more than they produce. Nonetheless, a little personal public relations is often necessary to see that your efforts are recognized by those in positions of power within your company. Otherwise, those less capable who excel at self-promotion may pass you by in the climb up the corporate ladder.

Q: I'm starting off in a new supervisory position and would like to know how to get off to a fast start with my new boss.

A: As the cliché goes, "First impressions are lasting ones." Nowhere is that truer than in the business world. Anytime you start a new job, it pays to display your skills early and often. Adhere strictly to the rules, at least until you get a feel for your boss's likes and dislikes. In fact, more than a few successful careers have been started by creating a strong initial impression.

Caution is also critical when you're the new kid on the block, since little things can make a big difference. Ordinarily, something as simple as getting tied-up in a traffic jam is a legitimate excuse for being late for work. But when it happens the first week on a new job, it may be treated with suspicion, and that's because you have no track record that indicates you're seldom late.

As a new supervisor, you're much more likely to be singled out for the boss's attentive eye. Your initial performance can cut both ways. It can either single you out for stardom, or spotlight you as a potential problem. Of course, over a period of time either view may be altered, but it takes a while to change an initial perception.

Q: Are there any tried and true techniques to gain recognition without doing a lot of apple polishing, since that's not my style?

A: There are several different angles you can try:

1. *Do some volunteering.* Becoming a stand out at work can be a speedy process if you're willing to volunteer for projects that others shun. Just make sure they're not "can't win" assignments.

At the same time, there's risk involved, since if you botch up an important task, no one remembers that you only volunteered for the job after everyone else turned it down. In short, there's both upside gain and downside loss if you take on a tough assignment that isn't your responsibility.

Planning any volunteering depends to a great extent on the specifics of where you work and what your job is. One thing to consider is the visibility you can gain from taking on an unwanted task. The most obvious benefit is the gratitude of your boss for your cooperation. Any advantage this confers depends upon (1) how badly the boss needs the job done, and (2) is your boss the type that shows appreciation when pay reviews roll around?

2. *Take on thankless tasks.* Some otherwise thankless tasks are worthwhile when they give you a chance to broaden your contacts throughout the company. This type of project allows you to meet and work with people from other departments. If they get to like you, this could eventually lead to a future position in another area within the company.

For example, committee assignments are often a good way to meet the movers and shakers in your company. There's no quicker opportunity for someone buried in the bureaucracy of a large corporation to get to know senior executives.

But even if that's not possible, any assignment that provides for interaction with other departments can be beneficial. If your boss is a bottleneck to your advancement, then you should place added significance on any possibility to work for someone else.

3. *Expand your duties.* You can increase your value to the company within your own department. Simply pick up the slack that exists all around you, by expanding the duties of your job. It's easy enough to do by just assuming some of your boss's duties. All you have to do is say "Can I help you out?" He may decline, but just the fact that you asked is to your advantage.

4. *Become a resident expert.* Another effective means of expanding the powers of your position is by filling the gap when new procedures or equipment are introduced. People resist change and avoid involvement when anything new is introduced.

This creates an opportunity for you to become the resident expert on new equipment and procedures. It doesn't matter whether it's computers in the office, a revised reporting procedure for sales people on the road, or a different technique for controlling inventory in a manufacturing plant. If you dig in and familiarize yourself with the change, you'll probably become the unchallenged authority on the subject.

This places you in a great position, since if your boss relies on your expertise you increase the power of your position; not only vis-à-vis your peers, but also your boss. And who knows? If your new-found expertise is significant to the operation of the company, a revised job description, job title, and salary increase may result.

10.9 HOW TO NEUTRALIZE BOSSES' PETS

If you believe that qualifications and hard work are the sole criteria for success, let's burst that bubble right now. We all have our favorite friends, along with an enemy or two. These human traits carry over into the workplace. Subjectivity does enter into pay and promotion decisions, although good managers attempt to be objective in their evaluations.

Q: I know for a fact that another supervisor – let's call her Susan – got a higher pay raise than I did. I'm not happy to say the least.

A: Look at the variables, since there may be a rational explanation, even if you're not feeling very calm at the time. Perhaps Susan was hired below the going market rate, and is being given a larger raise to bring her in line with everyone else.

The flip side of the coin is that Susan has been given a bigger raise because she gets along better with the boss. If that's so, it boils down to living with the fact, and working smarter instead of harder in the future, and/or searching for greener pastures.

Q: How can I compete against the duck walkers we have in my company who ape every move the boss makes. Every time he comes to a sudden stop someone's in danger of breaking their nose.

A: How do you compete against duck walkers? Simply by being competitive professionally and yourself personally. Not every boss succumbs to the tactics of duck walkers. Secure, self-confident managers know their own abilities. They're insightful enough to recognize flattery for what it is, and in the workplace, it's usually an attempt to compensate for poor performance.

Pay raises and promotions will soon tell you if your boss is susceptible to fawning by duck walkers. If they get the good raises and promotions, then the best thing you can hope for is a new boss.

10.10 LEARNING HOW THE BOSS PLAYS OFFICE POLITICS

Although most managers practice some degree of social diplomacy, the politicians of the working world consider it to be the solitary path down the road of success. In fact, they may, at least partially, owe their jobs to the use of ego-flattering techniques. From your vantage point, it's vital to be aware of how significant the game of office politics is to your boss's agenda.

Q: My boss plays office politics to the hilt. What bothers me is that he doesn't want to hear anything negative, or discuss the pros and cons of how the job is done. What's the best way to deal with this?

A: The truth is that some managers like to be surrounded by "yes" people. It heightens their sense of self-importance, and reassures an insecure manager that a subordinate poses no threat to their position.

When a politician tells you that something has to be done right away, the chances are that he's made a commitment to higher-ups. So although the particular task may not seem very important, it's best to make it your own top priority.

If you work for an overt politician, you'll never be in the dark about what top management is thinking, because this kind of boss sticks strictly to the party line. As long as you're a team player, an office politician type of boss will usually support you. The main danger with this type of boss is that their loyalties can change faster than tires at an Indianapolis 500 pit stop.

Office politicians may, or may not, know what they're doing, but they always know how to make the right moves. They carefully conceal any weaknesses they have, and play everything according to the rules of their constituency – which is top management. As long as you recognize a boss is doing this, then you should be able to cope with it. On the other hand, if your plight is intolerable, it's best to start searching for a job somewhere else.

NOTE: See Sec. 11.5 for more on office politics in the context of it being practiced by those other than your boss.

10.11 MAKING THE BEST OF AN INCOMPETENT BOSS

Working for an incompetent boss can be a trying experience. Fortunately, most bosses know their jobs and perform them adequately. However, if you do have the misfortune to work for an ineffective boss, it's prudent to be cautious in dealing with that fact.

Q: My boss is a real dud. How do people like this get their jobs?

A: Usually, incompetents are the result of trying to put a square peg in a round hole. One of the failures of management in general is a lack of attention when they place people in management positions.

In some instances, people become managers by virtue of time on the job. Everyone else may have long since left, or been promoted, so Sam Seniority gets the open slot by default. Actually, Sam may have been an excellent worker in his previous position, but just doesn't have the ability to manage people and other resources effectively.

An out-and-out incompetent may be able to disguise his inadequacies. He may be lucky enough to have good people working for him – including you, or a friendly personality that tends to compensate for his weaknesses.

Working for an incompetent boss may mean you get stuck doing unnecessary work, as he bumbles his way through life. Never expect to get a direct answer – so don't waste time looking for one. Incompetent bosses can hurt you in other ways.

First of all, if you're doing a good job, they'll take all of the credit. Since they don't believe in rocking the boat, they won't push you for pay raises and promotions. They may also be prone to nit-pick. This means changing something here and something there in everything you do.

The only advantage in working for an incompetent is that it's easy to look good by comparison. However, be careful not to make an enemy by openly capitalizing on the incompetent's lack of knowledge. After all, no one likes to be thought of as stupid.

Q: I have a boss who knows his job, but is an unbearable dictator. What can I do?

A: Just as the term implies, dictators state what they want, and won't take "No" for an answer. They're usually very critical and love docile employees. If piety isn't your strong suit, you have several options.

First, hope that your boss accepts a job offer in Iceland. Since that's not likely, work your butt off and get promoted away from the tyrant. If that will take longer than a potential nervous breakdown, then find another job quick, either within the company or elsewhere.

Employee turnover is often high in a department headed by a dictator. However, it's not as great as might be expected, since dictators operate best in a company that pays well and has good benefits. That makes it harder for employees to upchuck and leave. The dictator knows that and can operate accordingly.

You can handle a dictator if you produce. In fact, if push comes to shove, stand up for your rights. A bully in a suit and tie is still a bully, and they'll back down if they know you refuse to be pushed around. Dictators respect aggressive behavior and will gravitate toward easier fish to fry. But if you're basically mild mannered, keep a résumé circulating. Life is too short, and if you wanted barracks discipline you could have joined the Marines.

CAUTION: Don't be too quick to peg your boss as an incompetent. Once in a while, someone has a boss with whom they have a personality clash. Just because personalities differ, that doesn't mean a boss is incompetent. After all, in most cases a manager had to have something on the ball to get where he or she is.

10.12 THE DO'S AND DON'TS OF DEALING WITH A NEW BOSS

The arrival of a new boss is always accomplished by rumors, fond hopes that soon fade, and fears that soon look foolish. Despite the hype and hoopla about the virtues and vices of a new boss, the claims are usually exaggerations and not much really changes, at least initially.

Q: I'm getting a new boss who was hired from outside the company. How can I ensure that I start off on the right foot in this relationship?

A: The one major difficulty with a new boss is that you're starting off fresh again, no matter how long and capably you have been doing your job. Conversely, if things didn't go so well with your former boss, then you have a chance to start anew. In short, the way to cope with a new boss is to adopt a business as usual attitude. Remain alert and attentive, and adjust to revisions in operating methods as they become apparent. A few clues on adapting to a new boss are as follows:

1. Be helpful, but not overbearing, about your knowledge of how things are done within the company.
2. Don't adopt an attitude of, "We always did it this way." But don't intentionally let a new boss screw up because of not knowing company procedures. Just be sure to give advice in a non-threatening manner.
3. Be alert for signs of how your new boss operates. The quicker you learn the nuances, the better off you'll be.

4. Don't make negative comments about the company or other employees. You'll be pegged as a griper.
5. Don't overwhelm a new boss with problems that need resolution. New bosses need time to get their bearings before being besieged with complicated issues.
6. Be careful about leaving a new boss out of the loop. This can be done unwittingly by assuming it's quicker to work around a new boss than to explain everything in detail.

11

Problems You Don't Want – But Can't Avoid

In striving to be an effective supervisor, you must come to grips with a wide range of problems which go beyond the basics of getting the work out. You have to protect your own interests when interdepartmental wrangles erupt, combat prejudice and overcome sexism within your group, and cope with office politics.

Beyond this, you must be successful in doing your job within the constraints imposed by company policy, as well as sidestep the ill effects of mistakes made along the way.

All in all, supervision is seldom dull, occasionally frustrating, but nevertheless a rewarding experience if you don't let it overwhelm you. Let's look at some problems you wish you didn't have, but that you can capably conquer with a little bit of imagination and a lot of effort.

11.1 CORPORATE CULTURE: WHAT IT IS AND WHAT IT MEANS

Every job has certain controls imposed upon it. These include the broad-based rules that cover everyone in the organization, such as working hours, vacation policy, and pay. Then, there are additional procedures covering the specific department you supervise, such as who does what job and how they're supposed to do it.

Beyond these day-to-day operating procedures is an overall company image that is embodied in rules – written and unwritten – which gives a company individuality. This is the stuff of which dress codes, long working hours, and a host of other things become the standard fare of what is commonly called "corporate culture."

Q: I was just hired for a supervisory position with a large corporation. My boss told me that all managers, including first-level supervision on the factory floor, were required to wear suits and ties. It wasn't like that in my previous job where everything was pretty informal. My boss says an emphasis on appearance is part of the "corporate culture." How come?

A: "Corporate culture" is neither mysterious, nor hard to understand. It's simply the established practices and traditions that are unique to a particular company.

Actually, as a supervisor, your only concern with "corporate culture" is to recognize there are certain values, practices, and traditions followed within your company that differentiate it from similar businesses. You, and other employees, are expected to adhere to these customs. Otherwise, you'll be pegged as a nonconformist who isn't part of the team.

11.2 THE CHALLENGE OF MANAGING PEOPLE WITHOUT PREJUDICE

Managing a group of workers involves dealing with prejudices; perhaps open and undisguised, or else subtle and subsurface. Controlling discrimination at work is imperative, not only because it's the proper thing to do, but also because of its disruptive effects on your group.

Q: I have a diverse group of people working for me and on occasion I sense subsurface hostility. It's nothing that I can put my finger on, but I don't like it. What can I do about this?

A: Open and overt discrimination should of course be dealt with firmly and fast in accordance with established company procedures.

The real challenge is to quell the veiled prejudice that may lurk beneath the surface.

It's unreasonable to expect that you can singlehandedly wipe out ingrained prejudices that people have formed over a lifetime. However, you can and should keep them from surfacing at work. The following basics for doing this consist of:

- Set the standard by your own behavior. Equality can only exist when it's practiced as well as preached. Let your subordinates know that prejudicial behavior won't be tolerated.
- Struggle to overcome your own opinions and preferences when you interact with others.
- Discourage prejudice disguised as humor. When someone says, "Did you hear the one about the...," respond with, "No, and I don't want to hear it."
- Don't be condescending. People aren't looking for sympathy – only fair and equal treatment.

11.3 WHY YOU SHOULD SOMETIMES IGNORE COMPANY POLICY

Policies are set by companies to identify corporate goals, and procedures are then established to implement this policy. As a supervisor, it's your job to follow these policies and procedures. Still, there may be times when it's best to deviate from the rules.

Q: I just received a new procedure covering rework of defective parts. To make a long story short, it can't be implemented without fouling everything up. How can I handle this?

A: Anytime a policy or procedure is unworkable, take it up with your boss so that it can be altered. Don't just ignore it without consulting upper management, since that will leave you high and dry if a flap occurs.

There are several reasons why policies and procedures can't always be followed. These are

1. The procedure is outdated. For example, an existing procedure may become outmoded because of changes in operating methods that haven't yet been formalized.
2. Exceptional demands – for example, a rush job – sometimes can't be met without deviating from existing procedures.
3. A new procedure may be introduced which ignores the realities of how the work is actually done. For instance, the procedure itself may be in error, or else it may be based on incorrect assumptions.
4. A policy or procedure may be subject to various interpretations. This may be by mistake or by intent. In some instances, policies and procedures are left deliberately vague so that sufficient flexibility is maintained for everyone to operate within the guidelines.

CAUTION: As a member of the management team, it's your responsibility to follow company policy. Except for unusual conditions, that's the standard that should be followed, and in no event should you side with subordinates and encourage them to ignore company policy. This was discussed at length in Sec. 4.1.

11.4 HOW TO AVOID THE ILL-EFFECTS OF MISTAKES

In the course of doing your job, it's inevitable that mistakes will be made. In most cases, these will be of minor significance. Still, there may be occasions when, for one reason or another, you're put on the spot because of an error, and when this happens, it's necessary to minimize the damage.

Q: To put it mildly, my boss doesn't suffer fools lightly. When the slightest mistake is made, he's all over someone's back. How can I avoid his wrath?

A: Needless to say, a boss who displays intolerance when errors are made isn't an easy person to work with. Therefore, about all you can do is deflect the criticism that may come your way. How this is done will depend upon your job, the boss's quirks, and the overall working environment.

Many mistakes are attributable to nothing more complex than poor communications. Always make sure that you know what the boss wants. On occasion, you may find that the boss himself isn't sure of what needs to be done. If despite your best efforts you're left with a vague assignment, that spells potential trouble.

To protect yourself, always try to confirm in writing how you intend to proceed. Do this in the form of an informational memo to the boss and others involved in the project. That way, at least, no one can turn around later and say that they didn't know what you were doing.

One of the most common ways to provoke the wrath of a boss is by missing deadlines. Frequently, this is beyond your control because of one or more of the following reasons:

- An unreasonable deadline. Sometimes deadlines are set that can't be met. When this happens, establish this fact at the outset. For example:

You: "Boss, this date can't be met."
Boss: "Do the best you can."

If your boss is the type who backs his people, then no further action is necessary. However, if you have a boss who looks for scapegoats, sit down and write him a memo outlining a realistic date for the job to be done. You may still be held to the original date, but if it isn't met at least you have evidence in the form of your memo that defends your position.

- Lack of cooperation. Deadlines are often missed because of the failure of other departments to furnish their inputs on time. If this happens, inform your boss right away. For example.

You: "Boss, we didn't get the engineering drawings today. Every day of delay means a day of slippage in our delivery date."

Here again, depending upon the nature of your boss, you may, or may not, want to put this in writing.

- Unforeseen event. All sorts of unexpected events can intervene and cause missed deadlines. For instance, supplies may be delivered late by a vendor. As before, the key is to document the failure.

In the final analysis, don't worry about your mistakes. If you're doing the best you can within the limits imposed by your job, that's all you can do. However, if you are occasionally unfairly criticized, avoid anger or resentment. Remember, that those who make the fewest errors are often those who do the least amount of work.

POINTER: Correcting mistakes is only half of the equation for success in this area. Equally, if not more important, is to figure out why the error was made and to take steps to prevent a repetition.

11.5 AVOIDING THE HAZARDS OF OFFICE POLITICS

One of the hardest realities of the workplace for many folks is reacting to the role that politics play within a company. A skillful politician can often succeed where others fail by virtue of the use of pure political smarts. So whether you're an active participant in this regard, or primarily a passive observer, it's imperative to know how to avoid the pitfalls of organizational politics.

Q: I'm not much for playing office politics, but I also don't want to play second fiddle just because I don't cozy up to every top dog in the company. How can I hold my own in this regard?

A: Whether or not you choose to play the political game at work is a judgment that only you can make. When it comes to office politics, folks tend to fall into one of three categories which are:

1. Nonplayers. At one extreme are people who either ignore, or fail to recognize, the political games that are played at work.
2. Duck walkers. These are folks who practice politics to the hilt and are recognizable back-slappers. These were discussed briefly in Sec. 10.9.
3. Middle-of-the roaders. This type of person isn't ignorant of the role that office politics can play, but on the other hand, doesn't tend to pander to those in positions of power.

If your personality is such that you aren't big at backslapping, a good avenue to achieve personal success is to follow the self-promotional tips outlined in Sec. 10.8. It's also valuable to be aware of your boss's attitude and practices when it comes to office politics. (See Sec 10.10.)

Nevertheless, whatever your perspective is, it's imperative to be aware of what's going on around you. That means essentially knowing who the power people are within the organization, cultivating – or at least not offending – key people, and finally, not upstaging upper-level managers. For instance, if Mr. Oneway, a senior manager, wants something done, pointing out the stupidity of his request is accomplished at the risk of alienating him to your own detriment.

The essence of success when it comes to office politics is that a little bit of savvy is a sensible tactic for survival. Therefore, even if you don't want to play the game, at least learn the rules and be an informed spectator.

11.6 HOW TO SIDESTEP GETTING CAUGHT IN THE MIDDLE

One of the common hazards you face as a supervisor is being placed in the middle of a predicament that you didn't have anything to do with. Yet, despite your innocence, it's often necessary to do a little dancing to get yourself off the hot seat.

Q: Now and then, my boss goofs and I'm put in the position of defending myself for something I didn't do, or else fingering my boss as the culprit. How can I casually get off the hook?

A: Naturally, if you're being blamed for something that wasn't your fault, the simplest way out is to identify the responsible party. But regrettably, the easiest path out of a dilemma isn't always the wisest choice. This is particularly true if extricating yourself means placing the blame on your boss. Consequently, the trick is to vindicate yourself without convicting anyone else. The common sense approach is to be creative in coming up with a plausible excuse. Let's look at how this can be done.

Background

Mr. Brown, a senior-level manager, corners Helen, a supervisor, to find out why an order was fouled up. What Brown doesn't know is that Benny, Helen's boss, hadn't told her about a change in customer requirements which is what caused the error.

Mr. Brown: "Helen, how come the Moo Doo order is fouled up?"

Helen: "The order was completed before the change order came through. It was too late to stop the line, so we're reworking the items."

Or another possible reply

Helen: The order went into production Wednesday morning. I was in the design shop working on the McPherson priority order at the time. Mr. McGuire (Benny, her boss) left the message on my desk, but I didn't see it until I returned just before lunch. The order was already in process. The rework to incorporate the change will only take four hours."

As in these examples, the primary prerequisite for success at shielding your boss – or a subordinate – from blame, while still protecting yourself, is to use an alibi that has a ring of validity to it.

CAUTION: It's not always possible to think of a ready-made excuse. When it isn't, you still may be better off by accepting the blame for what went wrong, and offering to resolve the problem. After all, you have to live with your boss on a daily basis. Besides, it's a display of loyalty that a boss can appreciate and reward at some later date.

11.7 COPING WITH PEOPLE'S PERSONAL PROBLEMS

From time to time, your subordinates may encounter major personal problems. Sometimes, it's best to ignore these situations as discussed in Sec. 2.3. However, beyond that, there are a whole host of minor personal difficulties that can cause people to ask for time off. For the most part, you have to respond as an efficient – yet sympathetic – boss.

Q: My people frequently present me with requests for time off to attend to personal business. Going strictly by the book means saying "No," but that isn't always realistic. What's the proper approach to take when I'm presented with these requests?

A: There is no hard and fast rule. Each individual request should be dealt with on its merits, taking the following considerations into account:

- The demands of the job. What will be the impact of granting the request?
- The worker's record. Does this employee try to take advantage of you?
- The nature of the request. Is it a real emergency, or is it something that can be done during nonworking hours?
- Overall company policy. You can be a lot more flexible if you're granting a request that is commonly approved by others. (See Sec. 5.9 for more on this.)
- Approval level required. Some requests require approvals in addition to your own. For example, a worker who wants to shift from full-time to part-time work.

11.8 SEXUAL HARASSMENT: YOU BETTER KNOW IT WHEN YOU SEE IT

Sexual harassment is an area where you are the front line of attack in confronting the problem. One of the major reasons that sexual harassment survives in the workplace is an attitude of "Ignore it until there's a complaint." However, success in eliminating this abusive practice requires an active rather than a reactive approach.

Q: What constitutes sexual harassment?

A: The law is constantly evolving in this as well as in other areas. Title VII of the Civil Rights Act was the initial federal law prohibiting sexual harassment. In addition, there are state laws covering various forms of discrimination which may also be applicable. Also, ongoing court cases at any given time can result in further refining the definition of sexual harassment. As far as a strict legal interpretation goes, that fall within the province of lawyers and other experts in the field.

From a practical standpoint, sexual harassment consists of (a) requests for sexual favors, (b) unwelcome sexual advances, and (c) other physical or verbal conduct of a sexual nature, if the behavior is linked to employment decisions, or the conduct effects a person's work performance or creates a hostile working environment.

Q: What are my responsibilities in this area?

A: You should take immediate action when you become aware of any conduct that constitutes sexual harassment. Report any complaints promptly to your superiors and the personnel office.

TIP: Whether a particular act or acts is or isn't prohibited conduct isn't always easy to decide, so avoid making these determinations on your own. Take it up with those responsible for setting company policies and procedures in this area.

Q: As a supervisor, what can I do to deter sexual harassment within my department?

A: First of all, set an example by your own conduct. Treat everyone with equal respect and dignity. In addition, refuse to condone sexist remarks, lewd comments, and obscene jokes. It's all too easy to look at some conduct and wink at it as harmless. However, no conduct is harmless if it's offensive to someone – which is a point that should be emphasized with your subordinates.

Q: A couple of other supervisors and an upper-level manager have asked me out for dinner in the past. Although I always say "No" the invitations keep coming. What's the best way to fend off unwelcome invitations?

A: "Thanks, but no thanks." Any unwelcome attention should be responded to with a polite but firm, "No thank you." Answers such as, "Not tonight," or "Perhaps some other time," or "I'm busy after work," may lead to another invitation at a later date. In fact, a large part of the problem in the area of sexual harassment lies in the unwillingness of some men to take "No" for an answer.

11.9 HOW TO SHORT CIRCUIT OFFICE FLIRTS

Flirts flitting around your work area are not only a nuisance, but also a disruptive influence. What's even more serious is the fact that what a perpetrator may consider to be harmless flirting, may be offensive and unwelcome attention to the person who is the object of such behavior. So it pays to discourage such activity to the maximum extent possible.

Q: What's wrong with a little flirting here and there? Besides, how can I control it?

A: Flirting can cause all kinds of trouble. First of all, folks floating around flirting aren't being very productive workers. From an even more serious standpoint, flirting can lead to a charge of sexual harassment if and when it's carried too far.

Obviously, you can't conquer romance at its various stages. However, from a practical position, you should neither encourage it or condone it when it interferes with the business of your department.

The most effective weapon you have against flirting is the attitude you convey to subordinates. If you have a businesslike demeanor, this in itself helps to keeps things from getting out of hand. Furthermore, don't be hesitant in admonishing your subordinates to limit their socializing when it's conflicting with their duties.

In addition, if you have persistent pests from other departments invading your territory on a regular basis, chase them out promptly. If that doesn't discourage them, then a well-placed comment to their supervisor can get the job done. Say something like, "Say Mark, if Joe's short of work, why not transfer him to me. He's always hanging out in my department anyway." That sort of a message usually gets through without too much difficulty.

11.10 PUTTING SEXIST ATTITUDES OUT TO PASTURE

One aspect of employee interaction that's not easy to control is sexist remarks. Yet, when they go unchallenged, they create an atmosphere of open hostility or silent resentment that destroys working relationships, and may lead to more serious problems such as sex discrimination and sexual harassment charges.

Q: I obviously can't control what people say, but I don't want anyone in my unit to make sexist remarks. How can I discourage this?

A: The most effective way for you to discourage sexist remarks is to openly demonstrate to subordinates that you won't tolerate such behavior. Frequently, you'll find that one or two individuals are responsible for such conduct. Tell them bluntly that (a) it's rude to offend people, (b) they're in no position to comment on anyone's abilities, and (c) ability is judged on performance – and you're the judge.

Point out plainly that sexist remarks are not only offensive to the person at whom they're directed, but also to you. This type of tactic will let your subordinates know where you stand on the issue, and should lead to elimination of this behavior.

11.11 A SHORT LIST OF SEXIST "NO-NO'S"

Some folks are reluctant to accept change in any form. In the workplace, this has meant an unwillingness by some people to recognize that women are an integral part of the work force. These laggards at accepting reality are sometimes prone to couch their hostile attitudes in terms of sexist remarks. A sampling of such language includes

- "Not a bad job for a woman."
- "This is men's work," or "That's women's work."
- "You ought to be home with your kids instead of working."
- She's just a dumb blonde."

Attitudes that result in this type of remark shouldn't be tolerated. In the workplace, supervisors – by virtue of their management position – have a critical role in keeping discrimination from rearing its ugly head in any of its myriad forms. When it comes to discouraging workers from engaging in antisocial behavior, controlling the lesser abuses is the foundation for preventing more serious forms of discrimination.

11.12 WHY FLEXIBILITY IS THE BUZZWORD FOR THE FUTURE

In your position as a supervisor, you may have to cope with future organizational adjustments within the company, as well as adapt to constant changes in technology and the resulting impact on your operations.

Beyond these internal factors, eternal events can indirectly influence your future as a supervisor. For example, worldwide competition will require operating efficiency gains in order for companies to remain competitive. This can result in additional demands upon you as a supervisor. Coping with these challenges means that you'll have to be increasingly flexible in adjusting to the requirements of your job.

Q: How can I best be prepared to cope with future changes at work?

A: You really need to do a little planning as you see various changes taking place. In terms of specific areas, let's look at how to approach and deal with change.

1. *Automation.* Look at the introduction of new equipment and procedures as a means of making your job easier. Get involved as early as possible in planning the orderly introduction of new equipment. Your outlook is important in influencing how your subordinates relate to change.

For example, a supervisor who constantly makes remarks such as, "This new equipment causes more problems than it solves," will encourage a negative reaction by workers. Instead, emphasize the positive such as, "Once we get this equipment up and running, we'll eliminate a lot of our drudgery."

2. *Participative Management.* As more and more companies realize the value of increasing the participation of workers in deciding how they do their jobs, you, as a supervisor, will be more involved in the decision-making process. This makes your position as the front-line link between workers and top management more crucial than ever. Therefore, it's of value to improve your communication skills to the maximum extent possible. Therefore, avail yourself of training opportunities, and if company-sponsored training isn't available, take the initiative to enroll in courses on your own.

3. *Work force relationships.* With an increased emphasis on productivity gains becoming a key goal of any business striving to remain competitive, well-trained and motivated workers will be essential for success. From

your perspective, that may mean increased pressure on you to get the most out of your people. To do this successfully, you may have to go that extra yard in your supervisory capacity. That means being flexible in relating to employee concerns, battling to get your people the proper training, and doing everything within your power to reward performance.

4. *Your own career.* Not only will you have to be flexible in adjusting to organizational and operational change in the future, but you also have to view your working life as being subject to change. Companies will grow, shrink, spin-off, and reorganize, all of which will have employment implications.

You may be a super supervisor, but that's of little solace if cutbacks cost you your job. Therefore, it pays to be always looking down the road in terms of your own future. This requires that you be ready to take advantage of opportunities when they arise, as well as getting the necessary training and experience you might need to achieve your personal goals.

To do this successfully, ask yourself "What if...?" in teams of losing your job or being stuck in a dead-end position. Answering this question will tell you what you have to do to be prepared for a career move. And whatever needs to be done shouldn't be left until circumstances force you to take action.

Start preparing now, and you won't have your back against the wall in the future. It may require something as simple as sketching out a draft résumé, or it may require you to invest in additional training. Whatever it is, you're better off planning now, rather than panicking later.

11.13 TEN SHORTCUTS TO SUCCESS AS A SUPERVISOR

There are no simple formulas for success as a supervisor. Managing people in the pursuit of a common goal requires you to stretch both your talents and patience to the limit. "Take two tablets and you'll feel better in the morning," may work for a headache or some other physical ill, but unfortunately, there are no similar "quickie cures" for many of the problems you have to resolve in your supervisory role. Nevertheless, there are a number of broad-based concepts to keep in mind that will help you in your supervisory responsibilities. These are as follows:

1. Treat everyone with respect. A company is only as good as its lowest level employee. You can't manage subordinates like second class citizens, if you expect first class performance from them.

2. "Do unto others…" Reflect on your actions as if you were the one on the receiving end.

3. Fight for your people the way you would like your boss to fight for you. Don't shortchange your subordinates just because your boss treats you poorly.

4. When a worker has a complaint, handle it promptly. Even when you can't resolve a problem to the employees' satisfaction, take the time to give a full explanation. People will accept "No" for an answer if they have been treated fairly.

5. Keep employees fully informed as to what's going on. This instills trust and avoids damaging rumors.

6. Be accessible to employees and let them know that you care about their concerns.

7. Keep your temper in check. If your personality is such that you're impatient and/or tense, work at controlling these impulses.

8. Maintain your personal ethical standards. Be yourself and not what you think others expect you to be.

9. Don't let your work overwhelm you. Take your vacations when scheduled and don't dwell on job-related problems in your leisure time. Being relaxed and well-rested better prepares you for the challenges of the job.

10. Don't neglect your career. You can't predict the future, but that doesn't mean you should ignore it. You may be happy in your current job, but circumstances – many of which are beyond your control – can change that. Therefore, it's prudent to be prepared to move on to another position, either with your present employer, or elsewhere.

Supervisory Career Planning Guide

INTRODUCTION

There are all kinds of reasons for changing jobs. It may be a voluntary decision to move on, or one that is forced upon you by corporate cutbacks. Unfortunately, many folks do little advance planning to guide their career. Consequently, they either take another job based upon a short-term decision of their own, or hastily scramble to look for employment when the corporate ax falls.

For others, career opportunities are missed because they're comfortable in their current job. They know what to expect – both good and the bad – and are reluctant to face the unknowns of a new position. Admittedly, changing jobs isn't an easy thing to do. It means adjusting to everything from a new boss to a different commute – or perhaps even relocation far from family and friends.

All of these complications can easily lead you to shunt any ideas about a new job to the back of your mind, with only passing thoughts of a career change at the end of a bad day at work. However, whether you're happy with your present position, or actively looking for work elsewhere, it's necessary to plan your future, and the place to begin is by looking at where you stand in your current job.

ASSESSING YOUR FUTURE PROSPECTS

The job demands of a supervisor don't leave you with much time to ponder your career prospects. In fact, if you think about it, a lot of your effort is instead directed toward responding to subordinate's questions about their future. Yet, somewhere along the line, it's necessary to sit down and think about where you stand in terms of your own career possibilities. Generally, it's easier to do this if you consider each of the separate elements that can affect your career. These include:

- Your relationship with your boss
- The organizational structure of the company
- The future growth possibilities of the company
- How your company treats employees
- Your degree of job satisfaction
- Your near- and long-term career goals
- Being happy as a supervisor

Let's look at these one-by-one.

Your Relationship with Your Boss

Working relationships are complex and it's easy to generalize how we feel about them. However, it's worthwhile to look beyond the simple day-to-day interactions with the boss when considering your career. For example, you may have a boss who is very easy to work with, but isn't the type who is likely to promote your cause when it comes to promotional opportunities.

On the other hand, you may work for someone who isn't the easiest person in the world to satisfy. Perhaps he or she has a bad temper. Yet, this individual may readily recognize and reward achievement.

To some extent, you have to balance competing interests. Are you better off working for a boss you're happy with, knowing your promotional opportunities will be nil, or for a demanding individual who isn't easy to deal with, but will go to bat for you when the time comes?

Obviously, these are two extremes and the range of possibilities is endless. But the bottom line comes down to deciding how helpful your boss will be in furthering your advancement within the company.

Often, other than your gut feeling, there is little to go on besides the boss's track record. This includes considerations such as

1. Has the boss been supportive in getting other supervisors promoted in the past?
2. Conversely, are there people being held back from advancement because your boss hasn't pushed them for promotion – including yourself?
3. Does your boss encourage you to pursue training that will help you move ahead?
4. Has the boss held discussions with you about your future prospects
5. Does the boss give you assignments that allow you to increase your potential for promotion?

The Organizational Structure of the Company

You can be the most productive and promotable supervisor in the world, but if there's no position for you to move up to, then ultimately you either have to accept that fact, or decide to look for a job elsewhere.

In making this assessment, look at who presently occupies the positions that you would most logically be promoted to. Is that person, or persons, likely to remain in that position for the foreseeable future? Obviously, your evaluation is mostly conjecture. However, there are signs that signal an unlikelihood that a position will be opening up. For instance, if the position is occupied by someone who has been with the company for many years, but is still a long way from retirement, then it's a fair bet they're not going anywhere anytime soon.

It's also of value to consider what has happened in the past within your company. Have others before you stalled in their climb up the corporate ladder? How flexible has the company been in expanding the responsibilities of positions and/or creating new positions to give folks promotions, rather than leaving them blocked from moving up.

The Future Growth Possibilities of the Company

Closely aligned with the opportunities and obstacles for promotion presented by the organizational structure are the future prospects for company growth. A growing company greatly enhances advancement opportunities for everyone.

Naturally, it's impossible for you to be able to crystal ball the future prospects of your employer. However, if you've been with a company for a few years and it's showing few signs of growth, it's unlikely that expansion will occur – at least in the near term.

NOTE: If you work for a company where cutbacks in the work force are likely to occur, that doesn't necessarily mean you should scramble about looking for a new job. Sometimes, cutbacks can lead to new opportunities for those remaining after the dust has settled. Of course, that's not to say that you should ignore the realities of the situation. However, don't panic needlessly when you hear the first rumor about possible cutbacks.

How Your Company Treats Employees

Every supervisory position presents enormous potential for conflict between yourself and others. Disagreements can arise over pay, promotions, or workload to name just a few. Your relationships with bosses, other supervisors, and subordinates can range from close friendship to barely concealed contempt. Balancing personal desires against the demands of the job can be as tricky as walking on a high wire of wet noodles.

In addition to possible personality clashes, there are organizational demands that require conformity to the rules and practices of the company. These rules – formal or informal – impose a degree of rigidity on you in terms of working hours, mode of dress, and much more. However, you have individual needs and desires of your own, as well as a personality that doesn't necessarily square with the organization's requirements.

The biggest problems surface when companies with rigid rules square-off against the needs of employees. Something has to give, and it's always the employee, since the company writes the rules. To some extent, how far an employee is willing to bend to satisfy employer demands determines the future success of the employee. From the first day on a new job, you're forced to put personal preference in your pocket in deference to a paycheck.

Dissatisfaction at work can range from basic concerns to such moral dilemmas as whether or not to report fraud or other illegalities. However, it's fundamentals such as fair treatment, recognition, various forms of subtle discrimination, and overall working conditions that spawns most of the discontent in the workplace. Although some of these factors may be beyond the control of your immediate boss, others can be readily resolved.

On the other hand, many managers simply adopt a policy of, "That's the way it is, and that's the way it's going to be." Rather than dealing with employee concerns, these managers avoid them by pointing to corporate policies and procedures. This may make their job simpler, but it leads to resentment, low productivity, and high turnover, all of which make your job as a supervisor more difficult than it has to be.

Within this working environment, you're expected to be a team player. However, your day-to-day treatment by upper management may not give you any sense of being part of a team. Instead, you're more likely to be given second-class status, and when business is bad, you're as likely to be laid off as the subordinates you supervise.

In fact, except for senior executives, most managers are in the same boat as a newly hired mail clerk. In short, when push comes to shove, you're as dispensable as a disposable diaper. Dealing with that reality starts with an open-eyed assessment of what you can expect to happen if and when bad times hit your company.

Your Degree of Job Satisfaction

The most personal and subjective career considerations are your own feelings about your job in particular and the company in general. There's an obvious comfort factor associated with any job, as opposed to the unknowns of a new position in unfamiliar surroundings. After all, you know what you're dealing with in your present position. To some extent, even the unpleasant aspects of your present position may be easier to accept than the unknowns awaiting you at a new job.

Your own personality comes into play here. Some folks find it easier to accept change than others. That makes it simpler to pick-up and move on to a different job. In fact, there are people who are prone to move on for purposes that really don't involve any more practical reason than their own restlessness. When it comes to gauging your own level of satisfaction with your present position, about all that can be said is to make any judgments based on your own priorities.

Your Near- and Long-Term Career Goals

Where do you want to be in terms of your career two or three years from now? From a longer term perspective, what are your goals for five to ten years down the road? Naturally, the further ahead you look the more difficult it is to visualize both what you want as well as the path you have to follow to get there. Understandably, many unforeseen events in both your personal and professional life will intervene and cause you to alter your objective.

However, even though it's impossible to predict the future, that doesn't mean it should be ignored. This is especially true if your future objectives require the completion of additional requirements. If, for example, a college degree will make your goals more attainable, it doesn't help to continually postpone getting started. Often, the biggest hurdle in the way of expanding your horizons is avoiding taking that first step that will start the process rolling.

CAUTION: If you're relatively happy with what you're doing, don't be needlessly seduced by the lure of more money or status in another position. There's no point in putting yourself in a "career at all costs" position if that isn't what you really want.

Being Happy as a Supervisor

Many people don't spend their careers in the same line of work. Career changes may come about because of a deliberate decision to switch career fields, or perhaps just a fortuitous event that results in a different job.

As a supervisor, you know first-hand the pressures associated with supervising people. Perhaps you may be dissatisfied with having to handle one problem after another with subordinates. Therefore, you may well be thinking about getting away from a job with supervisory responsibilities. For example, stop for a moment and picture what happened to someone we'll call Frank.

Frank was happily married with two young children. He was a supervisor for XYZ Corporation. Much of his spare time was spent fishing, or as an active participant in the company bowling league. Six months after Frank was promoted to his supervisory position, his physical and emotional well-being started to suffer. Periodic stomach pains bothered him, and his family life started to deteriorate. He gave up fishing and quit the company bowling league.

After several medial consultations, it became apparent that Frank's job was the cause of his physical and emotional problems. Frank had always been a conscientious worker, was well-liked, and never took his work home with him. However, after becoming a supervisor, Frank was faced with decisions involving pay raises, job assignments, discipline, and so forth. It seemed that every decision he made resulted in someone being unhappy.

Frank worried about this constantly, and he was also irritated when his fellow workers kidded him about being a boss. Was all of this aggravation worth the additional money Frank was getting? Not for him, and perhaps it isn't for you if you're unhappy with your supervisory responsibilities.

Here are a few questions you can think about to help decide whether or not your supervisory position is right for you:

1. Are you supervising workers with whom you now socialize? A close friendship with a subordinate can lead to frustration and resentment by other workers. Perhaps, you'll be accused of favoritism by jealous subordinates.

    In addition, can you treat everyone equally? The people you supervise have varied backgrounds, interests, desires, and personalities. Do you have inborn prejudices which are deep-seated? If so, can you overcome them? Whatever your feelings in this regard, the important point to remember is that you can't let personal feelings enter into job decisions.

2. Can you communicate effectively? Many people overlook the fact that communication is accomplished in several ways. First and foremost, can you listen and perceive what others say just as readily as you verbalize your own thoughts? Many people fail miserably in this regard.

   Effective listening requires concentration on what the speaker is saying. When dealing with grievances, you must try to project how you would feel if you were in the complainant's shoes.

   How's your writing ability? If written reports and memoranda are a considerable part of your duties, then you need to be able to write clearly and concisely.

   In addition to speech and written communication, there is also expressive communication. This consists of gestures and expressions that convey meaning to people. This includes an upraised eyebrow, frowning, and various other signals that can silently disclose displeasure with a subordinate.

3. What are your personality traits? Are you decisive, as well as consistent, in your treatment of subordinates? Are you a worrier who takes work problems home? Are you overly sensitive? As you know, a supervisor has to make decisions that may not be popular.

4. Are you content with the additional responsibility that goes along with the supervisory role? As you're well aware, you not only have your own performance to worry about, but also face the task of being judged on the performance of your subordinates.

   One of the most important things to recognize is that you are the front line of management. Higher level management decisions on policy and procedure are implemented by you. It's your responsibility to explain new procedures, answer employees' questions, and provide feedback to top management.

Now that you have thought about these questions, there is one more thing you can do. Take a piece of paper and draw a line down the middle. List all of the advantages offered by your supervisory position on one side of the paper, and opposite these list all of the disadvantages.

After completing this self-analysis, you will be better able to make an informed decision on your desire to remain in a supervisory capacity. If your decision is in the affirmative, you will be following in the path of many others who achieved career success as a supervisor.

On the other hand, if thinking about the subject reinforces doubts in your mind about continuing in a supervisory capacity, give the matter some further thought. After all, it makes little sense to be miserable doing a job that's not to your liking. It's admittedly difficult to reach this conclusion – especially if you've been in a supervisory position for some time – but it's a decision that's better off being faced sooner rather than later.

CAUTION: If you're unhappy in your present position, don't arbitrarily blame it on your supervisory responsibilities. Be honest with yourself in pinpointing why you don't like your job. It may be something that's temporary in nature, or perhaps it's more permanent, such as an overbearing boss. Whatever it is, consider what adjustments have to be made to eliminate the cause of your discomfort. That may mean deciding to look for a new job somewhere else if it's a situation you can no longer tolerate.

In summary, assessing your future job prospects is an all-encompassing endeavor. It includes not only objective factors, such as how good an employer you work for, but also your personal feelings and attitudes about changing jobs. Frankly, it's a topic that's tough to deal with, since it's not easy for many folks to pick up and move on unless they're forced to because of losing their job, or extreme dissatisfaction makes their present position unbearable.

Nevertheless, it's prudent to keep yourself mentally tuned to developments at work that may affect your job status. That way, even though you have no present intention of looking for another job, at least you'll be ready to make a move should conditions change. One of the most important considerations to be resolved if you decide to change jobs is whether or not you'll accept a position that requires you to relocate. Let's look at the pros and cons of relocation, to better prepare you for a go/no-go decision if that becomes necessary.

THE PROS AND CONS OF RELOCATION

Picking up and moving to another part of the country for a new job isn't easy to do. In fact, a lot of people dismiss such a possibility without even giving it any thought. However, as difficult as relocation is for some people to accept, it's that much harder if it's thrust upon you without warning. Even if your present position is such that you aren't even considering relocation, it's worthwhile to explore the pros and cons of moving. Should disaster strike in the form of job loss, you'll at least be able to make a sound judgment on whether or not you will or won't relocate.

In fact, it's impossible to plan your career beyond the immediate future without considering job relocation. That's because although relocation might be out of the question right now, that might change in the event of a corporate cutback, or poor economic conditions developing in your part of the country. Rather than simply saying, "Heck no, I won't move under any circumstances," you're better off at least considering the possibility with an open mind. Of course, if in the final analysis your decision is to continue living in your present locale, at least that judgment can be made with the knowledge that you've given it sufficient thought.

For other people, relocation may be an unrealized dream that hasn't been explored in detail. For a few supervisors – especially those employed by large corporations – relocation may be a foregone conclusion if you're in a position that requires periodic moves for career advancement. All in all, whether or not you're open-minded about relocation, it's a topic that can't be ignored when considering your career.

The Dual Career Dilemma

For many couples, relocation means considering dual careers. That means a joint strategy is needed, since any potential move must weigh the effect it will have on the long-range goals of not one, but two careers. So preplanning can minimize the difficulties that arise when relocation is under deliberation by families where both spouses work.

This may be an irksome issue, but it's by no means an insurmountable obstacle. The important thing to remember is that career couples should sit down and discuss their career objectives long before being faced with the reality of job transfers. The ultimate answers may not always be as simple as they seem. Superficial decisions just based on adding up dollars don't make sense. What's vital is that the potential for long-term career advancement for both marriage partners be weighed – not the immediate career gain of one by accepting a job transfer.

Personal Priorities

Personal priorities also influence job transfers. The impact of leaving family, friends, and off-the-job interests receive great weight when folks consider job offers that require a change of residence. All of which means that it's not easy for many people to pack up and move when a job offer beckons.

The first and controlling consideration in some relocation decisions are personal preference. At the two extremes are those who will readily move anywhere, while other people will never relocate, no matter how lucrative an offer they receive. Most people fall somewhere between these two viewpoints, and for them a decision can only be made by carefully reviewing all aspects of a potential move.

Of course, the specifics of individual situations will vary. For instance, how permanent will any move be? Obviously, if it's relatively short term the personal pressure is less severe. Of equal importance is the reason for relocating. Is your present employer transferring you, or are you considering moving on for a better opportunity?

In any event, never decide to resettle for the wrong reasons, such as marital or financial problems. Doing this can only lead to a negative perspective about your new environment. The ultimate outcome may be that you not only fail to solve your personal problems, but actually intensify them by your unhappiness in a new locale.

Always consider your own personality when you think about making a move. Do you tend to make friends easily, or are you essentially a loner? If you're married these deliberations, of necessity, involve your family. In fact, their ability to make friends is probably more important, since your job will be a ready-made source of new acquaintances for you.

There are many other noneconomic factors to be weighed. For example, what are the continuing education possibilities in the new area? If you plan to seek specialized training, do the educational institutions offer the required courses? Children present additional difficulties, both in terms of their reluctance to leave friends in their present setting, as well as the quality of schools in your new community.

In the final analysis, any decision on relocating will be determined by your own individual circumstances. If periodic moves are a requirement of your employer, it's not easy to say you won't relocate. On the other hand, if you're looking for a new position on your own, you have a great deal more latitude in terms of where and when to move. This lets you concentrate on your job search in areas of geographic preference. However, realism reigns, so be practical, since the best career opportunity isn't likely to be in your favorite resort area.

Whatever the reason, the fact remains that a relocation decision is a very personal one. If you relocate just because you think it's necessary for career advancement, you may not be able to adjust to, much less enjoy your new place of residence. While folks with families may find it more difficult to reach an initial decision to relocate, this may be compensated for by making the adjustment on the other end a little easier. Whatever your circumstances, ultimately it will all boil down to not letting your emotions get in the way of your decision – either one way or the other.

Weighing the Risks of Relocation

Almost anywhere is a great place to live for someone, but that person may not be you. Relocation decisions go far beyond the salary and perks of a good job offer. So a well thought-out decision can't ignore your lifestyle.

Someone who says, "I'll move anywhere there are sidewalks," may unhappily discover that paved pathways don't make cities similar. In the same vein, they may find that close proximity to their family and friends can't be replaced by any combination of fattened finances and fancy fringe benefits.

Given the optimism that often accompanies a lucrative offer to relocate, one point is often overlooked, and that's the relative ease or difficulty of moving back to your old community if things don't work out at planned at your new location. Therefore, it's important for you, along with family members, to sit down and figure out your own hometown comfort factor.

What it really comes down to is risk assessment. That is, what are the chances that your relocation will be unsuccessful, either from a career and/or personal standpoint? If you determine that it's relatively high, then you had better appraise the relative ease or difficulty of returning from an unsuccessful move. Obviously, it's always prudent not to burn your bridges behind you in the job you're leaving. Even after you move, it's sensible to keep in contact with your network of business associates.

In addition, don't forget to consider the financial expense of an unsuccessful relocation. For instance, if you've owned your own home for a few years, you may have a nice capital gain on the sale, but don't forget that if you return, you'll be buying back into the local housing market at current prices.

All of which means that a financially conservative approach may be practical when you first move on to a new locale. It's wise not to pump any home sale profits into a new sports car – or otherwise upgrade your standard of living – until you're sufficiently certain that you're permanently settled in your new hometown. Otherwise, you may subconsciously compensate for dissatisfaction with your new location by going on a spending spree. This may initially overcome unhappiness, but in the long run will do little to aid the adjustment process.

Researching Relocation Sites

Naturally, your relocation decision will be largely influenced by the environment in the city you are considering. The best way to evaluate the pros and cons of the new area is to do as much research as possible. Local Chambers of Commerce can provide information about their individual localities. In addition, statistical facts of one kind or another can be garnered from a wide variety of published sources.

One of the most valuable tools in researching a new area is the local newspaper. Read it thoroughly for information on real estate prices, local politics, entertainment, sports, and the local social scene. Many cities also have regional general interest magazines which will give you a perspective on the lifestyle in the city of your choice. In many communities of any size, the regional business publication can fill you in on the business pulse of the community.

Of course, it's always useful to take advantage of both vacation trips and business travel to get a firsthand picture of an unfamiliar city. Talk with local residents in the community you are considering. The more people you talk with the better, since a wider sampling will eliminate individual bias. If you're lucky enough to know other people who have moved there, you can take advantage of their knowledge to ease your task.

TIP: A great source of potential contacts in a distant city is through your membership in social and civic organizations that are national in scope. Perhaps the local chapter can put you in contact with members in another city. This has the added advantage of giving you a leg-up on assimilating yourself into a new environment if you do relocate.

CAUTION: It's important not to place excessive weight on derogatory remarks about an area by someone who may have lived there for a short while and didn't like it. Some folks are pretty parochial, and tend to be negative about any place that's more than five miles from their place of birth. In the same vein, factor out the advice of self-appointed experts on cities they know nothing about. For instance, a short vacation in San Francisco doesn't qualify someone from the East Coast as an authority on the advantages and disadvantages of living in California – or for that matter San Francisco itself.

When researching an area, it's important to remember that every place has its good points and bad points. There's a lot of adventure involved in moving to another part of the country. It can present a vista of new opportunities, and if you don't expect utopia, then you won't be disappointed.

On the other hand, an attitude approximating, "We'll give it a try," is fine for sampling restaurants – not relocation. So, unless you're pretty positive about relocation, you might be better off staying put.

The Financial Side of Relocation

You just received a job offer with a hefty pay raise, but there's only one hitch – it's a long way from home. However, the money is good, so if the personal considerations fall into place then relocation should be no problem. Wrong! The financial aspects of relocation go far beyond an increase in salary. A pay raise that looks great if you're staying put in Peoria isn't a bargain if you're on your way to San Jose.

There are many up-front costs whenever you relocate, and even worse, the hidden costs of relocation can nick you long after you've settled down in a new town. This makes it imperative to analyze all of the financial particulars before you say "Yes" or "No" to a job offer.

First of all, your minimum acceptable salary should take into account the cost-of-living in a new locale, since there are significant regional differences. Your initial step is to be sure that your income will be sufficient to at least maintain – and hopefully improve – your standard of living.

There are several sources of cost-of-living data which provide city-by-city comparisons. As a starting point you might want to contact the Chamber of Commerce in the city where you plan to relocate; not only for cost-of-living data, but also a wide range of facts and figures on the community at large.

Many relocation firms also perform cost-of-living studies for their clients. If your employer is relocating you, the firm they do business with can provide you with a wealth of data. Of course, any cost-of-living comparison is influenced by the approach and method of data collection. Furthermore, although they are a good general guide as to regional cost differences, surveys can't provide specific answers for any individual situation.

For instance, average housing costs for a given metropolitan area can be deceptive. If the best housing bargains are in one section of town, and your job is in another part of the area, you might have to make a trade-off between housing costs and a lengthy commute.

Although living costs include many variables, housing and taxes are the two that matter most. In short, the cost of peanut butter is pretty much the same everywhere, and even where there are differences in food costs, it's often because of local price wars or other competitive factors which are temporary in nature. Therefore, concentrate your cost comparisons on housing and state and local taxes.

Of course, if you're being relocated by your employer, it's important to establish what expenses will be paid for by the company. House hunting trips, mortgage interest differentials, and moving expenses are a few of the common costs.

Most large businesses have a standard relocation policy setting forth what they'll cover. That doesn't mean you can't or shouldn't ask them to pay for items not included in their package. They might just agree. However, the important thing to remember is that these benefits vary widely, so make sure of what kind of assistance you'll receive.

When you plan your house hunting in a distant city, it's important to pin down the setting you want to live in, since there are wide variances in both housing and schools within metropolitan areas. One way to do this is to use your present home in establishing the criteria you set. The closer you come to approximating your present environment, the more comfortable you're likely to be in your new surroundings.

Along with housing, taxes are a major financial factor in relocation decisions. Tax considerations can include a gain or loss on the sale of your present home, the tax status of relocation benefits, and the impact of state and local taxes in the new area.

Incidentally, don't minimize the importance of state and local taxes when you consider relocation. There are wide disparities both in levels of taxation and the methods used to raise revenues. Since local property taxes can vary widely from community to community, take this into account when you go house hunting.

NOTE: The trend of taxes may be more important than present rates. Therefore, don't rely on outdated information as to where taxes are high or low.

TIP: If you don't plan your move carefully, you may find yourself saddled with expenses that surface after you've settled in at your new location. For example, if you're unhappy with the school system, you may end up footing the bill to send your children to private school – an expense that can quickly eat away any pay increase you may receive.

Once you've left the old homestead behind, nostalgia may set in. Although reminiscing alone won't cost you anything, it could evolve into lengthy long distance phone calls, and numerous trips to your former home to see family and friends.

In the end, successfully dealing with relocation hinges upon your assessment of how you will profit from both financial and personal perspectives. To help in making this determination try rating the following factors by assigning point values from 0 to 10.

#	FACTOR	CONSIDERATIONS	POINT RANGE
1	Salary and Fringe Benefits	How much is the increase?	1-10
2	Relocation Costs	Who pays for what?	1-10
3	Cost-of-Living	What's the cost-of-living vs. where you live now?	1-10
4	Climate	How different from current area?	1-10
5	Housing	Availability, cost, proximity to work?	1-10
6	Taxes	Are state and local taxes higher or lower?	1-10
7	Schools	How good are the schools?	1-10
8	Shopping and Leisure Time Activities	Downtown and/or suburban malls? Easy to get to? Participation and spectator sports? Social scene?	1-10
9	Cultural and Medical Facilities	What kind? Diversity? Distance from new home?	1-10
10	Public Services	Police/fire/public transportation? How far to the airport?	1-10

The higher the score, the more favorable is your relocation potential for a move to the city under consideration. Of course, you can fine-tune your assessment by adding items that may be important to you, or changing the assigned values to more closely reflect your interests.

RESUMÉ TIPS FOR THE TIMID

Résumé Preparation Is a Continuing Process

One of the most common failings when it comes to job hunting occurs long before folks contemplate looking for a new job. The fact is that even though you're perfectly content in your present job, it's still necessary to keep your options open concerning the future. To do that successfully means doing the little things on a continuing basis, so that if and when you do enter the job market, you can do so without scrambling about in a panic.

All too often, people take the first job that comes along, simply because they didn't lay the groundwork for job hunting success. Although you may not be looking for a job at the present time, let's look at a couple of actions you can take to be better prepared should that eventuality arise.

First of all, you should always have a résumé sketched out, which you need to periodically update whenever there is any significant change in your duties. This greatly simplifies the task of putting a formal résumé together when the time comes.

As a part of this process, it's useful to keep a folder in which you can insert notes about on-the-job accomplishments as they occur. The purpose of this is two-fold. One, it eliminates the necessity of relying on memory alone when it's time to sit down and put a résumé together.

Second, in the conduct of day-to-day activities, it's easy to overlook accomplishments, and/or shrug them off as just being part of your job as a supervisor. That may be true, but it's these very achievements that can ultimately make your résumé stand out from the pack.

Therefore, get in the habit of writing a note to yourself when your boss says something such as, "Nice going on that rush job." That's the time to jot down the details of what you did that caused the boss to express his appreciation.

TIP: Don't be bashful about what you include in your accomplishments file. If you know you did a good job in handling a tough assignment, make a note of it. Don't just include items that your boss and/or other managers have complimented you on. If you do that, you may have a pretty thin file, since some bosses can tend to be long on criticism and short on praise.

Furthermore, there may be reasons known only to you as to why a particular task was handled well. In short, include every achievement – large or small – in this file. Don't forget, in the future you may have to prepare a résumé to place your accomplishments in competition with other job candidates who are more than willing to engage in personal public relations. Remember, you don't see "help wanted" ads in the newspaper listing "shy and reserved" as required qualifications.

Putting Your Résumé Together

One of the best investments you can make is to have a professional résumé service prepare your résumé. It's not only time-saving, but it also guarantees that your qualifications will be presented in the best possible light.

However, that doesn't negate the necessity for you to dig up the relevant information. The best résumé writers in the world can't help if you don't give them the proper information to work with. If you keep a draft résumé up-to-date – as mentioned in the previous section – your task is simplified.

In preparing your draft, use action words to describe your accomplishment, and be specific in describing your duties. A few samples of good and bad ways to present your qualifications follow:

BAD: ... supervisory responsibilities

GOOD: ... supervise twelve electronic technicians

BAD: … helped reduce product defects

GOOD: … recommended procedure that cut product defects 20%

BAD: … maintained good employee relations

GOOD: … highest productivity rate and lowest employee turnover
          rate among 10 supervisors in department

It may seem like wasted effort to go through this exercise if your résumé will be prepared by someone else. However, the more precise the information you furnish, the less time will be wasted in ferreting out your background. Furthermore, when you're questioned by the person who is preparing your résumé, you may not remember certain details at that time. So the greater the effort in background preparation, the better the final product.

Résumé Do's and Don'ts

- Listing your job objective. Your résumé should be as specific as possible in listing your job objective. Why? Quite simply, personnel people aren't going to take the time to try and figure out what kind of position you're seeking. Obviously, this means you may have to prepare alternative résumés with different job objectives. Nevertheless, the extra effort and expense is preferable to sending out a résumé with a generalized job objective.
- Be honest in stating your qualifications. You want to put your best foot forward, but that doesn't mean embellishing a résumé so as to turn fact into fiction.
- Check your résumé over carefully after it's completed – even if it's prepared by a résumé service. All a prospective employer will see is what's on the résumé, and errors may be interpreted to mean you're careless.
- Cover letters and résumés can get separated, so don't put anything in a cover letter that should have been included in the résumé.

Once you have a satisfactory résumé prepared, you're ready for the next step in your job search, and that's getting your qualifications in front of the people who are in a position to offer you the job you want. Let's consider not only how to go about circulating your résumé, but also what to do when you have an interview.

WINNING WAYS FOR THE INTERVIEW GAME

Getting Your Résumé into the Right Hands

A successful job search starts long before you ever get to your first interview. Once you have a résumé prepared, the next step is to circulate it so that you get the maximum response. Some job seekers think that means blindly mailing résumés to as many companies as possible. Often, this is done randomly with little thought given to targeting the mailing, both to the right companies, as well as the proper person within that company.

Other folks take an entirely different tack than those who flood the market with résumés. They simply contact a single employment agency and rely exclusively on whatever opportunities the agency can turn up. Needless to say, the success of this approach depends entirely on the competence of the agency.

In addition, some agencies tend to specialize in certain professions, and even those that generalize are sometimes more adept at placement in specific fields. Suffice it to say, that if you're going to use an agency, check carefully to make sure they have a good track record in placing people in the type of job you're seeking.

The best tactic to take in circulating your résumé is to use a variation of the technique that direct marketers use, and that's to target your résumé to those companies that offer the best prospects for your job search. Doing this isn't as difficult as it seems if you do your homework.

Targeting Your Job Market

One of the best ways to be prepared for a future job search is to keep a file of potential contacts. Sure, you may have no interest in looking for a job at the present time, but circumstances change, and when they do it helps to be ready. There are a variety of methods you can use to build a contact list. These include

- keeping in contact with supervisors who have moved on to jobs with other companies.
- meeting other managers at conferences and training courses you attend.
- your membership in professional and social organizations.
- family and friends.
- clipping the names of people from promotion announcements in the business pages of your daily newspaper, and/or from the local business magazine or newspaper.

In short, use every avenue you can think of to gather the names of individuals who may be valuable contacts in landing a future job. This not only assists in gathering a list of good companies to work for, but it can also help eliminate those you want to avoid. For example, if over a period of time several people have less than pleasant things to say about the company they work for, then that should give you second thoughts about applying for a job there.

It's also useful to clip "help wanted" ads from the newspaper on a regular basis. It stands to reason that if a company is currently advertising for someone with your type of qualifications, then that company is likely to have future requirements for the same type of job.

Once you decide that it's time to look for another position, you need only pull out your file and compile a mailing list for your résumé. Of course, you will likely have the names of several people you can contact by phone to check on vacancies with their company. However, even if you get a couple of hot leads over the phone, don't arbitrarily decide to hold up on mailing résumés to other possibilities on your contact list.

Instead, make this decision purely on the basis of why you're looking for a job. If you're out of work, about to be, or dissatisfied to the point of distraction, don't sit back and wait to see if a promising lead pans out. If it falls through, you'll have wasted time in pursuing other opportunities.

There's another advantage to sending a résumé to every possible source at once. You may have the good fortune to receive more than one job offer before you have made a commitment to anyone. This gives you a better chance to select the job you want, and it also puts you in a better negotiating position if you want to do a little bargaining over salary.

TIP: Anytime you have the name of an operating manager, it's worthwhile to send a résumé to that person, rather than the personnel office. This is particularly true when you're interested in future possibilities, as opposed to applying for an immediate opening.

Nevertheless, for any specific advertised vacancy, you should send your application to the appropriate personnel office. Otherwise, you run the danger of your résumé not being considered for the present opening. Furthermore, you also risk alienating someone in the personnel office, which certainly doesn't help your chances of getting the job.

If you're responding to a solicitation for an advertised vacancy, you may still want to send a résumé directly to a hiring manager. But let the person know in your cover letter that you've also applied directly through personnel.

There are a couple of reasons why it's advantageous to send your résumé to an operating manager. First of all, it gets individualized attention, since it doesn't arrive from personnel along with a batch of other applications. Furthermore, even when there's no immediate opening, the manager may hold your résumé for future use when a vacancy arises. If lightning strikes, your qualifications may have enough appeal to create a job where none existed.

Job Application Cover Letters

A cover letter transmitting your résumé should be short and to the point. The following is one example.

LLL Corporation
Attn: Ms. Patricia Humphrey
Human Resources Department
55 Magnolia Boulevard
Dayton, OH 45401

Dear Ms. Humphrey:

The attached résumé is submitted in response to your solicitation for a Supervisor of Warehouse Operations. I would be most interested in discussing this position with you at your convenience.

You can contact me at either my home or office number listed on my résumé. Your consideration of this application is appreciated, and it is hoped that a long and productive association with the LLL Corporation will result.

Very truly yours,
Sammy Suave

NOTE: Never put any information in your cover letter that you want to have considered as part of your application. There are two reasons for this. First, the cover letter may be separated from the résumé. Second, even if it isn't, the letter may not be read, since there's a presumption that it's only for transmittal purposes.

Preparing for the Interview

In preparing for a job interview, there are several points to consider. These are:

1. Human nature being what it is, many folks are deeply immersed in their work on Mondays after a weekend of

rest and relaxation. And at the other end, some people are less than attentive to their duties on Fridays, as they look ahead to a couple of days off. These traits are as true for those involved in hiring new employees as they are for anyone else.

With that in mind, if at all possible, try to avoid scheduling an interview on those days. Obviously, it's not something to dwell on at length, but if the opportunity is available, schedule any interviews during the middle of the week. Every little detail might make the difference, so if it's avoidable there's no sense in interviewing with someone who may have their mind somewhere else.

2. Once you have an interview scheduled, try to learn as much as you can about the company beforehand. It makes a good impression on people when they realize you're familiar with their company.

3. Dress in appropriate business attire for the interview. A little spit and polish may not win you the job, but it will certainly keep you from losing it based on a bad impression.

4. If there's one thing you want to avoid, it's being late for an interview. Plan for the unexpected, such as heavy traffic and/or detours, and allow extra travel time to get to your appointment. You may arrive early by doing this, but it's preferable to starting off an interview with an apology for being late.

5. Bring along any documentation you may have that demonstrates your competence. It may be a congratulatory note on a job well done, a well-written memo on a difficult project, or anything else that show you're as good as your résumé implies. Most people don't do this, but it's very reassuring to an interviewer to see first-hand evidence of your abilities.

Interviewing Do's and Don'ts

In terms of your general demeanor during an interview, attempt to project an air of self-confidence. That may be difficult if your prior experience in interviews has been on the sweaty palms side of the ledger. However, if you stop to think about it, no one knows more about your background than you. That knowledge alone puts you – not the interviewer – in the driver's seat.

Furthermore, many hiring managers don't have a great deal of expertise in interviewing job applicants. Frankly, their interest may lean toward filing the vacancy as soon as possible, so if you appear relatively relaxed, that in itself can work in your favor.

Although it's important to be self-confident, don't be overly ambitious in this regard. In the end, the best approach is to be yourself – not what you think others are looking for. After all, you'll have to be yourself after you're hired, so you might as well project that very image during the interview. If that's not what your potential boss is looking for, you're both better off realizing it before you're hired.

Finally, during the interview process, someone may try to throw you off guard to test your temperament under pressure. Therefore, be sure to maintain your composure no matter how trying the circumstances may be. That's not likely to happen, but if it does – either deliberately, or through inadvertence – keeping a cool head will give you the hot hand in the competition for the job.

Fielding Questions with Finesse

After any interview, folks often worry about how well they did in answering the questions that were posed to them. Most interviews cover the same general ground consisting of

- open-ended questions about your background
- skill-specific questions to test how your expertise matches up with the job opening
- employment-related questions such as your salary requirements

- an opportunity for you to ask questions.

Let's consider some typical questions and appropriate responses:

Q: "Give me an idea of what you do on your present job?"

A: "My most important duties consist of.."

POINTERS: Briefly outline your duties, and in doing so weave specific accomplishments into your answer. Also use this opportunity to highlight personal traits such as loyalty and dedication.

Don't get bogged-down in a blow-by-blow account of everything you do on a daily basis. You'll accomplish little other than boring the interviewer. Remember, they've seen your résumé, so if they didn't think you were qualified, you wouldn't have been invited for an interview.

What interviewers are trying to establish with questions about your current job are whether what you say is consistent with the résumé, as well as how that experience relates to the available job. Therefore, concentrate your efforts in answering this type of question on demonstrating your skills in resolving people problems which, after all, is the guts of any supervisory position.

CAUTION: Another advantage of being brief in outlining your duties is that it prevents you from being tripped up in multiple interviews. One of the main purposes of having different people interview you is to compare notes on whether or not you gave different versions of your duties to the various interviewers.

Q: "What do you consider to be your strengths?"

A: "I don't like to toot my own horn, so that's a tough question to answer. I'll try to be objective by covering some areas that my superiors have complimented me on."

POINTERS: The fact is that you want to toot your horn as loud as you can, but try to do it with a dash of humility sprinkled in. That way, you not only score points for your accomplishments, but you also let the interviewer know that you're not overly impressed with yourself.

This counts for a lot, since in the final analysis people hire someone they want to work with. If you can successfully tout your triumphs, while simultaneously leaving the interviewer thinking, "What a nice person," you're in good shape.

HINT: When you get a, "What are you good at?" type of question, answer it in terms of your job. The interviewers aren't interested in your biggest fish story, your half-finished novel, or your vacation in Greenland.

Q: "What is your biggest weakness?"

A: "I can't relax until all my work is done." Or, "I'm a perfectionist."

POINTERS: This type of question doesn't mean it's time for true confessions. Not matter how you do it, what you want to respond with are strengths disguised as weaknesses. The answers above could be interpreted to imply that you're a workaholic, and if true, they may not be the best thing in the world, for either your health or your personal life. However, from the perspective of a potential employer, it's nirvana. After all, what employer doesn't want someone who worries about getting the job done right?

Q: "Can we contact your current employer?"

A: "Yes, if a definite job offer is to be made after your inquiry."

POINTERS: Most people don't want their present employer to know they are job hunting. Therefore, there's a hesitancy in consenting to an employer being contacted. However, bluntly refusing permission to query your current employer is often enough to take you right out of contention for the job.

The best way to handle this dilemma is to tell the interviewer that you would prefer your employer not be contacted, unless it's reasonably certain that a job offer will be forthcoming. Hopefully, this will discourage any inquiry being made as part of a general screening, where there's less likelihood of a job offer resulting.

Q: "If you come to work for us, what would you like to be doing three or four years from now?"

A: "More important than any specific job, I'd like to be able to look back and see that I helped contribute to the growth of the company."

POINTERS: This type of question traditionally leads to answers such as, "I'd like to be a department manager," or some other position that signifies the candidate expects to be promoted. The theory is that this illustrates drive and ambition, with the assumption being that these are traits that the potential employer is looking for. Yet, there are several pitfalls in answering such a question in that manner. These are as follows:

1. An applicant isn't usually familiar enough with the organizational structure of the company to determine the length of time it takes to be promoted to the next management level. As a result, the answer may be unrealistic in terms of the employee's expectations.
2. An applicant who appears overly ambitious may – in the eyes of the interviewer – be someone who will readily job hop for further career advancement.
3. The hiring manager is looking for someone who can be counted on to fill the vacant position for the indefinite future. Therefore, those doing the hiring are unlikely to have any interest in a candidate who implies that the job is only a quick pit stop on the road to success.
4. The folks doing the hiring may well know that advancement opportunities are slim to none within the company. Consequently, they may be looking for signs that a candidate isn't looking beyond the current job opening. That's why an answer that emphasizes the contribution you hope to make in the open job may be preferable.

Let's say you do that, and a canny interviewer presses you further with a follow-up question such as, "Well, what I really want to know is what your long-term career goals are in terms of promotions?" Simply score more points by saying something such as "I believe in doing whatever job I have to the best of my ability, and by doing that I feel the future takes care of itself." By handling this type of question in this manner, you've conveyed an impression of someone who is both hard working and loyal. That's what employers are looking for – not people with pie-in-the-sky aspirations.

NOTE: If, during an interview, you're hit with a question that's hard to answer, don't fumble about. Instead, do what a lot of skilled politicians do when served a hardball query. Just answer the question you want to answer, rather than the one that was raised.

Of course, try to keep the reply within the same ballpark as the question. That way, it may be assumed that you did answer properly. Naturally, the interviewer may not think so, and will follow-up with the same or a similar question. Nevertheless, you're still ahead of the game, because you've had time to think of an appropriate response.

The important point in this regard is to avoid stumbling around with your answers. Another alternative is to readily admit you don't have the answer, but even here, try to give a convincing reason why. For example, "That type of machine has been updated since I last worked on it two years ago."

Q: "Why are you leaving your current position?"

A: "I want to change my job, so I can further develop my people-handling skills. Things are pretty stable where I work now which is fine, but it's limiting my opportunity to learn and grow as a supervisor."

POINTERS: Actually, there are many factual answers that can be given to this question which are dictated by your personal circumstances. A few examples are

- "The company is shutting the plant down."
- "The company is undergoing a reorganization."

- "The product line I supervise is being phased out."

In essence, if there's a readily understandable reason for you to be job hunting, just state the facts.

On the other hand, if you're looking for a better opportunity, or wanting to get away from a bad situation, some variation of an "I want to expand my horizons," answer works well. What you want to imply is that you're reasonably happy where you are, but your skills aren't being fully utilized.

WARNING: Never, under any circumstances, criticize your current employer, either generally, or specifically in terms of individuals such as your boss. It just signals "sour grapes" no matter how logical and detailed an explanation you give. Although most people exercise good judgment in this regard, implications can be cast during an extended interview if you're not careful.

Getting Answers to Your Questions

It's easy to forget that an interview is a two-way street. And just as the potential employer wants to learn as much as possible about your background, you too should be seeking answers. Let's look at a few of the most common areas that a job candidate should cover during an interview.

- Get all of the details you need to evaluate the fringe benefits offered by the company. This is an important consideration from a financial standpoint. Incidentally, request this information from the personnel representative you talk with – not the manager who is filling the vacancy. You want to confine your discussions with the latter to details of the job, and your qualifications to fill it.
- Find out why the position you're interviewing is vacant, as well as why it's being filled from outside the company. The answers can be very revealing. For instance, it may be a new position created because of growth, which is a good sign for the future. The fact that the job is being

filled from outside the company might just mean that there's no one qualified to fill it internally.

On the other hand, it may be an undesirable job which no one wants. Actually, the likely answer you'll get is that no one was qualified, but it never hurts to ask, because you never know when you'll get a revealing answer.

- Ask about the future growth potential of the company. You don't want to join a company that is going downhill fast. There's nothing quite as demoralizing as discovering shortly after you start a new job, that the reason you were hired was because everyone else is deserting a sinking ship.
- Get all of the facts you can about the job itself. How many people will you supervise? What happened to the previous supervisor? Is there a lot of overtime worked on a regular basis?

Don't be shy about asking these types of questions. If you don't get this information, you can't make an informed judgment about the job. All too often, folks see a solid pay raise in the offing, only to discover later that the money wasn't the bargain it appeared to be.

NOTE: Don't ask about salary during an initial job interview. If possible, leave salary discussions until the company makes you an offer.

TIP: You might want to refer back to Sec. 7.1 to 7.5 of Chapter 7 which cover interviewing from the point of view of a hiring supervisor. It can help to prepare for an interview by looking at it from the other side of the desk.

Post-Interview Tips

After you leave a job interview, usually with the standard, "We'll get back to you," farewell, there are still a couple of worthwhile chores to perform. These are

1. Promptly send a "thank you" note to the interviewers, thanking them for their time and attention. Also include the fact that you were really impressed with the company, and look forward to working with them. Very few people bother to do this, and that's precisely why it's effective.
2. Think about what took place during the interview. Did you genuinely like the people you interviewed with, or did they make you feel uneasy? Were they enthusiastic about the company, or did they appear to be just going through the motions?

In addition, what are your instinctive feelings toward your potential boss? If you're uneasy now, it doesn't bode well for the future. For instance, was he critical of existing employees at any time? If so, that's a style you can expect to face if you take the position.

BARGAINING FOR BUCKS AND BENEFITS

Establishing a Target Salary

The one item that job hunters tend to think about the most is what their starting salary will be. Unfortunately, these thoughts are rarely translated into a plan which can give job seekers a fighting chance at achieving their salary goals.

Instead, they rely on the salary offer being sufficiently above what they're currently earning in their present position. This benign neglect can lead to accepting a salary that's several though dollars a year less than what could have been realized by careful bargaining. Also, that monetary loss is compounded for years to come, since future salary increments will be computed from a lower salary base.

The starting point for success in salary negotiations is to first establish the minimum salary you'll accept. This can be done long before you even have your first interview. But remember, whatever that figure is, you may want to revise it during the interview process. That's because in the course of discussing a job opening, certain aspects of that job may warrant asking for a higher – or lower – minimum starting salary than you had originally contemplated.

For example, if a position will require longer hours for which you won't get paid, then you might want to increase your salary demands. This can happen in operations that require substantial overtime on a regular basis.

Playing the Negotiating Game

The procedure for getting the best salary deal you can is fairly simple, but it requires you to follow a basic strategy. The first consideration is an understanding of how the employer plays the game. To simplify it, let's list the realities from the company negotiator's standpoint and who, incidentally, is usually from the personnel office.

- The job has a salary range, and anything outside of this range is unacceptable as far as the company is concerned.
- All things considered, the company wants to hire you for as low a figure within that range as is possible.
- The company negotiator knows your salary. You were either asked for a salary history in the "Help Wanted" ad you responded to, or on a company application form, or during the interview.
- The negotiator will ask you what your salary requirements are. As we'll discuss shortly, you want to hedge as long as possible about giving a figure.
- The negotiator will offer you a salary based on what minimum percentage above your current salary he or she thinks you'll accept. Alternatively, if you've given them a desired salary figure that's substantially above your present earnings, they'll point to the fact as justification for offering less than you're asking for.

Now, let's look at how you should proceed to win this game.

- Do as much research as necessary to find out what comparable jobs pay for someone with your experience and qualifications. If possible, try to establish whether the company you're interviewing with pays better or worse than the average.
- When you furnish a current salary figure, make sure it includes all types of compensation. That means adding bonuses, overtime, and any other compensation to your base salary.

NOTE: Some applicants succumb to the temptation to arbitrarily inflate their current earnings. It's wrong, it's risky, and it's unnecessary, since you can do just as well without the risks by being honest.

- Don't mention the salary you're looking for until the interviewer brings it up. Then, try to get the company representative to make the first move. For example:

Interviewer: "What are you looking for in terms of salary?"
You: "It's negotiable. What's the salary range for the job?"

NOTE: A sharp interviewer may bounce the ball back into your court by saying, "We're flexible, what are you looking for?" If this is done, and you haven't found out the salary range, give a figure of 10% more than you expect to get. (For example, if you're making $47,000 and will accept $55,000, add 10% to that and quote $60,500.) This gives you flexibility in the event you're underestimating the range for the job.

- Don't panic if the interviewer expresses surprise at your salary figure. It's a common negotiating ploy to get you to lower your figure. Most people think they'll lose the job because they're too high, and blurt out something such as, "Well, I'm flexible, what did you have in mind?" Instead, do this

Interviewer: "Your acceptable figure is a little high."

You: (Don't say anything. Several seconds of deafening silence will force the interviewer to continue, taking one of the following three courses.)

Interviewer: (a) "Well, let me see what I can do." (That implies they can meet your figure.)

(b) "I'm sorry, but that's beyond the range for the position." (You're too high, but now you can ask what the range is.)

(c) "That's 30% more than you're making now. I don't know how I could justify it." (It's open for negotiation, and it's up to you to give reasons as to why you're worth the money.)

If you're challenged as to why you want a significant increase over your current salary, give factual reasons such as a longer commute, longer working hours, more responsibility, and so forth.

Incidentally, long before you talk salary, make sure you know the specifics of the fringe benefit package. This translates into real dollars. For instance, if your new medical plan will cost you more out of your own pocket than the plan provided by your current employer, take this into consideration when negotiating salary. Also, something such as a lengthy commute is not only more expensive, but it's eating up your leisure time.

In essence, if you think everything over carefully, you can come up with plenty of good arguments to support your salary request. As long as you're within the salary range for the job, you have a good shot at getting your figure if you play the game right.

Finally, planning your career, all the way from assessing your future prospects with your present employer, to saying "Yes" to a job offer, requires some effort on your part. However, if you make the necessary investment in time to keep your career on track, the benefits will justify the effort.

References

Argyris, Chris (2000). *Flawed Advice and the Management Trap*. New York: Oxford University Press, Inc.

Batstone, David (2003). *Saving the Corporate Soul & (Who Knows?) Maybe Your Own*. San Francisco: Jossey-Bass.

Bennis, Warren G. and Thomas, Robert J. (2002). *Geeks and Geezers: How Era, Values, and Defining Moments Shape Leaders*. Boston: Harvard Business School Press.

Beyerlein, Michael M., Freedman, Sue, McGee, Craig, and Moran, Linda (2003). *Beyond Teams: Building the Collaborative Organization*. San Francisco: Jossey-Bass/Pfeiffer.

Blanchard, Kenneth and Johnson, Spencer (1981). *The One Minute Manager*. LaJolla, CA: Blanchard-Johnson.

Bossidy, Larry and Charan, Ram, with Charles Burck (2002). *Execution: The Discipline of Getting Things Done*. New York: Crown Business.

Cascio, Wayne F. (2003). *Responsible Restructuring: Creative and Profitable Alternatives to Layoffs*. San Francisco: Berrett-Koehler.

Christensen, Clayton M. and Raynor, Michael E., and Scott D. Anthony (2003). *The Innovator's Solution: Creating and Sustaining Successful Growth*. Boston: Harvard Business School Press.

Collins, James, C. (2001). *Good to Great: Why Some Companies Make the Leap . . . and Others Don't*. Cambridge, MA: Harvard Business School Press.

Conger, Jay A., Lawler III, Edward E., and David L. Finegold (2001). *Corporate Boards: Strategies for Adding Value at the Top*. San Francisco: Jossey-Bass.

Covey, Stephen R. (1989). *The Seven Habits of Highly Effective People: Restoring the Character Ethic*. New York: Simon and Schuster.

Csikszentmihalyi, Mihaly (2003). *Good Business: Leadership, Flow, and the Making of Meaning*. New York: Penguin Putnam.

Dannemiller Tyson Associates (2001). *Whole-Scale Change: Unleashing the Magic in Organizations*. San Francisco: Berrett-Koehler.

Deming, W. Edwards (1986). *Out of the Crisis*. Cambridge, MA: MIT Press.

Frost, Peter J. (2003). *Toxic Emotions at Work: How Compassionate Managers Handle Pain and Conflict*. Boston: Harvard Business School Press.

George, Bill (2003). *Authentic Leadership: Rediscovering the Secrets to Creating Lasting Value*. San Francisco: Jossey-Bass.

Gladwell, Malcolm (2000). *The Tipping Point*. Boston, MA: Little, Brown, & Co.

Goleman, Daniel, Boyatzis, Richard, and McKee, Annie (2002). *Primal Leadership: Realizing the Power of Emotional Intelligence*. Boston: Harvard Business School Press.

Hackman, J. Richard (2002). *Leading Teams: Setting the Stage for Great Performances*. Boston: Harvard Business School Press.

Johnson, Spencer, M. D. (1998). *Who Moved My Cheese?* New York: Putnam Books.

Joyce, William, Nitin Nohria, and Bruce Roberson (2003). *What (Really) Works: The 4 + 2 Formula for Sustained Business Success*. New York: Harper Collins.

Kanter, Rosabeth Moss (2001). *Evolve! Succeeding in the Digital Culture of Tomorrow*. Boston: Harvard Business School Press.

Kaplan, Robert S. and Norton, David P. (2001). *The Strategy-Focused Organization*. Cambridge, MA: Harvard Business School Press.

Katzenbach, Jon R. (2003). *Why Pride Matters More than Money.* New York: Crown Business.

Katzenbach, Jon R. (2000). *Peak Performance: Aligning the Hearts and Minds of Your Employees.* Cambridge, MA: Harvard Business School Press.

Kouzes, James M. and Posner, Barry Z. (1993). *Credibility.* San Francisco: Jossey-Bass.

LaFasto, Frank and Larson, Carl (2002). *When Teams Work Best: 6,000 Team Members and Leaders Tell What It Takes to Succeed.* Thousand Oaks, CA: Sage Publications.

Lawler III, Edward E. (2000). *Rewarding Excellence.* San Francisco: Jossey-Bass.

Lawler III, Edward E. (2003) *Treat People Right! How Organizations and Individuals Can Propel Each Other into a Virtuous Spiral of Success.* San Francisco: Jossey-Bass.

Lawrence, Paul R. and Nohria, Nitin. (2002). *Driven: How Human Nature Shapes Our Choices.* San Francisco: Jossey-Bass.

Lundin, Stephen C., Paul, Harry, and Christensen, John (2000). *Fish!* New York: Hyperion.

Maccoby, Michael (2003). *The Productive Narcissist: The Promise and Peril of Visionary Leadership.* New York: Broadway Books.

Maslow, Abraham H. (1998). *Maslow on Management.* New York: John Wiley & Sons.

McGregor, Douglas (1960). *The Human Side of Enterprise.* New York: McGraw-Hill.

Meyerson, Debra E. (2003). *Tempered Radicals: How Everyday Leaders Inspire Change at Work.* Boston: Harvard Business School Press.

Miller, Frederick A. and Katz, Judith H. (2002). *The Inclusion Breakthrough: Unleashing the Real Power of Diversity.* San Francisco: Berrett-Koehler.

Mitroff, Ian I. with Anagnos, Gus (2001). *Managing Crises Before They Happen.* New York: American Management Association.

Murnighan, J. Keith and Mowen, John C. (2002). *The Art of High-Stakes Decision-Making: Tough Calls in a Speed-Driven World.* New York: John Wiley & Sons.

Nutt, Paul C. (2002). *Why Decisions Fail: Avoiding the Blunders and Traps that Lead to Debacles.* San Francisco: Berrett-Koehler.

Peters, Thomas J. and Waterman, Robert H. Jr. (1982). *In Search of Excellence.* New York: Harper and Row.

Porter, Michael E. (1985). *Competitive Advantage: Creating and Sustaining Superior Performance.* New York: Free Press.

Robbins, Peter Thayer (2001). *Greening the Corporation: Management Strategy and the Environmental Challenge.* London: Earthscan Publications.

Seligman, Martin E. P. (2002). *Authentic Happiness: Using the New Positive Psychology to Realize Your Potential for Lasting Fulfillment.* New York: Free Press.

Senge, Peter M. (1990). *The Fifth Discipline.* New York: Doubleday.

Stiglitz, Joseph E. (2002). *Globalization and Its Discontents.* New York: W.W. Norton & Company.

Thomas, Kenneth W. (2000). *Intrinsic Motivation at Work.* San Francisco: Berrett-Koehler.

Ventrice, Cindy (2003). *Make Their Day: Employee Recognition That Works.* San Francisco: Berrett-Koehler.

Weick, Karl E. and Kathleen M. Sutcliffe (2001). *Managing the Unexpected: Assuring High Performance in an Age of Complexity.* San Francisco: Jossey-Bass.

Made in the USA
San Bernardino, CA
24 May 2017